BRITAIN'S *Best*
PUBS 2012
PERFECT PLACES TO EAT & DRINK

Typeset by AA Lifestyle Guides
Printed and bound by DZS Grafik, d.o.o, Slovenia
Editorial contributor: Philip Bryant

A CIP catalogue record for this book is available from the British Library

ISBN: 978-0-7495-7214-3

Published by AA Publishing, which is a trading name of AA Media Limited, whose registered office is:
Fanum House, Basing View, Basingstoke,
Hampshire RG21 4EA
Registered number 06112600

theAA.com/shop

A04800

Contents

Welcome

Britain's Best Pubs is for anyone who enjoys eating and drinking well in formal or informal surroundings. Where stars have been awarded, you can relax in the knowledge that accommodation has been inspected and rated by the AA.

Britain's Best

In this fully updated and revised guide to Britain's Best Pubs you'll find a selection of pubs and hostelries from cosy inns on old coach routes to smart gastro-pubs in towns and cities. Though very different in conception and setting, they all share a commitment to providing refreshment and serving good food based on fresh (and local where possible) produce cooked to order. Hospitality is warm and welcoming, and real ales and well-known brands are offered alongside decent wines. The index and map sections at the back of this guide will help you to find a wide range of towns and villages to visit in search of an authentic pub experience. To help you make the most of your visit we've included recommended places to see in the area of your choice.

A place to stay

Room prices for single and double occupation are shown where the accommodation has been inspected and rated by the AA under our Hotel and Guest Accommodation Schemes. Many places will also offer variable rates and special offer breaks so it's worth asking when you book.

Accommodation varies from pubs with two or three rooms, to much grander inns and hotels with all the extras (although most of the places included in this guide have fewer than 20 rooms). Whatever their size or style, all the places selected for inclusion in Britain's Best Pubs have the same best qualities in common: good food, beer served in relaxed and inviting surroundings and great value for money.

How to use the guide

The main section of the guide is divided into three parts, covering England, Scotland and Wales. The counties within each of these sections are ordered alphabetically as are the town or village locations (shown in capital letters as part of the address) within each county. Finally, the establishments are listed alphabetically under each location name. Town names featured in the guide can also be located in the map section at the back of the guide.

❶ Grading and awards

If the accommodation is rated by the AA under either the AA Hotel Scheme or the AA B&B Scheme the rating is shown. For full details see page 10.

Egg cups 🍳 & **Pies** 🥧 Breakfasts and/or dinners are particularly special. For full details see page 12.

Rosettes ◉ The AA's award for food excellence. For full details see page 12.

❷ Designator

For full details see page 11.

❸ Address details

❹ Contact details

For further details see page 8.

❺ Map reference

Map page number followed by a 2-figure National Grid reference. For full details see page 8.

❻ Directions

Brief details of how to find the pub.

❼ Opening times

The opening times of the establishment and, if appropriate, the dates when it might be closed for business.

Bar meals 🍴

The times and days when bar food can be ordered.

Restaurant 🍽

The times and days when restaurant food can be ordered. Please note that last orders can vary by up to 30 minutes.

❽ Rooms

Bedroom information is only shown if the accommodation has been rated by the AA. For full details see page 8.

Prices

These are indications only. Please check before booking. Charges shown are per night unless otherwise stated. **S** (single): Bed & breakfast per person per night. **D** (double): Bed & breakfast for 2 people sharing a room.

❾ Facilities

For further details see page 8.

❿ Notes

Details relating to the pub's status, children, dogs, number of wines by the glass and beer festivals. For further details see page 8.

⓫ Description

Includes background information, beers and drinks, the eating options and, where relevant, information about the accommodation.

⓬ Recommended in the area

Local places of interest, activities and potential day trips.

The Old Passage Inn

★ ★ ★ ★ ⊛⊛ 🍴 RESTAURANT WITH ROOMS

Address: Passage Rd, ARLINGHAM, GL2 7JR
Tel: 01452 740547
Email: oldpassage@btconnect.com
Website: www.theoldpassage.com
Map ref: 2 SO71 **Directions:** A38 onto B4071
through Arlingham to river **Open:** 10-3 7-finish
🍴 **L** Tue-Sat 12-2, Sun 12-3 **D** Tue-Sat 7-9 🍴 **L** Tue-Sat
12-2, Sun 12-3 **D** Tue-Sat 7-9 Booking required in bar &
restaurant **Closed:** 25 Dec, Jan-Feb Tue & Wed eve, Sun
eve & Mon **Rooms:** 3 en suite
S £60-£130 **D** £80-£130 **Facilities:** Garden Parking
Wi-fi **Notes:** ⊞ FREE HOUSE ⁙ ⁙ ☗ 12

The 'old passage' in the name refers to the ford and later ferry service that crossed the River Severn here. The rich harvest of salmon and elvers that once came from the river is now sadly depleted, but chef Mark Redwood's seafood menu features local, sustainable ingredients, such as freshwater crayfish, whenever possible. Fresh lobster from Pembrokeshire (sometimes from Cornwall) is always available from the tank, and freshly shucked oysters and fruits de mer are specialities. The simple but innovative menus often change daily to reflect what is available, but might include such dishes as roast tranche of turbot served with parsley new potatoes and hollandaise. The large dining room has a fresh and airy appeal, and in summer you can eat out on the garden terrace, with views across a bend in the river towards Newnham-on-Severn and the distant Forest of Dean. The three stunning en suite bedrooms enjoy the same views and enable guests to enjoy not only an exceptional breakfast, but also take full advantage of the excellent wine list at dinner, which includes plenty of half bottles and wines by the glass, and features wines from the Three Choirs Vineyard at Newent.

Recommended in the area
Wildfowl & Wetlands Trust, Slimbridge; Owlpen Manor; Berkeley Castle

Key to symbols

★	Black stars (see page 10)	
★	Red Stars (see page 10)	
★	Yellow Stars (see page 10)	
%	Hotel Merit Score	
⊛	AA Rosette (see page 12)	
🍴	Breakfast Award in Guest Accommodation scheme	
🍴	Dinner Award in Guest Accommodation scheme	
3 TQ28	Map reference	
S	Single room	
D	Double room
⁙	Children allowed
⁙	Dogs allowed
Wi-fi	Wireless network connection
🍴	Bar meals
🍴	Restaurant meals
L	Lunch
D	Dinner
⊞	Pub status (Chain or Free House)
☗ 30	Number of wines available by the glass
🍺	Beer festival

How to use the guide continued

Contact details

The pub address includes a locator or place name in capitals (e.g. NORWICH). Within each county, entries are ordered alphabetically first by this place name and then by the name of the establishment.

Telephone numbers, e-mail and website addresses are given where available and are believed correct at the time of going to press but changes may occur. The latest establishment details can be found at **theAA.com**.

Map reference

Each establishment is given a map reference – the map page number and two-figure map reference based on the National Grid.

For example: **Map 5 SU48**
5 refers to the page number of the map section at the back of the guide
SU is the National Grid lettered square (representing 100,000sq metres) in which the location will be found
4 is the figure reading across the top and bottom of the map page
8 is the figure reading down each side of the map page
Maps locating each establishment and a route planner are available at **theAA.com**.

Rooms

Room information is only shown where accommodation has been inspected by the AA. The number of letting bedrooms with a bath or shower en suite are indicated. Bedrooms that have a private bathroom adjacent may be included as en suite. Further details on private bathroom and en suite provision may also be included in the description.

Always phone in advance to ensure that the establishment has the room facilities that you require.

Facilities

This section lists a selection of facilities offered by the pub such as garden details or children's play area. If you have young children it may be worth checking what facilities are available.

Additional facilities, such Wi-fi, or notes about other services (e.g. if credit card details are not accepted) may be listed here.

Parking is listed if available. Other types of parking (on road or Park and Ride) may also be possible; check the descriptions for further information. Phone the establishment in advance of your arrival if unsure.

Notes

This section provides specific details relating to:

Pub Status:

⊕ This symbol is followed by text that indicates the name of the brewery to which the pub is tied or the company which owns it, or where the pub is a free house and independently owned and run.

Children:

ⁱ⁺ This indicates that the pub is child friendly and might provide a children's menu or portions, a play room area or a family room.

Dogs:

🐕 All establishments should accept assist/guide dogs. (Under the Equality Act 2010 access should be allowed for guide dogs and assistance dogs). Some places that do accept dogs may restrict the size and breed, where dogs are allowed on the premises, and the rooms into which they can be taken. Please check the policy when booking.

Wines:

♉ This indicates the number of wines available by the glass.

Beer festivals:

◀ This indicates that the pub organises a beer festival.

Complaints

Readers who have any cause to complain about accommodation, food and drink or service are urged to do so on the spot. This should provide an opportunity for the proprietor to correct matters. If a personal approach fails in connection with accommodation, readers can write to the editor of the guide at AA Lifestyle Guides, Fanum House, Basingstoke, Hants RG21 4EA.

The AA may at its sole discretion investigate any complaints received from guide users for the purpose of making any necessary amendments to the guide. The AA will not in any circumstances act as a representative or negotiator or undertake to obtain compensation or enter into any correspondence or deal with the matter in any other way whatsoever. The AA will not guarantee to take any specific action.

AA Ratings

Star ratings shown in Britain's Best Pub guide indicate where the accommodation available has been inspected by the AA under either its Guest Accommodation or Hotel Schemes.

Guest Accommodation and Hotel Schemes

The AA inspects and rates establishments under two different accommodation schemes. Guest houses, B&Bs, farmhouses, inns and restaurants with rooms are rated under the Guest Accommodation Scheme and hotels are rated under the Hotel Scheme. Establishments recognised by the AA pay an annual fee according to the rating and the number of bedrooms. This rating is not transferable if an establishment changes hands.

Common standards

A few years ago, the accommodation inspection organisations (The AA, VisitBritain, VisitScotland and VisitWales) undertook extensive consultation with consumers and the hospitality industry which resulted in new quality standards for rating establishments. Guests can now be confident that a star-rated B&B or a hotel anywhere in the UK and Ireland will offer consistent quality and facilities.

The system of ratings also uses descriptive designators to classify the establishment – see the opposite page for a fuller explanation.

★ Stars

AA Stars classify accommodation at five levels of quality, from one at the simplest, to five at the highest level of quality in the scheme.

★ Red stars highlight the best hotels in each star rating category within the AA Hotel Scheme.

☆ Yellow stars indicate that the accommodation in the Guest Accommodation Scheme is in the top ten per cent of its star rating. Yellow stars only apply to 3, 4 and 5 star establishments.

Check **theAA.com** for up-to-date information and current ratings.

The inspection process

Establishments applying for AA recognition are visited by a qualified AA accommodation inspector as a mystery guest. Inspectors stay overnight to make a thorough test of the accommodation, food and hospitality. After paying the bill the following morning, they identify themselves and ask to be shown around the premises. The inspector completes a full report, resulting in a recommendation for the appropriate star rating. After this first visit, the establishment will receive an annual visit to check that standards are maintained. If it changes hands, the new owners must re-apply for a rating.

Guests can expect to find the following minimum standards at all levels:

- Pleasant and helpful welcome and service, and sound standards of housekeeping and maintenance
- Comfortable accommodation equipped to modern standards
- Bedding and towels changed for each new guest, and at least weekly if the room is taken for a long stay
- Adequate storage, heating, lighting and comfortable seating
- A sufficient hot water supply at reasonable times
- A full cooked breakfast. (If this is not provided, the fact must be advertised and a substantial continental breakfast must be offered.)

Designators
(Guest Accommodation)

All AA rated guest accommodation is given one of six descriptive designators to help potential guests understand the different types of accommodation available in Britain.

INN: Traditional inns often have a cosy bar, convivial atmosphere, good beer and pub food. Those listed in the guide will provide breakfast in a suitable room, and should also serve light meals during licensing hours. The character of the properties vary according to whether they are country inns or town establishments. Check arrival times as these may be restricted to opening hours.

B&B: Accommodation is provided in a private house run by the owner and with no more than six guests. There may be restricted access to the establishment particularly in the late morning and the afternoon.

GUEST HOUSE: Provides for more than six paying guests and usually offers more services than a B&B, for example dinner, which may be served by staff as well as the owner. London prices tend to be higher than outside the capital, and normally only bed and breakfast is provided, although some establishments do provide a full meal service. Check on the service and facilities offered before booked as details may change during the currency of this guide.

FARMHOUSE: A farmhouse usually provides good value B&B or guesthouse accommodation and excellent home cooking on a working farm or smallholding. Sometimes the land has been sold and only the house remains, but many are working farms and some farmers are happy to allow visitors to look around, or even to help feed the animals. However,

you should always exercise care and never leave children unsupervised.

The farmhouses are listed under towns or villages, but do ask for directions when booking.

RESTAURANT WITH ROOMS: These restaurants offer overnight accommodation with the restaurant being the main business and open to non-residents. The restaurant usually offers a high standard of food service, and often has been awarded an AA Rosette.

GUEST ACCOMMODATION: Establishments that meet the minimum entry requirements are eligible for this designator.

Designators (Hotels)

All AA rated hotels are given a descriptive designator to identify the different types of hotel available.

HOTEL: The majority of establishments in this guide come under the category of Hotel.

TOWN HOUSE HOTEL: A small, individual city or town centre property, which provides a high degree or personal service and privacy

COUNTRY HOUSE HOTEL: These may vary in size and are located in a rural area.

SMALL HOTEL: Has less than 20 bedrooms and is managed by its owner.

AA Rosette Awards

Out of the many thousands of restaurants in the UK, the AA identifies some 2,000 as the best. The following is an outline of what to expect from restaurants with AA Rosette Awards. For a more detailed explanation of Rosette criteria please see **theAA.com**

⊚ Excellent local restaurants serving food prepared with care, understanding and skill, using good quality ingredients.

⊚⊚ The best local restaurants, which aim for and achieve higher standards, better consistency and where a greater precision is apparent in the cooking. There will be obvious attention to the selection of quality ingredients.

⊚⊚⊚ Outstanding restaurants that demand recognition well beyond their local area.

⊚⊚⊚⊚ Amongst the very best restaurants in the British Isles, where the cooking demands national recognition.

⊚⊚⊚⊚⊚ The finest restaurants in the British Isles, where the cooking stands comparison with the best in the world.

♨ Egg cups and ⌣ pies

Awarded only to establishments rated in the AA's Guest Accommodation Scheme.

These symbols indicate that in the AA's opinion the breakfasts and/or dinners at this establishment are really special, and have an emphasis on freshly prepared local ingredients.

⁀ Children
Child-friendly pubs have a symbol at the end of the entry under Notes. When booking a meal you would be advised to check that children are welcome.

⁀ Dogs
Some establishments that accept dogs may restrict the size and breed of dogs permitted. Under the Equality Act 2010 access should be allowed for guide dogs and assistance dogs.

Facilities for disabled guests
The Equality Act 2010 provides legal rights for disabled people including access to goods, services and facilities, and means that service providers may have to consider making adjustments to their premises. For more information about the Act see: www.equalities.gov.uk. or www.direct.gov.uk/en/DisabledPeople/RightsAndObligations/DisabilityRights/DG_4001068

The establishments in this guide should be aware of their obligations under the Act. We recommend that you always phone in advance to ensure that the establishment you have chosen has appropriate facilities.

Fire precautions and safety
Many of the establishments listed in the guide are subject to the requirements of the Fire Precautions Act of 1971. All establishments should display details of how to summon assistance in the event of an emergency at night.

Smoking regulations
Smoking in public areas is banned in England, Scotland and Wales. Many pubs provide an outdoor covered area or outbuilding for smokers. The proprietor can designate one or more bedrooms with ventilation systems where the occupants can smoke, but communal areas must be smoke-free.

theAA.com
Go to theAA.com to find more AA listed guest houses, hotels, pubs and restaurants – there are around 12,000 establishments on the site.

- The AA's easy-to-use route planner in on the home page.

- Simply enter your postcode and the establishment postcode given in this guide and click 'See your Route'. You will have a detailed route plan to take you from door-to-door.

- Use the Travel section to search, either by name or location, for Hotels, B&Bs and Restaurants and Pubs.

Bank and Public Holidays 2012

New Year's Day	1st January
New Year's Holiday	3rd January (Scotland)
Good Friday	6th April
Easter Monday	9th April
Early May Bank Holiday	7th May
Spring Bank Holiday	4th June
Diamond Jubilee Holiday	5th June
August Holiday	6th August (Scotland)
Summer Bank Holiday	27th August
St Andrew's Day (Scotland)	30th November
Christmas Day	25th December
Boxing Day	26th December

Why not spend less and relax more on UK breaks?

cottages4you
property ref: GRL

Make AA Travel your first destination and you're on the way to a more relaxing short break or holiday.

AA Members and customers can get great deals on accommodation, from B&Bs to farmhouses, inns and hotels.

You can also save up to 10% at cottages4you, enjoy a 5% discount with Hoseasons, and up to 60% off the very best West End shows.

Thinking of going further afield?

Check out our attractive discounts on car hire, airport parking, ferry bookings, travel insurance and much more.

Then simply relax.

These are just some of our well-known partners:

Visit theAA.com/travel

ENGLAND

River Duddon, Lake District National Park

Berkshire

The Goring Gap

The Hinds Head

◎◎

Address: High St, BRAY, Maidenhead, SL6 2AB
Tel: 01628 626151
Email: info@hindsheadbray.com
Website: www.hindsheadbray.com
Map ref: 3 SU97 **Directions:** M4 junct 8/9 take
Maidenhead Central exit. Next rdbt take Bray/
Windsor exit. 0.5m, B3028 to Bray
Open: all wk 🍴 🍽 **L** Mon-Sat 12-2.30, Sun 12-4
D Mon-Sat 6.30-9.30
Closed: 25 Dec
Facilities: Parking
Notes: ⊕ FREE HOUSE ♦♦ ♟ 15

Some say it was a royal hunting lodge, others that it was built for the Abbot of Cirencester. But that was long ago and today there is no doubt about the role of this 15th-century building, a hostelry for 400 years, and neighbour of Heston Blumenthal's world famous Fat Duck restaurant. Heston owns this too but, contrary to what you might expect given his celebrity, the Hinds Head remains a village local, albeit one that is highly regarded and with a string of accolades to boot. Inside, oak panelling and sturdy beams confirm its Tudor origins, while leather chairs and real fires supply the modern, day-to-day comforts. The main dining area is on the ground floor, as are the bar and several little alcoves; upstairs are two private dining rooms.

Heston's kitchen offers modern, traditional and historic British dishes on daily-changing menus, with some, such as powdered goose, mutton ham, oxtail and kidney pudding, and the intriguing-sounding quaking pudding dessert, inspired by his time spent with food historians, in part at the Tudor kitchens of Hampton Court Palace. Alongside a list of wines from around the world are beers from Britain, including Marlow's Rebellion brewery's IPA, Czech Pilsner Urquell and Stargazer Somerset cider.

Recommended in the area

Cliveden (NT), Taplow; Windsor; Dorney Court, Eton

The Chequers Brasserie

Address: Dean Ln, COOKHAM DEAN, SL6 9BQ
Tel: 01628 481232
Email: info@chequersbrasserie.co.uk
Website: www.chequersbrasserie.co.uk
Map ref: 3 SU88
Directions: From A4094 in Cookham High St
towards Marlow, over rail line. 1m on right
Open: all day all wk 11-11 🍴 **L** Mon-Sat 12-2.30,
Sun 12-9.30 **D** Mon-Thu 6.30-9.30, Fri-Sat 6.30-10,
Sun 12-9.30
Facilities: Garden Parking Wi-fi
Notes: ⊕ FREE HOUSE ⚑ ♟ 14

The Chequers is a popular gastro-pub in this pretty Thames Valley village, where *Wind in the Willows* author Kenneth Grahame spent his childhood, and where artist Stanley Spencer was born and spent most of his working life. Both would have been familiar with the encompassing wooded hills and Victorian and Edwardian villas surrounding the village green. Open the pub door to the small intimate bar area and you are greeted by oak beams, maybe an open fire, comfortable seating and real ales from Marlow's Rebellion and Adnams breweries, and Cotswold Brewing's speciality lagers. Dining takes place in either the main part of the building, the Conservatory, a private dining room or outside on the small lawned area. A good-value lunch blackboard lists dishes such as free-range Cumberland spiced sausages with Cheddar-mashed potato and onion gravy. The main and specials menus change regularly to feature warm salad of smoked chicken, chorizo and black pudding topped with soft-poached duck egg; seared calves' liver and smoked bacon with sage-mashed potato, caramelised baby onions and red wine sauce; and dressed Cornish crab with Marie Rose sauce, and lemon and dill mayonnaise. The all-day Sunday roast has been claimed to be the best in Berkshire.

Recommended in the area

Cliveden (NT); Burnham Beeches; Bekonscot Model Village

The Queen's Arms Country Inn

★★★★ INN

Address: EAST GARSTON, RG17 7ET

Tel: 01488 648757

Email: info@queensarmshotel.co.uk

Map ref: 3 SU37

Directions: M4 junct 14, 4m onto A338 to Great Shefford, then East Garston

Open: all day all wk 🍺 🍴 **L** all wk 12-2.30 **D** all wk 6.30-9.30

Rooms: 8 en suite (1 GF)

Facilities: Garden Parking Wi-fi

Notes: ⊕ FREE HOUSE 🚶 🐴

Situated in a picturesque village this inn evokes a bygone era and England's rural traditions. There are warm and welcoming bars full of locals, many of whom have links to the horseracing industry which continues to thrive in the Lambourn Valley. The food, created by head chef Gary Burns, is made from the freshest seasonal produce available, with the constantly evolving menus offering such innovative dishes as pan-seared sea trout with crushed truffle purple potatoes and caviar cream; spiced loin of venison with cauliflower and almond purée; roast partridge crown and braised legs, red cabbage, game chips and bread sauce. Much of the ingredients is sourced from the surrounding farms so you're just as likely to bump into the

farmer who produced the beef as you are the stalker who supplied the venison. Don't overlook the desserts – perhaps jam roly poly and custard; or rice pudding with mulled winter fruits. A range of local and task ales are proudly offered alongside a list of interesting and good value wines. The terrace and large garden are popular in the warmer months. Horses almost outnumber people in this area, so why not spend a day riding on the country bridleways?

Recommended in the area

Uffington White Horse; Ashdown House (NT); Ridgeway National Trail

The Swan Inn

★★★★ ⛉ ⛵ INN

Address: Craven Rd, Lower Green, Inkpen,
HUNGERFORD, RG17 9DX **Tel:** 01488 668326
Email: enquiries@theswaninn-organics.co.uk
Website: www.theswaninn-organics.co.uk
Map ref: 3 SU36 **Directions:** S on High St, past rail
bridge, left to Hungerford Common, right signed Inkpen
Open: all wk 12-2.30 7-10 (Sat 12-11 Sun 12-4)
🍴 **L** all wk 12-2 **D** Mon-Sat 7-9.30 🍽
L Wed-Sun 12-2.30 **D** Wed-Sat 7-9.30
Closed: 25-26 Dec **Rooms:** 10 en suite **S** £70-£80
D £85-£105 **Facilities:** Garden Parking Wi-fi
Notes: ⊕ FREE HOUSE 👥

Organic beef farmers Mary and Bernard Harris
preside over this rambling award-winning 17th-
century free house, which stands in fine walking
country just below Combe Gibbet and Walbury
Hill. An attractive terraced garden sets the scene
for alfresco summer dining, in contrast to the
heavily beamed interior with its old photographic
prints and open winter fires. Almost everything
on the menu is prepared using their own fresh
produce; meats – 100% organic and butchered on
the premises – can be bought from the farm shop.
The bar offers well kept ales and traditional English
favourites, with beef and classic Italian dishes. Fresh
pasta and bread are cooked daily on the premises,
and even the wine is organic. Try perhaps Cozze
in Crema – mussels in white wine, cream, onion
and garlic; or home-made smooth chicken liver
pâté to start, followed by one of the Inkpen Beef
inspired dishes - chilli con carne; beef Strogonoff;
or homemade sausages to name but three. Then
there's beer battered cod and chips; ricotta and
spinach cannelloni; mixed seafood risotto; and Thai
green curry among the many other choices. There is
a farm shop and butchery attached to the pub (Soil
Association registered), and en suite bedrooms are
available.

Recommended in the area

Kennet and Avon Canal; Newbury Racecourse;
Avebury Stone Circle

The Dundas Arms

Address: 53 Station Rd, KINTBURY, Hungerford, RG17 9UT
Tel: 01488 658263
Email: info@dundasarms.co.uk
Website: www.dundasarms.co.uk
Map ref: 3 SU36
Directions: M4 junct 13, A34 to Newbury, A4 towards Hungerford, left to Kintbury. Pub 1m
Open: all wk 11-2.30 6-11 🍽 🍽 **L** Mon-Sat 12-2 **D** Tue-Sat 7-9
Closed: 25 & 31 Dec, Sun eve
Facilities: Parking
Notes: ⊕ FREE HOUSE ⏱

When an inn with a 200-year history has been in the same family for more than 45 years, it seems reasonable to conclude that it has discovered the formula for success. The family in question is the Dalzell-Pipers and current landlord David Piper has worked and cooked here throughout that near-half century. The pub stands by a lock on the now fully restored Kennet and Avon Canal, and the River Kennet itself, making it an ideal spot for an hour or two's gongoozling (that is, idly watching expert and not so expert boatcraft) over lunch or dinner on the river patio. The simple elegance of the restaurant has been likened to that of a French auberge and, as in such establishments, you can expect fresh, locally sourced food, examples here being baked salmon with fennel and saffron risotto; steak and kidney pie; fried calves' liver with crispy bacon and mash; roast Creedy Carver duck breast with cider and apple sauce; and spinach and red pepper lasagne. An extensive, worldwide wine list shows a clear fondness for bins from France, while the bar offers a selection of real ales and a good choice of food from the blackboard.

Recommended in the area

Antique shops in Hungerford; Highclere Castle & Gardens; Living Rainforest, Hampstead Norris

Buckinghamshire

South African monument, Ellesborough

The Crooked Billet

Address: 2 Westbrook End, Newton Longville,
nr BLETCHLEY, MK17 0DF
Tel: 01908 373936 **Email:** john@thebillet.co.uk
Website: www.thebillet.co.uk
Map ref: 3 SP83 **Directions:** M1 junct 13, follow
signs to Buckingham. 6m, signed at Bottledump rdbt
to Newton Longville **Open:** noon-2.30 5-11 (Sun
noon-4 7-10.30) ㋡ **L** Tue-Sat 12-2, Sun 12-4
D Mon-Sat 7-9 ㋡ **L** Tue-Sat 12-2, Sun 12-4 **D** Mon-
Fri 7-9.30, Sat 6.30-10 **Closed:** 27-28 Dec, Mon L
Facilities: Garden Parking
Notes: ⊕ GREENE KING ⋔ ☗ 200

While it retains much traditional charm, with original oak beams, open log fires and a large garden, the top attraction is the food and wine offered by husband-and-wife team John and Emma Gilchrist. Emma's weekly-changing menus are based on the finest ingredients, local when possible, and the suppliers are all acknowledged in print. On offer is a range of sandwiches, wraps, burgers and goodies on toast, and a seven-course 'whole table only' tasting menu. Falling somewhere between these two extremes are main menu starters of garlic roasted hand-dived scallops with butternut squash purée, crisp sage and lardons; house-cured sliced duck breast, pecorino shavings, white honey truffle, purple fig and thyme. Then might come mild monkfish and king prawn curry, lemon and coriander rice with onion fritter; or overnight roasted crispy pork belly braised Puy lentils, tarragon and baby onions. Desserts include Muscat poached pear, tonka bean ice cream and a bar of 'Fruit & Nut'; or apple, blackberry and almond tart, rosehip flavoured custard with blackberry ice cream. The cheese board has won heaps of awards, as has John Gilchrist for compiling 'best wine' lists, including his 300-bin selection here.

Recommended in the area

Woburn Abbey; Bletchley Park; Leighton Buzzard Railway

The Royal Oak

Address: Frieth Rd, BOVINGDON GREEN, Marlow, SL7 2JF

Tel: 01628 488611

Email: info@royaloakmarlow.co.uk

Website: www.royaloakmarlow.co.uk

Map ref: 3 SU88

Directions: A4155 from Marlow. 300yds right signed Bovingdon Green. 0.75m, pub on left

Open: all day all wk 11-11 (Sun 12-10.30)

L Mon-Fri 12-2.30, Sat 12-3, Sun 12-4

D Sun-Thu 6.30-9.30, Fri-Sat 6.30-10

Closed: 26 Dec **Facilities:** Garden Parking Wi-fi

Notes: SALISBURY PUBS LTD 22

Drive up the hill out of Marlow and you'll soon come across this old whitewashed pub. Sprawling gardens, fragrant kitchen herbs and a sunny terrace suggest that it is well looked after. Red kites, which were re-introduced to the Chilterns in 1989, frequently soar majestically overhead. The interior is both spacious and cosy, with a snug with wood-burning stove, a rose-red dining room and rich dark floorboards. Plush fabrics and heritage colours create a warm background for the early evening regulars gathered around a cryptic crossword, or playing a tense game of cards. The imaginative British food is a big draw, not least because it derives from fresh, seasonal and, as far as possible, local produce. Fish, of course, has to travel, but a belief in good food ethics means choosing new and interesting varieties from sustainable sources. Other menu suggestions might include veal and rosemary sausage casserole with Boston baked beans; and crispy pork belly with pig's cheeks on sticky red cabbage and cider gravy. Real ales from Rebellion Brewery in Marlow Bottom keep beer miles to a minimum.

Recommended in the area

Cliveden (NT); Burnham Beeches; Hughenden Manor (NT)

The Swan Inn

Address: Village Rd, DENHAM, UB9 5BH
Tel: 01895 832085
Email: info@swaninndenham.co.uk
Website: www.swaninndenham.co.uk
Map ref: 3 TQ08
Directions: A40 onto A412. 200yds follow 'Denham village' sign. Through village, over bridge, last pub on left
Open: all day all wk 11-11 (Sun 12-10.30)
⅃ **L** Mon-Fri 12-2.30, Sat 12-3, Sun 12-4
D Sun-Thu 6.30-9.30, Fri-Sat 6.30-10
Closed: 26 Dec **Facilities:** Garden Parking Wi-fi
Notes: ⊕ SALISBURY PUBS LTD 🍴 🐕 🍷 22

The Swan is probably everyone's idea of the traditional country inn – Georgian, double-fronted and covered in wisteria. The surprise, though, is that the secluded village of Denham is really no distance at all from the bright lights of both London and its premier airport at Heathrow. The interior is cosily welcoming, with a large log fire and pictures picked up at local auctions, while outside is a sunny terrace, and gardens large enough to lose the children in (only temporarily, of course). Though The Swan is still very much a pub, the quality of the food is a great attraction, with fresh, seasonal produce underpinning a menu that reinvigorates some old favourites and makes the most of market availability with daily specials. For a starter or light meal look to the 'small plates' section, where you'll find Marlow Rebellion (a local beer) steamed mussels with garlic herbs and onion rye bread; and pan-fried balsamic chicken livers on 'eggy bread' brioche with crispy pancetta. Among the main meals there is plenty of variety, from slow-cooked Chiltern lamb shoulder on smoked potato mash to Indian-spiced mackerel.

Recommended in the area

Burnham Beeches; Cliveden (NT); Dorney Court

The Black Horse

Address: Windmill Ln, FULMER, SL3 6HD
Tel: 01753 663183
Email: info@blackhorsefulmer.co.uk
Website: www.blackhorsefulmer.co.uk
Map ref: 3 SU98
Directions: A40 E of Gerrards Cross. Follow
Fulmer/Wexham signs. Pub in 1.5m
Open: all day all wk 🍴🍽️ **L** Mon-Fri 12-2.30,
Sat 12-3, Sun 12-4 **D** Sun-Thu 6.30-9.30, Fri-Sat
6.30-10 **Closed:** 26 Dec
Facilities: Garden Parking Wi-fi
Notes: ⊕ SALISBURY PUBS LTD 🧍 🐾 🍷 22

A simple village pub, as it has been for some four centuries. But being just a village pub is no guarantee of success these days, so what's on offer here? For a start, its atmosphere is seductive. It's warm and comfortable, with bars that make you feel you belong, and a warren of little rooms filled with antique furniture and pictures from local salerooms, set off by rich Zoffany fabrics and heritage colours. The dining room is tucked away at the back, and there's a delightful garden. And of course, there's the food, British Colonial in style, such as Buckinghamshire pheasant with white pudding and apple parcel, celeriac purée and elderberry jus; pan-roasted coley fillet with braised fennel and creamy vermouth sauce; chicken and ham pie, kale colcannon and pearl onion jus; grilled Tamworth pork loin chop with tomato, harissa and haricot bean ragout. Game comes from around Marlow and the chefs themselves often forage for other local produce, beginning in the spring with wild garlic. And for vegetarians there could be Indian spiced butternut squash, aubergine and cauliflower with basmati rice. And last, but by no means least, are the wines, all European, but still offering a good choice, and the imaginative spirits selection.

Recommended in the area

Cliveden (NT); Bekonscot Model Village & Railway; Chiltern Open Air Museum

The Nags Head

★★★★ ◉ INN

Address: London Rd, GREAT MISSENDEN, HP16 0DG
Tel: 01494 862200
Email: goodfood@nagsheadbucks.com
Website: www.nagsheadbucks.com
Map ref: 3 SP80
Directions: N of Amersham on A413, left at Chiltern
hospital into London Rd signed Great Missenden
Open: all day all wk ⓑ ⓘⓞⓘ Booking required
L Mon-Sat 12-2.30, Sun 12-3.30 **D** all wk 6.30-9.30
Rooms: 5 en suite **S** £80-£120 **D** £90-£130
Facilities: Garden Parking Wi-fi
Notes: ⓦ FREE HOUSE ⓘ ⓡ ♈ 19

Situated in the valley of the River Missbourne in the glorious Chilterns, the inn is ideally situated within walking distance of the picturesque village of Great Missenden, yet near major road and rail networks. The inn has been appointed to a high standard, retaining the many original 15th-century features including low oak beams and a large inglenook fireplace, plus a large garden. The building comprises an award-winning gastro-pub and restaurant together with beautifully furnished double and twin bedrooms. The Nags Head has played host to a variety of TV series and has been visited by many famous names, including prime ministers and the children's author Roald Dahl; a replica of the inn featured in the film animation of his book *Fantastic Mr Fox*. The English and French fusion dishes on the extensive menu, and daily specials board, use the highest quality, locally sourced produce whenever possible; expect home-smoked fish, saddle of lamb from a nearby farm, and locally made cheeses. To accompany, there's a carefully selected, global wine list, as well as beers and local ales on tap.

Recommended in the area

Roald Dahl Museum; Bekonscot Model Village; Whipsnade Zoo

The Hand & Flowers

@@@

Address: 126 West St, MARLOW, SL7 2BP
Tel: 01628 482277
Email: theoffice@thehandandflowers.co.uk
Website: www.thehandandflowers.co.uk
Map ref: 3 SU88 **Directions:** M4 junct 9, A404
to Marlow, A4155 towards Henley-on-Thames. Pub
on right **Open:** 12-2.30 6.30-9.30 (Sun 12-3.30)
 L Mon-Sat 12-2.30 **D** Mon-Sat 6.30-9.30 **L** all
wk 12-2.30 **D** all wk 6.30-9.30 Booking required for
all times **Closed:** 24-26 Dec, 1 Jan dinner, Sun eve
Facilities: Garden Parking Wi-fi
Notes: ⊕ GREENE KING ♦♦ ♟ 11

Seven years ago, Tom and Beth Kerridge reopened
this 18th-century, whitewashed pub just outside
Marlow, and there seems to be no stopping its
progress. The interior is an easygoing combination
of flagstone floors, beams, exposed stone walls,
neutral colours, leather banquettes and cloth-
free tables. Tom is the chef, and he's frequently in
the spotlight for his regularly changing, seasonal
menus of simple yet elegant modern British and
rustic French food. Among dishes which have
helped him earn three AA Rosettes are starters
of crayfish Scotch egg or truffled pork terrine with
toasted sour dough, and main course favourites
of slow cooked duck breast with Savoy cabbage,
duck fat chips and gravy, Weymouth plaice with
sweetcorn purée, girolles, brown shrimps and
Chablis shallots, or cutlet of lamb with lamb breast
and caramel poached chicory. Round off with tonka
bean pannacotta with mango and Pedro Ximenez
jelly, or passionfruit and white chocolate trifle. The
famous set lunch typically offers cream of celeriac
soup, followed by cassoulet and blackberry fool with
bramble jelly, while on Sundays there are roasts.
Two of the four stylish cottage suites have private
terraces with hot tubs.
AA Restaurant of the Year 2011-12.

Recommended in the area

Cliveden (NT); Burnham Beeches;
Hughenden Manor (NT)

The Old Queens Head

Address: Hammersley Ln, PENN, HP10 8EY
Tel: 01494 813371
Email: info@oldqueensheadpenn.co.uk
Website: www.oldqueensheadpenn.co.uk
Map ref: 3 SU99
Directions: From B474 into School Rd, 500yds, left into Hammersley Ln
Open: all day all wk 11-11 (Sun 12-10.30)
 L Mon-Fri 12-2.30, Sat 12-3, Sun 12-4
D Sun-Thu 6.30-9.30, Fri-Sat 6.30-10
Closed: 26 Dec
Facilities: Garden Parking Wi-fi
Notes: SALISBURY PUBS LTD   22

The Old Queens Head exudes bags of character and atmosphere. The Dining Room, originally a barn, dating from 1666, but with several later additions, now provides lots of cosy corners. Many hours have been well spent at local auctions finding sympathetic old furniture and pictures, while warm heritage colours blend with glowing dark floorboards, flagstones, rugs and classic fabrics. Although first and foremost a pub, it is just as ready to serve a light bite at lunchtime, or a fabulous dinner, special occasion or not. There's even free Wi-fi for those who have to work while eating. Experienced staff provide good service and plenty of good old-fashioned hospitality. The food balances classic with modern British, resulting in a menu with plenty of choice, such as Chiltern Hills venison and wild mushroom suet pudding on purple sprouting broccoli with girolle and game jus; and grilled plaice on lemon and thyme risotto with prawn beignet. A sunny terrace overlooks the large garden and the village church of St Margaret's. There are great walks nearby in the ancient beech woodlands.

Recommended in the area
Bekonscot Model Village; West Wycombe; Legoland

The Bull & Butcher

Address: TURVILLE, Henley-on-Thames, RG9 6QU
Tel: 01491 638283
Email: info@thebullandbutcher.com
Website: www.thebullandbutcher.com
Map ref: 3 SU79
Directions: M40 junct 5, follow Ibstone signs. Right at T-junct. Pub 0.25m on left
Open: all day all wk noon-11 (Sat noon-1am)
🛏 Booking required **L** Mon-Fri 12-2.30, Sat 12-3.30 Sun 12-4 **D** Mon-Sat 6-9.30
Facilities: Garden Parking
Notes: ⊕ BRAKSPEAR 👫 🐕 🍷 19

Fans of TV's *The Vicar of Dibley*, *Midsomer Murders* and *Goodnight Mister Tom* may recognise the pretty Chilterns village of Turville, which has often played host to many film crews. And it's not just the village either, because up on Cobstone Hill is the weatherboarded windmill that featured in *Chitty Chitty Bang Bang*. Built in the 16th century and licensed since the early 17th, the pub's two main areas, the Windmill Lounge and the Well Bar, both retain their original beams and large open fires. The 50-foot well is known to have still been in use during the Second World War, but then it was covered and not rediscovered until extension work in 1999. Appearing on the lunch and/or dinner menus might be haddock in real ale batter with mushy peas and fat chips; 'proper' chicken Kiev and skinny chips; homemade salmon fishcake; chargrilled rack of pork, crackling and chorizo roast potatoes; and wild mushroom risotto with fresh Parmesan. Lighter choices include sandwiches, ploughman's and burgers. Brakspear's full range of cask beers is joined by seasonal guests, while on the comprehensive wine list are some good rich reds and dry, fruity whites. Outside are patios and a sizeable garden.

Recommended in the area

Stonor House; The Hell-Fire Caves; Roald Dahl Museum & Story Centre, Great Missenden

Chequers Inn

★ ★ ★ 78% ⊛ HOTEL

Address: Kiln Ln, WOOBURN COMMON,
Beaconsfield, HP10 0JQ
Tel: 01628 529575 **Email:** info@chequers-inn.com
Website: www.chequers-inn.com
Map ref: 3 SU98 **Directions:** M40 junct 2, A40
through Beaconsfield towards High Wycombe. Left into
Broad Ln, signed Taplow/Burnham/Wooburn Common.
2m to pub **Open:** all wk noon-mdnt ⓑ **L** Mon-Fri
12-2.30, Sat 12-10, Sun 12-9.30 **D** Mon-Thu 6-9.30, Fri
6-10, Sat 12-10, Sun 12-9.30 †⊚**| L** all wk 12-2.30
D all wk 7-9.30 **Rooms:** 17 (8 GF) **Facilities:** Garden
Parking Wi-fi **Notes:** ⊕ FREE HOUSE ⋕ 🍷 14

Steeped in history, this family-run 17th-century
coaching inn is idyllically tucked away in The
Chilterns and is only 24 miles from London. With
oak beams, quiet corners and flagstone floors, The
Chequers Inn is a comfortable blend of old and new,
and full of charm and style. The newly refurbished
fine dining restaurant is renowned for its award-
winning classic French and English cuisine, and with
its understated elegance and relaxed ambience,
it is perfect for a quick business lunch or a long
romantic dinner. Fresh, seasonal produce is used
in dishes such as ballotine of foie gras, quince
jelly, green bean salad and toasted brioche; pea
and Taleggio risotto; and monkfish ceviche with
watermelon, avocado, pink grapefruit and light
curry cream followed by pan-fried loin of venison,
beets, pistachio purée, pommes noisettes and port;
cherry tomato tart Tatin, poached duck egg, rocket
and Grano Padano; or steamed fillet of sea bass,
crab risotto, pak choi and star anise butter. Leave
room for a dessert though, perhaps pomegranate,
elderflower and blackberry jelly, clotted cream and
blueberry coulis. There are 17 beautifully appointed
bedrooms so this makes an ideal base to explore
the Thames Valley and the delightful towns of
Henley, Marlow and Windsor.

Recommended in the area

Cliveden (NT); Burnham Beeches; Bekonscot Model
Village

Cambridgeshire

Grasshopper Clock, Corpus Christi College, Cambridge

The Crown Inn

Address: Bridge Rd, BROUGHTON, Huntingdon,
PE28 3AY
Tel: 01487 824428
Email: info@thecrowninnrestaurant.co.uk
Website: www.thecrowninnrestaurant.co.uk
Map ref: 3 TL27
Directions: A141 from Huntingdon towards
Warboys. Left to Broughton
Open: all wk Mon-Sat 11.30-3 6.30-11 (Sun
11.30-8) ﴾ ﴿ **L** all wk 12-2.30 **D** all wk 6.30-9.30
Facilities: Garden Parking
Notes: ⊕ FREE HOUSE ﴾﴿ ﴾﴿ ♟ 10

Horse chestnut trees surround the picturesque grounds of this family-run, 18th-century Grade II listed village pub situated in the hamlet of Broughton. In previous times it was a saddlery, stables and a piggery, but you wouldn't know any of this from the attractive bar and restaurant styled in traditional country pub with contemporary touches, providing a warm, comfortable and homely environment. On sunny days head outside to eat on the patio and enjoy the garden. Simple and hearty perfectly sums up the food ethos here, the kitchen using nothing but the finest, fresh local ingredients. This is complemented by a hand-picked wine list and a well-stocked bar complete with regularly changing guest ales. Since fresh, seasonal food is the best for flavour and quality, dishes are created and the menu changes as required so advantage can be taken of the best available produce. At lunchtime expect Cumberland sausage with mustard mash, Broughton burger, and roasted vegetable and mozzarella lasagne. The main menu might suggest pan-fried peppered duck breast, chargrilled rib-eye steak, or seared sea bass fillet. High levels of personal service makes The Crown the perfect venue for a business meeting dinner, intimate meal or a family get-together.

Recommended in the area

Huntingdon Racecourse; The Raptor Foundation;
St Ives

The Cock Pub and Restaurant

Address: 47 High St, HEMINGFORD GREY,
Huntingdon, PE28 9BJ
Tel: 01480 463609
Email: cock@cambscuisine.com
Website: www.cambscuisine.com
Map ref: 3 TL27
Directions: Between A14 juncts 25 & 26 follow
village signs
Open: all wk 11.30-3 6-11 ⏺ **L** all wk 12-2.30 **D** all
wk 6.15-9.30 **Facilities:** Garden Parking
Notes: ⏺ FREE HOUSE ⏺ ⏺ ⏺ 18 ⏺

Down-to-earth, but passionately run, this pub stands in the heart of a pretty village on the Great Ouse, the UK's fourth longest river. The traditional bar is separate from the bustling, country-style restaurant, and since food is not served in the pub area it is ideal for those who just want a pint of real ale from breweries all within an hour's drive, or village-brewed Cromwell cider. Service in the restaurant is professional and friendly, with food guided by the seasons, fresh and fully prepared on site. Lunchtime might offer beef, cinnamon and chilli stew with butter bean mash, or great sausages made by the chefs onsite. In the evening try a starter of spinach gnocchi, wild mushrooms, pinenuts and ricotta; or roasted fig, walnut and Stilton salad with green peppercorn dressing: then roast duck breast, potato bake, sprouting broccoli, beetroot and blackberries; or, from the daily changing fish board, monkfish with prosciutto, potato rösti, green vegetables, chorizo and red wine sauce. Speaking of wine, many are from the Languedoc, reflecting frequent research visits by the owners and staff. There is a delightful garden for summer dining. The August bank holiday weekend beer festival and barbecue is a cracking event.

Recommended in the area

Imperial War Museum Duxford; Grafham Water;
Houghton Mill (NT)

Christ's College gatehouse, Cambridge

Cheshire

Cholmondeley Castle

The Bhurtpore Inn

Address: Wrenbury Rd, ASTON, Nantwich, CW5 8DQ
Tel: 01270 780917
Email: simonbhurtpore@yahoo.co.uk
Website: www.bhurtpore.co.uk
Map ref: 6 SJ64 **Directions:** Just off A530
between Nantwich & Whitchurch. Turn towards
Wrenbury at x-rds in village
Open: all wk 12-2.30 6.30-11.30 (Fri-Sat 12-12, Sun
12-11) ⓑ ⓘ **L** Mon-Fri 12-2 **D** Mon-Fri 6.30-9.30
(Sat 12-9.30, Sun 12-9)
Closed: 25-26 Dec, 1 Jan
Facilities: Garden Parking
Notes: ⊕ FREE HOUSE ⁑ ⚲ ⓨ 11 ⬛

The George family has a bit of a thing about this
traditional village pub. In 1849 James George leased
it from the local Combermere estate, from which
descendant Philip George bought it in 1895, only
to sell it six years later to a Crewe brewery. Ninety
years later, in 1991, Simon and Nicky George
were looking to buy their first pub and came
across the boarded-up, stripped-out Bhurtpore.
Although it has been a pub since at least 1778, it
was the 1826 Siege of Bhurtpore in India, where
Lord Combermere had distinguished himself,
that inspired its current name. With eleven real
ales always available, a large selection of bottled
beers and seven continental beers on tap, it is
truly a free house. The food is fresh, home made
and reasonably priced, both in the bar and the
restaurant. Starters include spicy lamb samosas,
and pork and black pudding patties with coarse
grain mustard. Finish with spiced raisin and ginger
pudding with toffee sauce. Behind the pub is a lawn
with countryside views. At the centre of the local
community, the pub is home to an enthusiastic
cricket team, a group of cyclists known as the
Wobbly Wheels and folk musicians.

Recommended in the area

Cholmondeley Castle; Historic Nantwich; Stapeley
Water Gardens

The Pheasant Inn

★★★★★ 🍽 INN

Address: BURWARDSLEY, Nr Tattenhall, CH3 9PF
Tel: 01829 770434
Email: info@thepheasantinn.co.uk
Website: www.thepheasantinn.co.uk
Map ref: 6 SJ55
Directions: A41 (Chester to Whitchurch), 4m, left to
Burwardsley. Follow 'Cheshire Workshops' signs
Open: all day all wk 🛏 🍴 **L** all wk (no food Mon 3-6)
D all wk (no food Mon 3-6)
Rooms: 2 en suite (5 GF) **S** £75-£105 **D** £100-£155
Facilities: Garden Parking Wi-fi
Notes: ⊕ FREE HOUSE ⊪ 🐕 🚲

Sitting atop the Peckforton Hills, The Pheasant
enjoys magnificent panoramic views over the
Cheshire Plain. What began life as a sandstone and
half-timbered farmhouse and barn perhaps 300
years ago is nowadays a secluded and sophisticated
gastro-pub that also manages to cater for a passing
trade of walkers. Four real ales, usually drawn
from the local Weetwood Brewery, are always on
tap in the wooden-floored bar as well as a list of
well chosen wines. Drinks can also to be enjoyed
in the stone-flagged conservatory and flower-filled
courtyard and terrace. In winter, vast open fires
warm the cockles of the heart, perhaps quickened
by the racy menus that are strong on produce of
the local estates hereabouts. Various menus cater
for appetites ranging from nibble to blow-out,
with a strong nod to modern British and European
dishes. Choose perhaps a starter of local ham
hock and Cheshire cheese pressing with pommery
mustard dressing, then lemon and thyme encrusted
medallion of pork with dauphinoise potatoes and
mustard jus; or lamb shank served on mustard
mash with a Weetwood Bitter jus. Vegetarians can
enjoy spring onion, chilli and coriander potato cake
with poached egg and glazed hollandaise. Stay
overnight in the stylish accommodation.

Recommended in the area

Beeston Castle; Cheshire Candle Workshops;
Oulton Park

Albion Inn

Address: Park St, CHESTER, CH1 1RN
Tel: 01244 340345
Email: tommiesww1@albioninnchester.co.uk
Website: www.albioninnchester.co.uk
Map ref: 6 SJ46
Directions: In city centre adjacent to Citywalls & Newgate
Open: all wk 12-3, Tue-Fri 5-11, Sat 6-11, Sun 7-10.30, Mon 5.30-11 🛏 🍴 **L** all wk 12-2 **D** Mon-Sat 6-8.30
Closed: 25-26 Dec, 1-2 Jan **Facilities** Wi-fi
Notes: 🍺 PUNCH TAVERNS 🐕

The home fires still burn on winter nights at this living memorial to the Great War of 1914-18. With its splendid cast-iron fireplaces and original three-room layout, the pub is adorned with sepia photographs and prints, whilst leather sofas, enamelled advertisements and vintage artefacts complete the period look. The lounge wallpaper was designed on the first day of the Great War, and other objects of interest include a 1928 Steck Duo Art player piano. The Albion is the creation of Michael Mercer, who has run Chester's last Victorian street corner pub for over 40 years. 'Trench rations' are locally and regionally sourced wherever possible. Lunchtime choices include great British butties, both club and doorstep in concept, while Staffordshire oatcakes with various fillings, make for a lighter snack. Hot dishes range from boiled gammon, pease pudding and parsley sauce; McConichy's corned beef hash with pickled red cabbage; to lamb's liver, bacon and onions in a rich cider gravy; or fish pie with a mash and Parmesan cheese topping. Four cask ales are on tap, backed up by bottled organic cider from Westons, a good range of malts, and a decent list of New World wines. Please note that – in true wartime spirit – this is an adults-only pub. Two en suite bedrooms, and free parking, are available.

Recommended in the area

Roman Wall, Chester; Ness Gardens; Cholmondeley Castle

The Cholmondeley Arms

Address: CHOLMONDELEY, Malpas, SY14 8HN
Tel: 01829 720300
Email: info@cholmondeleyarms.co.uk
Website: www.cholmondeleyarms.co.uk
Map ref: 6 SJ55
Directions: On A49, between Whitchurch &
Tarporley
Open: all day all wk ⬛ **L** all wk 12-9.30
D all wk 12-9.30
Closed: 25 Dec
Facilities: Garden Parking Wi-fi
Notes: ⬤ FREE HOUSE ❖ ⛶ ♟ 10

Set in beautiful Cheshire countryside adjacent to
Cholmondeley Castle, the Cholmondeley Arms is
probably one of England's most unique pubs. It
occupies a former Victorian village schoolhouse
on Lord Cholmondeley's estate. Converted in 1988
it was the first public house on the estate for over
a century. The pub has won many accolades over
the years, building a great reputation for freshly
cooked food. The menu is quintessentially English in
style and includes such favourites as the traditional
pub sharing plate, handcrafted stalkers' venison
pie, and devilled kidneys on toast. In 2011 the
owners completed a wonderful restoration of the
property, and decor is now warm and inviting with
large mirrors, church candles, fresh flowers, open
fireplaces and interesting 'old school' furniture such
as the blackboards featuring the lunchtime specials.
The pub also has six en suite bedrooms situated
in the Headmaster's House opposite. Famous also
for offering over 40 different gins, plus malts, ports
and local ales brewed within a 30-mile radius, the
Cholmondeley Arms is truly a 'real pub', popular
with 'suits', 'Barbours' and a smattering of farmers.

Recommended in the area

Cholmondeley Castle Gardens; The Croccy Trail;
Beeston Castle; The Sandstone Trail

The Davenport Arms

Address: Congleton Rd, MARTON, SK11 9HF
Tel: 01260 224269
Email: enquiries@thedavenportarms.co.uk
Website: www.thedavenportarms.co.uk
Map ref: 6 SJ20
Directions: 3m from Congleton on A34
Open: noon-3 6-mdnt (Fri-Sun noon-mdnt)
 L Tue-Sat 12-2.30, Sun 12-3 **D** Tue-Fri 6-9, Sun
6-8.30 **L** Tue-Fri 12-2.30, Sat 12-9, Sun 12-8
D Tue-Fri 6-9, Sat 12-9, Sun 12-8
Closed: Mon L (ex BH)
Facilities: Garden Parking Wi-fi
Notes: ⊕ FREE HOUSE 9

As hereditary royal foresters, the Davenports once wielded considerable power, including the right to try, convict and execute highwaymen. Trials took place in an upstairs room of this old farm, those found guilty then hanged from a nearby gibbet. Today it's an independent free house with a traditional bar furnished with cushioned settles and leather sofas around a log fire, just the place to enjoy a pint of real ale on offer from a local microbrewery – Storm, Bollington, Howard Town and Brearton to name but a few. Food, right down to the chutneys and sauces, is all freshly made on the premises using locally supplied ingredients. Specials change daily and there's always a good fresh fish selection. Expect haddock with home-made chips; seabass fillets on pea and mint risotto with champagne sauce, braised shank of English lamb, roasted root vegetables, Marsala and rosemary sauce; or seasonal pheasant breast with red wine, bacon and shallot gravy. The large garden contains a discreet play area for children, although they may also want to see the Marton Oak in the village. Looking somewhat ravaged – not surprisingly after more than 1200 years – this is possibly the oldest surviving tree in England.

Recommended in the area

Quarry Bank Mill (NT); Capesthorne Hall (NT); Oulton Park

The Goshawk

Address: Station Rd, MOULDSWORTH, CH3 8AJ
Tel: 01928 740900
Website: www.thegoshawkpub.co.uk
Map ref: 6 SJ57
Directions: A51 from Chester onto A54. Left onto B5393 towards Frodsham. Into Mouldsworth, pub on left
Open: all day all wk noon-11 (Sun noon-10.30)
Closed: 25 Dec & 1 Jan
Facilities: Garden Parking
Notes: ⊕ WOODWARD & FALCONER PUBS ♦♦ ♚ 14

This sturdy old railway inn has a hint of Edwardian grandeur whilst benefitting from contemporary comforts; print-clad walls and dado rails, comfy sofas and open fires. Its village setting makes the most of the area's delights, including the many miles of footpaths, cycle trails and mysterious meres of nearby Delamere Forest, one of the largest in northwest England, whilst historic Chester is just one stop away on the train. The terrace and large grassy beer garden offer views across the heart of Cheshire, and the local motor museum is an interesting diversion. Cheshire ales from Weetwood draw an appreciative crowd of locals, whilst the wide-ranging menu is matched by an extensive wine list. Starters tempt with chicken liver pâté with apple and sultana chutney; and chicken satay with coriander and lime, mains include a wide choice of traditional favourites often with a twist: smoked haddock fillet, poached egg, creamed leeks and potato; chicken stuffed with haggis, wrapped in streaky bacon, with tatties, neeps and whisky cream sauce; and toad-in-the-hole, mash and onion gravy. There's a good range of vegetarian dishes and a choice of 21-day aged steaks. Desserts take in Pimms fruit jelly; banoffee Eton mess; and pear and cherry crumble.

Recommended in the area

Go Ape at Delamere Forest; Mouldsworth Motor Museum; Sail Sports Windsurfing Centre

The Bear's Paw

★★★★★ 🛏 INN

Address: School Ln, WARMINGHAM, CW11 3QN
Tel: 01270 526317
Email: info@thebearspaw.co.uk
Website: www.thebearspaw.co.uk
Map ref: 6 SJ76 **Directions:** M6 junct 18, A54,
A533 towards Sandbach. Follow signs for village
Open: all day all wk 🛏 🍴 **L** Mon-Thu 12-9.30, Fri-Sat
12-10, Sun 12-8 **D** Mon-Thu 12-9.30, Fri-Sat 12-10,
Sun 12-8
Rooms: 17 en suite **S** £79-£120 **D** £99-£140
Facilities: Garden Parking Wi-fi
Notes: 🏠 FREE HOUSE ⛱ 🐾 🍷 10

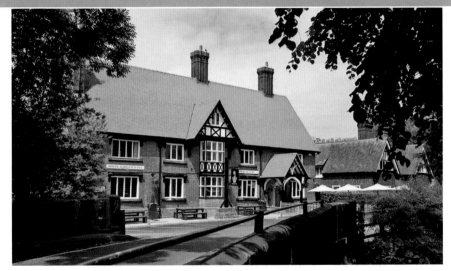

This charming yet stylish 19th-century gastro-pub reaches the heart of the community through the employment of good old-fashioned inn-keeping principles. The warm and friendly atmosphere is enhanced by the reclaimed antique oak flooring, two huge fireplaces surrounded by leather sofas, bookshelves and hundreds of pictures and archive photos lining the oak-panelled walls. The bar serves six real ales from local micro-breweries and a wide choice of wines from around the world. Whether you're sitting out front looking across to the churchyard or in the clubby interior, there is plenty of comfortable dining space in which to sample some wholesome food from a wide-ranging menu that cleverly blends classics with modern twists.

Take starters like ham hock terrine with home-made piccalilli, and main dishes as braised lamb shoulder with mustard mash, minted pea purée and juniper berry sauce; steak and Weetwood ale pie, or 28-day aged Bowland rib-eye steak with hand-cut chips. Great for sharing are the imaginative deli boards, which come laden with local cheeses, charcuterie or pickled and smoked fish. Upstairs, the stylish bedrooms are a real treat, with funky fabrics, contemporary art and wallpaper, and sleek bathrooms with rain showers.

Recommended in the area

Hack Green Secret Nuclear Bunker; Palms Tropical Oasis; Trent and Mersey Canal

Cornwall

Wheal Coates Tin Mine, St Agnes

The Halzephron Inn

Address: GUNWALLOE, Helston, TR12 7QB
Tel: 01326 240406
Email: halzephroninn@tiscali.co.uk
Website: www.halzephron-inn.co.uk
Map ref: 1 SW62
Directions: 3m S of Helston on A3083, right to
Gunwalloe, through village. Inn on left
Open: all wk 11-3 6-11 🍴 🍽 **L** all wk 12-2
D all wk 7-9
Closed: 25 Dec
Facilities: Garden Parking Wi-fi
Notes: 🍺 FREE HOUSE 🚶 ⛺ 🍷 8

The name of this ancient inn derives from 'Als Yfferin', old Cornish for 'cliffs of hell', and this is an appropriate description of its situation on this hazardous but breathtaking stretch of coastline. Once a haunt of smugglers, the pub is located close to the fishing village of Gunwalloe and stands just 300 yards from the famous South Cornwall footpath. The only pub on the stretch between Mullion and Porthleven, today it offers visitors a warm welcome, a wide selection of ales and whiskies, and meals prepared from fresh local produce. These may be served outside, with views of the surrounding fields to the back or the ocean to the front, or inside, in a number of dining areas, from cosy nooks to a separate dining area or a family room (there's a thoughtful junior menu). Lunch and dinner bring a choice of fresh Cornish fare, accompanied by home-made granary or white bread, plus daily-changing specials that might include roast monkfish tail wrapped in bacon on a seafood risotto, or seafood chowder. To follow there may be bread and butter pudding or hot chocolate fudge cake with Cornish cream. There's also a good wine list, with a choice of half-bottles. Dogs are welcome in the bar.

Recommended in the area

Lizard Lighthouse; Tate St Ives; RNAS Culdrose

The Crown Inn

★★★ INN

Address: LANLIVERY, Bodmin, PL30 5BT
Tel: 01208 872707
Email: thecrown@wagtailinns.com
Website: www.wagtailinns.com
Map ref: 1 SX05
Directions: Signed from A390. Follow brown sign approx 1.5m W of Lostwithiel
Open: all day all wk
Rooms: 2 en suite (7 GF)
Facilities: Garden Parking Wi-fi
Notes: ⊕ FREE HOUSE ♦♦ ♠

This charming pub was built in the 12th century for the men constructing St Brevita's church next door. Such great age means everything about it oozes history – its thick stone walls, granite and slate floors, glass-covered well, low beams, open fireplaces and distinctive bread oven. The bar serves beers from Sharps of Rock and Skinners of Truro, and ten wines by the glass from a reasonably priced wine list. With Fowey harbour not far away, the menu will undoubtedly offer fresh crab, scallops, mackerel and more, while other local produce includes meats from a butcher in Par, fruit and vegetables from a local grocer and dairy products from Lostwithiel. At lunchtime, try chef's smoked mackerel pâté, or a proper Cornish pasty. Dinner might begin with an appetiser of marinated olives and ciabatta bread, followed by a starter of locally smoked duck, Cornish charcuterie, or pan-seared scallops. Main courses include Greek-style salad; steaks with chips, onion rings and rocket and Parmesan salad; whole baked sea bass stuffed with lemon and fennel; and Laura's cheesy ratatouille. Some of the comfortable en suite rooms include children's beds, and in some dogs are welcome. The pretty front garden is lovely in warm weather.

Recommended in the area

Restormel Castle; Lanhydrock House (NT); China Clay Country Park

The Bush Inn

Address: MORWENSTOW, Bude, EX23 9SR
Tel: 01288 331242
Website: www.bushinn-morwenstow.co.uk
Map ref: 1 SS21
Directions: Exit A39, 3m N of Kilkhampton, 2nd right into Shop. 1.5m to Crosstown, pub on left
Open: all day all wk 11am-12.30am 🍴 🍽 **L** all wk **D** all wk
Facilities: Garden Parking
Notes: ⋔ ⊶ ♥9 ⬛

Said to be one of Britain's oldest pubs, The Bush Inn was originally built as a chapel in AD 950 for pilgrims en route to Spain. It became a pub some 700 years later and has provided sustenance for visitors for hundreds of years. Smugglers and wreckers were among them, drawn by the inn's dramatic and isolated clifftop location on the north Cornish coast; the views over the Tidna Valley and the Atlantic Ocean are just as stunning as they must have been then. The unspoilt interior features stone-flagged floors, old stone fireplaces, a Celtic piscina carved from serpentine set into a wall behind the cosy bar, and a 'leper's squint' – a tiny window through which the needy could grab scraps of food. Today the meals are very different, with the emphasis on fresh local produce, including beef from the inn's own farm. Local shoots provide the game, and seafood comes from home waters. In winter, warming dishes include red wine and blue cheese risotto and venison stew, all served with Cornish real ales and a variety of fine wines. In summer, diners can enjoy a plate of mussels or beer-battered pollock and chips in the garden. There are three bed and breakfast rooms and self-catering is also available.

Recommended in the area

Clovelly; Morwenstow Church & Hawker's Hut (NT); Boscastle

Driftwood Spars

★★★★ 🍽 GUEST ACCOMMODATION

Address: Trevaunance Cove, ST AGNES, TR5 0RT
Tel: 01872 552428
Email: info@driftwoodspars.co.uk
Website: www.driftwoodspars.co.uk
Map ref: 1 SW75 **Directions:** A30 onto B3285,
through St Agnes, left at Peterville Inn, follow
Trevaunance Cove sign **Open:** all day all wk 11-11
(Fri-Sat 11-1am, 25 Dec 11am-2pm) 🍴 **L** all wk 12-2.30
D all wk 6.30-9.30 (winter 6.30-8.30) 🍽️ **L** Sun 12-2.30
D all wk 7-9, (winter Thu-Sat 7-8.30) **Rooms:** 9 en
suite (5 GF) **S** £45-£66 **D** £86-£102 **Facilities:** Garden
Parking Wi-fi **Notes:** 🌐 FREE HOUSE 🚶 🐕 🍷 35 🍴

Around here the ancient Celtic landscape of
dramatic cliffs, crashing surf, small fields and
moorland abounds with legend and intrigue. Seek
out this family-run pub which occupies a 300-year-
old tin miners' store, chandlery and sail loft,
complete with its own smugglers' tunnel; it takes its
name from spars salvaged from nearby shipwrecks.
This award-winning establishment comprises a
dining room with sea view; two beer gardens; three
bars sparkling with real fires, old brass and lanterns;
a micro-brewery producing ten beers; a shop
and 15 en suite bedrooms. Across the three bars
seven hand-pulled real ales are offered alongside
a 40-bin wine list. On the seasonally changing
menus seafood figures strongly; typical dishes for
the autumn are grilled mackerel fillet with pickled
vegetables and horseradish crème frâiche; or deep
fried whitebait, lemon mayonnaise and rocket salad;
followed by River Exe mussels steamed with garlic,
onion and white wine; fricassée of local rabbit and
fresh egg tagliatelle; or wood pigeon (served rare)
and black pudding salad with mustard dressing.
Desserts shouldn't be overlooked, perhaps warm
saffron bread and butter pudding with vanilla and
clotted cream ice cream, or scoops of Callestick
Farm ice cream.

Recommended in the area

The Eden Project; Tate St Ives; South West Coastal
Path

The Victory Inn

Address: Victory Hill, ST MAWES, TR2 5DQ
Tel: 01326 270324
Email: contact@victory-inn.co.uk
Website: www.victory-inn.co.uk
Map ref: 1 SW83
Directions: A3078 to St Mawes. Pub adjacent to harbour
Open: all day all wk 11am-mdnt ⊯ **L** all wk 12-3 **D** all wk 6-9.30 ⑩ **L** all wk 12-3 **D** all wk 6-9.15
Facilities: Garden Wi-fi
Notes: ⊕ PUNCH TAVERNS ♦♦ ♦

Located near the harbour, this friendly fishermen's local is named after Nelson's flagship but adopts a modern approach to its daily lunch and dinner menus. You may eat downstairs in the traditional bar, or in the modern and stylish first-floor Seaview Restaurant (white walls, white linen and wicker chairs), with a terrace that looks across the town's rooftops to the harbour and the River Fal. High on the list of ingredients is fresh seafood - all from Cornish waters, of course - the choice changing virtually daily to include crab risotto; fisherman's pie; and beer-battered cod and hand-cut chips, with chicken breast cordon bleu; lamb shank provençale; and curry or casserole of the day among the other favourites. Children are provided with paper, crayons and their own menu; dogs are given treats too. Wines are all carefully chosen and excellent in quality, as are the real ales from Cornwall's own Roseland, Sharp's and Skinners breweries. There is outside seating with views over the harbour. Booking for meals is definitely advisable in the summer months. Ever popular St Mawes boasts lovely safe beaches, and if you choose to venture further afield the dramatic Cornish coastal scenery is close at hand.

Recommended in the area

The Eden Project; Falmouth Maritime Museum; St Mawes Castle

The Mill House Inn

Address: TREBARWITH, Tintagel, PL34 0HD
Tel: 01840 770200
Email: management@themillhouseinn.co.uk
Website: www.themillhouseinn.co.uk
Map ref: 1 SX08
Directions: From Tintagel take B3263 S, right after Trewarmett to Trebarwith Strand. Pub 0.5m on right
Open: all day all wk 11-11 (Fri-Sat 11am-mdnt, Sun noon-10.30) ⮑ **L** Mon-Sat 12-2.30, Sun 12-3 **D** all wk 6.30-8.30 🍽 **D** all wk 7-9
Facilities: Garden Parking Wi-fi
Notes: ⊕ FREE HOUSE ⋔ 🐾

The Mill House dates back to 1760, and was a working mill until the 1930s. It is situated on the north Cornish coast in a beautiful woodland setting, just half a mile from the surfing beach at Trebarwith Strand, and a short distance from King Arthur's legendary castle. The slate-floored bar with its wooden tables, chapel chairs and wood burning stove has a family friendly feel. You may also choose to eat on the partly-covered tiered terraces (with heaters) at the front, or in the restaurant that was designed to blend in with many existing features. The inn offers first-class food as in the traditional bar lunches such as snakebite-battered local haddock or a Cornish smoked fish platter, followed by selections on the evening restaurant menu such as duo of Tintagel duck served with swede and carrot purée or grilled local halibut with spinach and prawn ragout. Sharps and Tintagel Brewery local ales together with an imaginative wine list complement the regularly changing menus, which make use of the best locally sourced ingredients. The Mill House is licensed for wedding ceremonies and is a perfect location for receptions, parties and conferences.

Recommended in the area

Trebarwith Surfing Beach; Tintagel Castle; Delabole Wind Farm

The Springer Spaniel

Address: TREBURLEY, Nr Launceston, PL15 9NS
Tel: 01579 370424
Email: enquiries@thespringerspaniel.org.uk
Website: www.thespringerspaniel.org.uk
Map ref: 1 SX37
Directions: On A388 halfway between Launceston & Callington
Open: all wk noon-2.30 6-10.30 ⓑ ⓘ **L** all wk 12-1.45 **D** all wk 6.15-8.45
Facilities: Garden Parking
Notes: ⊕ FREE HOUSE ⓘ ⓘ

The creeper-clad walls of this 200 year-old free house shelter a cosy bar with high-backed wooden settles, farmhouse-style chairs and a wood-burning stove. You can bring your dog, join in with the chat, read the papers or cast an eye over the many books in the snug. Owner-managers Roger and Lavinia Halliday aim to provide the best that a traditional Cornish hostelry can offer - reliable ales, delicious food, fine wines and friendly service. In summer the landscaped, sheltered garden is a great place to relax with a pint of St Austell Tribute. The bar includes other local brews and guest ales. Food is a big draw here, with beef from the owners' neighbouring organic farm supplementing ingredients from the best local suppliers. Bar lunches range from the ever-popular ploughman's, and a selection of hot filled foccacias; to pub favourites like organic beef sausages and mash. Meanwhile a three-course meal might begin game and bacon terrine, before moving on to grilled coriander and lime chicken; or pan-fried local scallops with pancetta and white wine sauce. Desserts include Springer bread and butter pudding with creamy custard. The restaurant has flickering candles in the evenings adding to the romantic atmosphere. Children are always welcome.

Recommended in the area

Cotehele (National Trust); Mining Heritage Centre; Sterts Theatre, Upton Cross

Cumbria

Lake Buttermere, Cumbria

Drunken Duck Inn

★★★★★ ◎◎ ⚲ INN

Address: Barngates, AMBLESIDE, LA22 0NG
Tel: 015394 36347
Email: info@drunkenduckinn.co.uk
Website: www.drunkenduckinn.co.uk
Map ref: 6 NY30 **Directions:** From Kendal on
A591 to Ambleside, then follow Hawkshead sign. In
2.5m inn sign on right, 1m up hill
Open: all day all wk ⓑ **L** all wk 12-4 ⓘ **D** all wk
6-9.30 **Closed:** 25 Dec **Rooms:** 8 en suite (5 GF)
S £71.25-£172.5 **D** £95-£295
Facilities: Garden Parking Wi-fi
Notes: 🍺 FREE HOUSE ⅰ⅟ ♟ 17

This 17th-century inn is surrounded by 60 private
acres of beautiful countryside. In spring, you can
barely move for flowers, and all year round there
are striking views of fells and lakes. Under the same
family ownership since 1977, the Drunken Duck has
been appointed with a stylish mix of modern luxury
and old world charm. Expect plenty of sofas to
lounge in, a pretty residents' garden, and glamorous
bedrooms. The bar, with its antique settles and log
fires, serves beers from the inn's own Barngate
Brewery. These have been named after much loved
dogs: Cracker, Tag Lag and Chester's Strong and
Ugly. The award-winning candlelit restaurant offers
intelligent, modern British cuisine, with the same
menu offered at lunch and dinner, supplemented by
specials. Start with crab and shrimp tortellini with
prawn bisque and rocket; or duck and peppercorn
terrine, cherry jelly, pickled girolles and rye bread,
followed by braised belly pork and black pudding
with boulangère wilted lettuce; or lamb rump with
braised sweet red cabbage and Calvados apples.
Leave room for rhubarb and duck egg custard tart
with clotted cream; prune and Armagnac soufflé
with vanilla ice cream; or you could try the gourmet
cheese list.

Recommended in the area

Lake District Visitor Centre; Armitt Museum;
Windermere Steamboat Centre

The Sun, Coniston

Address: CONISTON, LA21 8HQ
Tel: 015394 41248
Email: info@thesunconiston.com
Website: www.thesunconiston.com
Map ref: 6 SD39
Directions: M6 junct 36, A590, A591 to Ambleside, A593 to Coniston. Pub signed in village
Open: all day all wk 11am-mdnt 🍴 **L** all wk 12-2.30 **D** all wk 5.30-8.30
Facilities: Garden Parking Wi-fi
Notes: ⊕ FREE HOUSE 🐾

With a peaceful location at the foot of the mountains, The Sun Coniston offers a unique mix of bar, diner and inn, with the kind of comfortable informality and atmosphere that many attempt but few achieve. The 16th-century pub is a favourite with thirsty walkers and tourists seeking peace from the village below. It boasts a wealth of classic Lakeland features including stone bar, floors and walls, exposed beams and a working range. The first-floor Boat Room is an eating and drinking area, which is also home to an exhibition of rare Donald Campbell photographs. But at its heart is a very special bar with eight guest real ales on hand-pull, four draft lagers, 20 plus malts and 30 plus wines. The menu has been created using locally sourced, seasonal ingredients to offer traditional British food as well as classic dishes with a twist. Perhaps start with devilled whitebait with paprika, horseradish and garlic mayonnaise, then follow with lamb shank with minted stout gravy, braised beef with red wine and caper sauce. Depending on your mood, the freshly prepared food can be enjoyed in the bar, in the conservatory and outside on the front terrace.

Recommended in the area

Brantwood; Steam Yacht 'Gondola' (NT); Ravenglass & Eskdale Railway

The Punch Bowl Inn

★★★★★ ◎◎ INN

Address: CROSTHWAITE, Nr Kendal, LA8 8HR
Tel: 015395 68237
Email: info@the-punchbowl.co.uk
Website: www.the-punchbowl.co.uk
Map ref: 6 SD49
Directions: M6 junct 36, A590 towards Barrow, A5074, follow Crosthwaite signs. Pub by church
Open: all day all wk ⓑ ⓘ Booking required **L** all wk noon-9 **D** all wk noon-9
Rooms: 9 en suite **S** £95-£221.25 **D** £120-£295
Facilities: Garden Parking Wi-fi
Notes: ⓦ FREE HOUSE ⦿ ⦿ ⓔ 14

Set near the head of the Lyth Valley amidst crimped limestone knolls, verdant pastures and damson orchards, this notable, destination dining inn has been awarded two AA Rosettes for the fabulous menu created by Richard Rose and his team. The elegantly furnished, light and contemporary interior; the slate bar-top, wood-burner stoves, fresh flowers and restrained decor reflect the care and attention to detail that ensure clients return time-and-again to this bolt-hole (with sumptuous, individually designed residential rooms available) just a few miles from Windermere's wooded shores. Drawing heavily on the area's estates, farms and nearby coastal villages for the raw materials, the carte menu is available throughout the bar and restaurant rooms; prepare to be tempted by starters such as wood pigeon and lentil casserole; or glazed Lancashire cheese soufflé, leading into Barnsley chop and kidneys, broccoli, capers and mint; roasted skate with shrimp and brown butter sauce; or a hearty dish of Cumberland sausages, mash and red onion gravy; finishing on lemon cream with poached rhubarb and cinder toffee; or hot cherry fondant and cherry sorbet. The owners are great supporters of Cumbrian micro-breweries, so expect bitters from Barngates and Hawkshead breweries.

Recommended in the area

Sizergh Castle; Beatrix Potter country; Cartmel Racecourse

The Highland Drove Inn and Kyloes Restaurant

Address: GREAT SALKELD, Penrith, CA11 9NA
Tel: 01768 898349
Email: highlanddrove@kyloes.co.uk
Website: www.kyloes.co.uk
Map ref: 11 NY53
Directions: M6 junct 40, A66 E'bound, A686 to Alston. 4m, left onto B6412 for Great Salkeld & Lazonby **Open:** all wk noon-2 6-late ⏹ **L** Tue-Sun 12-2 **D** all wk 6-9 **Closed:** 25 Dec & Mon L
Facilities: Garden Parking Wi-fi
Notes: 🍺 FREE HOUSE 👥 🐾 🍷 10

Father and son team Donald and Paul Newton have turned this 300-year-old country inn into the area's social hub. Deep in the lovely Eden Valley, it stands on the old drove road along which Kyloes, Highland cattle bred in the Western Isles, were once herded on their way to market. Maintaining its reputation for high quality food depends to some extent on the local game, meat and fish that go into the traditional dishes and daily specials. Thus, typical main dishes might be salad of crispy fried squid and spring onion in sweet chilli sauce; wild salmon and mussel tagliatelle in white wine saffron cream sauce; and roast beef-tomato stuffed with savoury couscous topped with goats' cheese. Always popular are desserts such as vanilla crème brûlée with shortbread and fruits of the forest compote; and sticky toffee pudding with butterscotch sauce and Chantilly cream. Locals come here to enjoy a great wine list and the real ales are chosen by Paul, sourced from Cumbria's micro-breweries.

Recommended in the area

Lake District National Park; Hadrian's Wall; Pennine Way

The Queen's Head

★ ★ ★ ★ ◎ INN

Address: Main St, HAWKSHEAD, LA22 0NS
Tel: 015394 36271
Email: info@queensheadhawkshead.co.uk
Website: www.queensheadhawkshead.co.uk
Map ref: 6 SD39
Directions: M6 junct 36, A590 to Newby Bridge,
1st right, 8m to Hawkshead
Open: all day all wk 11am-11.45pm (Sun 12-11.45)
🍽 🍴 **L** 12-2.30, Sun 12-5 **D** all wk 6.15-9.30
Rooms: 12 en suite (2 GF) **S** £45-£60 **D** £75-£130
Facilities: Garden Wi-fi
Notes: ⊕ FREDERIC ROBINSON 👫 🍷 16

This charming 16th-century inn sits in the heart of historic Hawkshead, the village where William Wordsworth went to school and Beatrix Potter created *Peter Rabbit*. Her husband William Heelis was the local solicitor and his old offices, now the Beatrix Potter Gallery, are full of her wonderful illustrations. The surrounding area is a haven for walkers, and Esthwaite Water is a stone's throw away. Inside, you'll find low oak-beamed ceilings, wood-panelled walls, an original slate floor and a welcoming fire. As well as a range of well-appointed en suite bedrooms, the inn offers everything you could need for relaxed wining and dining. There's an extensive wine list with many available by the glass and a selection of well kept real ales, plus a full à la carte menu and an ever-changing specials board. Enjoy timeless pub classics along with a more up-to-date, hearty repertoire with plenty of local colour. Dishes draw from the wealth of quality produce on the doorstep - organic trout from Esthwaite Water, wild pheasant from Graythwaite, traditionally cured hams and Cumberland sausage from Waberthwaite, and slow-maturing Herdwick lamb.

Recommended in the area

Hill Top (NT); Go Ape at Grizedale Forest Park; Brantwood House & Gardens; Tarn Hows

The Horse & Farrier Inn

Address: Threlkeld Village, KESWICK, CA12 4SQ
Tel: 017687 79688
Email: info@horseandfarrier.com
Website: www.horseandfarrier.com
Map ref: 10 NY22
Directions: M6 junct 40, A66 signed Keswick, 12m, right signed Threlkeld. Pub in village centre
Open: all day all wk 7.30am-mdnt
Facilities: Garden Parking Wi-fi
Notes: ⊕ JENNINGS BROTHERS PLC ⅋ ✦ ♇ 10

Within its thick stone walls lies all you would expect from a traditional Lakeland inn. Built in 1688 beneath 868-metre Blencathra, and with views towards Skiddaw in the west and Helvellyn to the south, it has slate-flagged floors, beamed ceilings and open fires. For the last ten years, under Ian Court's ownership, The Horse & Farrier has received numerous awards. A typical dinner might start with terrine of wild boar and venison, or seared trio of Morecambe Bay scallops, and continue with pan-griddled duo of Cumberland sausages with butterbean and chive mash; fillet of sea bass with a cassolette of chorizo, haricot beans, mushrooms and pasta shells; or, in the bar, a home-made curry or Mediterranean vegetable lasagne.

A house speciality is lamb shoulder slowly braised in Jennings Cumberland ale (this Cockermouth brewery's beers are a fixture in the bar, by the way) with chive mash and redcurrant and mint sauce. For dessert, a Swiss ice cream, perhaps, such as crunchy mint chocolate or parfait caramel. Stay overnight and enjoy a hearty Lakeland breakfast, then relax in the small beer garden and enjoy those magnificent mountain views.

Recommended in the area

Rheged Discovery Centre; Honister Slate Mine; Cumbria Way

The Inn at Keswick

★★★★ INN

Address: Main St, KESWICK, CA12 5HZ

Tel: 017687 74584

Email: relax@theinnkeswick.co.uk

Map ref: 10 NY22

Directions: M6 junct 40, A66 to Keswick town centre to war memorial x-roads. Left into Station St. Inn 100yds

Open: all day all wk ⓫ **L** Mon-Sat 11-9.30

D Sun 12-9

Rooms: 19 en suite **D** £70-£120

Notes: ⊕ THWAITES INNS OF CHARACTER ⛄ 🐾

Right in the heart of town, the former Keswick Lodge has been providing food and drink since the 18th century. Its closeness to Derwent Water, and because it serves food and drink from early until late, means that it attracts the many walkers, cyclists and other outdoor enthusiasts who visit the Northern Lakes. So where better to sit than by the roaring log fire in the bar and warm up after making what is regarded as the relatively easy ascent of 931-metre Skiddaw, or perhaps one of the inn's recommended walks? Watch Keswick life pass by through the windows of the dining room, where fresh, top quality food from local, ethical suppliers includes best-seller Fellside lamb hot-pot. Hot on its heels in the popularity stakes come chargrilled breast of chicken Caesar salad, and haddock in beer batter. Daily specials are based on what's available and in season. That climb up Skiddaw is recommended, since portions are hearty, although smaller plates are available for children. As a Thwaites house there is always a ready supply of cask ales, including its well-known Wainwright and seasonal Signature Range. There'll be water bowls for your dog too, even in the guest rooms.

Recommended in the area

Dove Cottage; Theatre by the Lake; Castlerigg Stone Circle

Queen's Head

★★★★ 🛏 INN

Address: Townhead, TROUTBECK, Windermere
LA23 1PW
Tel: 015394 32174
Email: reservations@queensheadtroutbeck.co.uk
Website: www.queensheadtroutbeck.co.uk
Map ref: 6 NY40
Directions: M6 junct 36, A590, A591 towards
Windermere, right at mini-rdbt onto A592 signed
Penrith/Ullswater. Pub 2m on left
Open: all day all week **Rooms:** 15 en suite (2 GF)
S £75-£90 **D** £120-£150 **Facilities:** Parking Wi-fi
Notes: ⊕ FREDERIC ROBINSON ⸙ ⤳ ♟ 8

Nooks and crannies, low beams stuffed with old pennies by farmers on their way home from market, and a log fire throughout the year make this smart 17th-century coaching inn hard to beat when it comes to old world charm. The lovely undulating valley of Troutbeck, with its maze of footpaths and stunning felltop views, is a magnet for ramblers. True to its roots, this inn offers sustenance and comfortable accommodation to the weary and footsore. The bar is perhaps its most remarkable feature, carved from a four-poster bed that once resided in Appleby Castle. Robinson's Brewery furnishes the likes of Cumbria Way, Old Tom and Dizzy Blonde at the pumps, while the chef's reputation for accomplished cooking is well established. The menu proffers hearty international fare ranging from crispy crabcakes, roasted red pepper dip with crayfish and caper mayonnaise; corned duck hash, poached duck egg, pancetta crisp and home-made brown sauce, followed by beef brisket braised in best bitter, horseradish dumplings, mushrooms, root vegetables and buttery mash; sausage of the day; or beer battered fish and chips. The freshly baked artisan baguettes, ploughman's and the seafood platter are also very tempting. Children will find lots to choose from too.

Recommended in the area

Brockhole National Park Visitor Centre; The World of Beatrix Potter; Lake Windermere

Lanercost Priory

Derbyshire

Dovedale, Peak District National Park

Old Hall Inn

Address: Whitehough, CHINLEY, SK23 6EJ
Tel: 01663 750529
Email: info@old-hall-inn.co.uk
Website: www.old-hall-inn.co.uk
Map ref: 6 SK08
Directions: B5470 W from Chapel-en-le-Frith. Right into Whitehough Head Ln. 0.8m to inn
Open: all day all wk ☕ ❍ Booking required **L** Mon-Sat 12-2, Sun 12-7.30 **D** Mon-Thu 5-9, Fri-Sat 5-9.30, Sun 12-7.30
Facilities: Garden Parking Wi-fi
Notes: ⊕ FREE HOUSE ♦♦ ♦ ♀ 12 ⬛

Prime Peak District walking country lies all around this family-run, 16th-century pub, which is attached to Whitehough Hall, an Elizabethan former manor house. The iconic landscape features of Kinder Scout, Mam Tor and Stanage Edge are all within easy reach. A strong supporter of local breweries, the popular bar showcases many of their beers every week, including Thornbridge's beefy Jaipur, and two hand-pulls dedicated to frequently changing traditional cider. The pub opens up into the Minstrels' Gallery restaurant in the manor house, where a short seasonal menu offers just-made pub food prepared from local produce, and daily specials, such as Chatsworth Estate venison with port and redcurrant sauce; homemade Gloucester Old Spot sausages, creamy mash with red wine and onion gravy; salmon and haddock fishcakes; and vegetarian moussaka. Desserts, some accompanied by Hilly Billy ice cream from nearby Blaze Farm, are all homemade, and there are some appealing cheese boards. Sandwiches are served at lunchtimes and if you're avoiding alcohol you can try one of the range of artisan teas and coffees. Clearly, this is a real community pub and there's usually something going on, including two great beer festivals each year.

Recommended in the area

Caverns & caves at Castleton; Lyme Park (NT); Peak District National Park

Devon

Watersmeet, Exmoor National Park

The New Inn

★★★★ INN

Address: COLEFORD, Crediton, EX17 5BZ
Tel: 01363 84242
Email: enquiries@thenewinncoleford.co.uk
Website: www.thenewinncoleford.co.uk
Map ref: 2 SS70 **Directions:** A377 from Exeter, 1.5m after Crediton left for Coleford, 1.5m to inn
Open: all wk 12-3 6-11 (Sun 6-10.30 winter)
🍺 🍽 **L** all wk 12-2 **D** all wk 6.30-9.30
Rooms: 6 en suite (1 GF)
Closed: 25-26 Dec
Facilities: Garden Parking
Notes: 🍺 FREE HOUSE 👬 🐾 🍷 20

In a peaceful conservation village between Dartmoor and Exmoor stands this pretty 13th-century free house. The Cole stream flows past its well-tended gardens, guarded by a stately weeping willow, eventually to join the Exe. Once inside, you'll be welcomed by Captain, an Amazon blue parrot who has been greeting visitors with cheeky comments for 29 years. Your surroundings - oak beams, slate floors, wood burners, old carved chests and cushioned stone wall seats – will be just what you hoped for. In the bar you'll find real ales from Devon and Cornwall, and plenty of wines by the glass to accompany fresh fish from Brixham, and game, meats, cheeses and other produce from surrounding villages and farms. Sandwiches and ploughman's platters are available at lunchtime, while fuller meals might start with Devonshire crab soup, or pan-fried, shell-off king prawns with garlic butter. Main dishes include home-made steak and ale pie; lamb's liver, bacon and mash with onion gravy; and grilled salmon with smoked salmon filling. Finish with orange marmalade bread and butter pudding, or mascarpone cheesecake with blackcurrant compôte. Comfortable overnight accommodation is guaranteed in the well-appointed bedrooms. Look out for the monthly hog roasts and live New Orleans jazz nights.

Recommended in the area

Castle Drogo (NT); City of Exeter; Tarka Trail

The Nobody Inn

★★★★ ⇔ INN

Address: DODDISCOMBSLEIGH, Exeter, EX6 7PS
Tel: 01647 252394
Email: info@nobodyinn.co.uk
Website: www.nobodyinn.co.uk
Map ref: 2 SX88 **Directions:** 3m SW of Exeter
Racecourse (A38) **Open:** all day all wk 11-11 (Sun
12-10.30) 🍴 **L** Mon-Sat 12-2, Sun 12-3 **D** Sun-Thu
6.30-9, Fri-Sat 6.30-9.30 🍽️ **D** Tue-Thu 6.30-9, Fri-
Sat 6.30-9.30 Booking required for bar & restaurant
Closed: 25-26 Dec, 1 Jan **Rooms:** 4 en suite
S £40-£65 **D** £60-£95 **Facilities:** Garden Parking
Wi-fi **Notes:** ⊕ FREE HOUSE 🚶 🚗 🍷 28

This 16th-century inn lies in rolling Devon countryside between the Haldon Hills and the Teign Valley. Although its history can be traced back to 1591, it was another two centuries before it became an inn and a further 160 years before it was renamed The No Body Inn, following an unfortunate episode involving a deceased landlord. You will be immediately transported back to the distant past by the low ceilings, blackened beams, inglenook and antique furniture, although in the interests of progress there have been some recent upgrades, mostly in the restaurant and guest rooms, and there's seating in the pretty garden. Seasonal dishes, with fish delivered daily from Brixham, are served in the bar and restaurant, where typical starters include pan-fried pigeon breast with rocket and walnut dressing, and baked scallops in Devon Oke cheese sauce. Among the mains might appear roasted vegetable and Sharpham Brie pie in herb pastry; venison steak with mandarin and orange sauce; and kiln-roast salmon on bubble and squeak. You can sample over 250 wines, 230 whiskies in addition to an ever-changing range of real ales. Rooms are all beautifully decorated and with a welcoming decanter of sherry.

Recommended in the area

Dartmoor National Park; Dart Valle Railway; Ugbrooke House & Park

California Country Inn

Address: California Cross, MODBURY,
Ivybridge, PL21 0SG
Tel: 01548 821449
Email: enquiries@californiacountryinn.co.uk
Website: www.californiacountryinn.co.uk
Map ref: 2 SX65
Directions: On B3196 (NE of Modbury)
Open: all day all wk ⓑ **L** Mon-Sat 12-2, Sun 12-2.30
D Mon-Sat 6-9, Sun 6-8.30 ⓞⓘ **L** Sun 12-2
D Wed-Sun 6-9
Facilities: Garden Parking Wi-fi
Notes: ⊕ FREE HOUSE ⓘⓘ ⓘ

An award-winning 14th-century country inn, locally noted for its food. Painted a rich cream outside, its atmospheric interior features exposed dry stone walls and old beams, with a dining room full of photos, fresh flowers, prints and brasswork. As a supporter of local food, the kitchen sources most of its produce from the fields of the South Hams and the nearby waters. At lunchtime or in the evening enjoy a bar meal from the extensive menu and specials board, with classics like lamb's liver on mustard mash with crispy onions and gravy; chargrilled pork loin with sautéed potatoes, Stilton and mushroom cream sauce; and beer-battered cod. For those preferring the polished cutlery, glassware and table cloths of the dining room,

the modern British cooking includes three-way Woolston pork (crispy belly, Parma ham and black pudding) with pear, Devon Blue cheese and sherry vinegar dressing, or roasted red pepper as a starter; followed by medley of monkfish, salmon, scallops and king prawns with chive pommes purée and white wine cream sauce; sticky honey and lemon chicken; or wild mushroom and asparagus risotto. In the summer months, enjoy a well-kept local real ale in the delightful landscaped garden.

Recommended in the area

South West Coast Path; Kitley Caves; Dartmoor Zoological Park

The Fox & Goose

Address: PARRACOMBE, EX31 4PE
Tel: 01598 763239
Website: www.foxandgooseinnexmoor.co.uk
Map ref: 2 SS64
Directions: 1m from A39 between Blackmoor Gate & Lynton. Follow Parracombe signs
Open: all day all wk 🍴 🍽️ **L** all wk 12-2 **D** Mon-Sat 6-9, Sun 7-9
Facilities: Garden Parking Wi-fi
Notes: ⊕ FREE HOUSE 👥 🐾 ⚲ 10

This imposing Victorian building was once just a couple of tiny thatched cottages serving the local farming community, but transformation into a hotel took place when a narrow-gauge railway arrived in 1898. Inside there's farm memorabilia, a scarf-wearing stag's head and photographs of villagers who now drink in more celestial surroundings; today beer drinkers have a choice of local Cotleigh and Exmoor, Otter from south Devon and local cider. Good home-made food comes from constantly changing blackboard menus that are likely to feature seasonal game from surrounding farms and estates, as well as fish and shellfish caught off the north Devon coast. Examples include bouillabaisse; pan-fried skate wing with brown shrimp and capers; brill fillets poached in red wine; and roast cod wrapped in bacon with Puy lentils. Among the meat choices are trio of venison sausages with creamy mash and gravy; fillet steak with sautéed mushrooms; and confit of duck with juniper and port sauce. For vegetarians there is pearl barley risotto with roasted squash and sage. To follow, perhaps brioche bread and butter pudding; or lemon posset. Children and dogs are welcome and, if they want, they can let off steam in the paved courtyard garden overlooking the river.

Recommended in the area

Exmoor Zoological Park; Arlington Court (NT); Exmoor National Park

The Harris Arms

Address: PORTGATE, Lewdown, EX20 4PZ
Tel: 01566 783331
Email: info@theharrisarms.co.uk
Website: www.theharrisarms.co.uk
Map ref: 1 SX48
Directions: From A30 at Broadwoodwidger/
Roadford Lake follow signs to Lifton then Portgate
Open: Tue-Sun ♿ 🍴 Booking required **L** Tue-Sun
12-2 **D** Tue-Sat 6.30-9
Closed: Mon & Sun eve
Facilities: Garden Parking
Notes: ⊕ FREE HOUSE ♦♦ ♨ ♟ 20

A 16th-century inn with wonderful views to Brentor, this establishment lives up to its promotional strapline: 'Eat Real Food and Drink Real Wine'. Located on the old A30 close to the boundary between Devon and Cornwall, it's an accessible spot for honest food with substance and style, plus real ales and excellent wines. Owners Rowena and Andy Whiteman have previously run vineyards in France and New Zealand, so their wine list, with over 150 wines, is both eclectic and extensive; twenty are served by the glass. The pub's excellent reputation, which reaches far beyond the local area, is built on robust cooking and locally-sourced, quality ingredients. Examples of starters are twice baked goats' cheese soufflé, tomato fondue and basil foam; and prawns piri-piri with brown bread, and main courses might be crispy confit of duck, haricot bean and chorizo ragout with gratin potato and red wine sauce; or braised beef cheeks with creamy garlic mash and red wine sauce; and pub classics such as home-cooked ham with eggs and chips. A children's menu is available. In warmer weather, enjoy a glass of Otter Best, Bay's Gold or Tamar Sauce or a meal outside on the decked patio that overlooks amazing countryside.

Recommended in the area

Dartmoor National Park; Lydford Gorge; Lawrence House Museum, Launceston

Jack in the Green Inn

◎◎

Address: London Rd, ROCKBEARE,
Nr Exeter, EX5 2EE
Tel: 01404 822240
Email: info@jackinthegreen.uk.com
Website: www.jackinthegreen.uk.com
Map ref: 2 SY09 **Directions:** M5 junct 29, A30
towards Honiton, left signed Rockbeare
Open: all wk 11-3 5.30-11 (Sun noon-11)
🔊 ⏏️ **L** Mon-Sat 12-2, Sun12-9 **D** Mon-Sat 6-9.30,
Sun 12-9 **Closed:** 25 Dec-5 Jan
Facilities: Garden Parking Wi-fi
Notes: ⊕ FREE HOUSE ☾ ♟ 12

There has been an inn on this site for several centuries, but since Paul Parnell took over some 20 years ago, it has become an award-winning beacon of good food in a contemporary and relaxed atmosphere. Within its whitewashed walls is a lounge bar furnished with comfy seating and dark wood tables, and a smart restaurant. The simple philosophy here is to serve real food to real people, with a firm commitment from the kitchen to sourcing the best and freshest local produce and preparing it to a consistently high standard. Typical dishes on the bar menu include home-made chicken liver parfait with redcurrant jelly; 'Posh' prawn cocktail with 'Bloody Mary' sauce; braised faggots, creamed potato and onion gravy; confit Creedy Carver duck leg with creamed haricot beans. Current cask ales include Otter Ale, Doom Bar and Butcombe Bitter plus three Devon ciders including St George's Temptation and Yarde Real Cider. Perfect for the summer months is the alfresco eating area for up to 80 people with full menu table service, and jazz fans should seek out the Friday night events. Dogs are welcome outside, with water provided and a field for walking them.

Recommended in the area

Bicton Park Botanical Gardens; Escot Park; Crealy Adventure Park

Blue Ball Inn

★★★★ INN

Address: Stevens Cross, Sidford,
SIDMOUTH, EX10 9QL
Tel: 01395 514062
Email: rogernewton@blueballinn.net
Website: www.blueballinnsidford.co.uk
Map ref: 2 SY18 **Directions:** M5 junct 30, A3052,
through Sidford towards Lyme Regis, inn on left
Open: all day all wk ⛻ †☺¶ Booking required
L all wk 12-2.30 **D** all wk 6-9 **Rooms:** 9 en suite (1 GF)
Closed: 25 Dec eve
Facilities: Garden Parking Wi-fi
Notes: ⊕ PUNCH TAVERNS †¶ ⌀ ⍨ 13

Run by the Newton family since 1912, but dating back to 1385, this thatched inn was destroyed by fire a few years ago and rebuilt with tremendous care to recapture its original atmosphere. There is a central bar and plenty of seating and dining areas, while outside is an attractive garden. The inn is keen to promote locally brewed ales such as Otter Bitter, Tribute and Doom Bar, and there are pub food favourites and more contemporary dishes on the menu, backed up by a weekly special board. Starters might include creamy Stilton and garlic mushrooms on ciabatta; Lyme Bay crab and avocado tian; seared pigeon breast with black pudding and pancetta, followed by pan-fried lamb's liver and bacon with bubble and squeak, buttered beans and onion and mustard sauce; wild mushroom risotto; Drews of Sidbury honey-glazed ham with Greendale Farm eggs, chips and peas; or local beer battered fish of the day, chips and peas. There are nine stylish bedrooms with crisp white linen, fluffy towels and power showers, including one twin, ground-floor room with a walk-in wet room. The inn is a popular choice for weddings, family celebrations and small conferences.

Recommended in the area

Crealy Adventure Park; Seaton Tramway; South West Coast Path

Dukes

★★★★ INN

Address: The Esplanade, SIDMOUTH, EX10 8AR

Tel: 01395 513320

Email: dukes@hotels-sidmouth.co.uk

Website: www.hotels-sidmouth.co.uk

Map ref: 2 SY18

Directions: Exit A3052 to Sidmouth, left onto Esplanade

Open: all day all wk **L** Sun-Thu 12-9, Fri-Sat 12-9.30 **D** Sun-Thu 12-9, Fri-Sat 12-9.30

Rooms: 13 en suite

Facilities: Garden Parking Wi-fi

Notes: FREE HOUSE 20

Situated at the heart of Sidmouth town centre on the Regency esplanade, a stone's throw from the sea, Dukes is a contemporary, family-friendly inn that successfully combines traditional values with an informal atmosphere. The interior is stylish and lively, with a relaxed continental feel in the bar and public areas, and there are comfortable en suite bedrooms to stay in, most of which have sea views and come with a range of home comforts, including Wi-fi. In fine weather, the patio garden, overlooking the sea, is the perfect place to bask in the sun with freshly ground mid-morning coffee, a pot of tea or a hot chocolate together with freshly baked scones and cakes; or on a chilly winter's evening choose to relax on the comfortable leather sofas. Branscombe Vale ales, Sandford Orchard ciders and award-winning Christopher Piper wines are on offer; all wines are available by the bottle or the glass. The seasonal menus and daily specials provide something for all tastes. Lunch and dinner options include a range of dishes showcasing local suppliers and feature fresh Lyme Bay fish and Devon-reared meat and game. Light snacks and traditional style pub favourites are also always available.

Recommended in the area

Jurassic Coast; Crealy Great Adventure Park; Exeter Cathedral

The Tower Inn

Address: Church Rd, SLAPTON, Kingsbridge,
TQ7 2PN
Tel: 01548 580216
Email: towerinn@slapton.org
Website: www.thetowerinn.com
Map ref: 2 SX84
Directions: Exit A379 S of Dartmouth, left at
Slapton Sands
Open: 12-2.30 (12-3 Summer) 6-11 ☎ ⊙ **L** all wk
12-2.30 **D** all wk 6.30-9.30
Closed: 1st 2wks Jan, Sun eve during Winter
Facilities: Garden Parking Wi-fi
Notes: ⊕ FREE HOUSE ♦♦ ✖ ◖

Visitors exploring Slapton Ley Nature Reserve and
Slapton Sands should venture inland to seek out
this ancient inn. Tucked away behind the church
and standing beside the dramatic, ivy-clad ruins of
the chantry tower, the 14th-century Tower Inn is a
truly atmospheric village pub, built to accommodate
the artisans working on the monastic college
next door, founded in 1373 by Sir Guy de Brian,
who was a standard-bearer to King Edward III. Six
hundred years on and guests continue to be warmly
welcomed and refreshed with local ales and a good
choice of modern pub food in the rambling bar and
dining rooms characterised by stone walls, open
fires, low beams, flagstone floors, and scrubbed
oak tables topped with church candles. Menus are
based around fresh local ingredients whenever
possible, including prime Devon beef, local game,
and fish from the nearby markets and Salcombe
Dairy ice cream. Dishes range from local crab
sandwiches, mussels in cider cream broth, and
Thai fishcakes at lunchtime to rabbit terrine with fig
chutney, pork belly and cheek stew; and at dinner,
pan-fried seabass fillets with fennel purée, confit
tomato, chorizo and charred aubergine. There's a
splendid landscaped garden with church and tower
views. Regular music nights are held.

Recommended in the area

Slapton Sands; Slapton Ley Nature Reserve;
Cookworthy Museum of Rural Life

Kings Arms

Address: Dartmouth Rd, STRETE, TQ6 0RW
Tel: 01803 770377
Email: kingsarms_devon_fish@hotmail.com
Website: www.kingsarms-strete.co.uk
Map ref: 2 SX84
Directions: On A379 (Dartmouth-Kingsbridge road), 5m from Dartmouth
Open: 11.30-3 6-11 (Sat-Sun 11.30-11)
Closed: Mon in winter
Facilities: Garden Parking
Notes: ⊕ HEAVITREE 👭 🐕

There's no missing this striking, 18th-century building, with its unique cast-iron balcony, as it stands beside the coast road, and the South West coast path passes the front door. Pop in for a pint of Otter Ale, bag a seat by the fire in the traditional, terracotta-walled bar, or head up the few steps into the light and airy contemporary-styled restaurant, replete with modern artwork and stunning views across Start Bay. Chef Rob Dawson's motto is 'keep it fresh, keep it simple' and on his daily lunch and dinner menus you'll find wonderfully fresh seafood, simply prepared with some modern twists, including crab, lobster and fish from a local boat (the boat trawls exclusively for the pub once a week). At lunch, tuck into delicious fish soup with saffron and rouille, a plate of smoked sprats, or smoked haddock and rocket fishcake with wholegrain mustard sauce. Evening choices extend to butternut squash, coconut & lemongrass soup; grilled sardine fillets with garlic butter; cod with local clams, peas and asparagus; red gurnard with scallion mash and roasted red pepper cream; and homemade steak and Otter Ale pie with a suet crust. In summer, dine alfresco overlooking the bay in the flower-filled garden.

Recommended in the area

Greenway (NT); Woodland's Family Theme Park; Cookworthy Museum of Rural life

The Golden Lion Inn

Address: TIPTON ST JOHN, Sidmouth, EX10 0AA
Tel: 01404 812881
Email: info@goldenliontipton.co.uk
Website: www.goldenliontipton.co.uk
Map ref: 2 SY09
Directions: Telephone for directions
Open: all wk 12-2.30 6-11 (Sun 12-2.30 7-10.30)
L all wk 12-2 **D** Mon-Sat 6.30-8.30, Sun 7-8.30
L all wk 12-2
Facilities: Garden Parking
Notes: HEAVITREE 12

Francois (Franky) and Michelle Teissier have been running their inviting village pub for quite a while now. It manages to retain that traditional pub feel with low wooden beams, stone interior walls and a blazing log fire and charmingly eclectic decor of art deco prints, Tiffany lamps and paintings by Devon and Cornwall artists. Franky and Michelle welcome customers with their extensive menu comprising the highest quality British, Mediterranean and rustic French cooking, such as lunchtime smoked duck salad with onion marmalade; home-cooked ham, egg and chips; and mussels, french fries and crusty bread. Dinner could begin with escargots de Bourgogne, or grilled goats' cheese crouton with Italian ham. To follow, try breast of chicken with light sherry and cream sauce; marinated lamb kebab in garlic and rosemary; or a blackboard special featuring fresh fish or seafood landed at nearby Sidmouth, such as sea bass stuffed with cream cheese and sage; monkfish kebabs; lobster in garlic butter; and Lyme Bay crab. Outside, a grassy beer garden shares the sun with a terracotta-walled terrace and tumbling grapevines. A pint of locally brewed Otter or a glass of cold Chablis tastes good in either on a warm day.

Recommended in the area

Cadhay, Elizabethan manor house; South West Coast Path; Exeter Cathedral

The Durant Arms

Address: Ashprington, TOTNES, TQ9 7UP
Tel: 01803 732240
Email: info@durantarms.co.uk
Website: www.durantarms.co.uk
Map ref: 2 SX86
Directions: A38, A381, A385 to Totnes. Take A381 towards Kingsbridge, 1m, left for Ashprington
Open: all wk Sat-Sun all day ⬛ ❏ **L** all wk 12-2 **D** all wk 7-9.15
Facilities: Garden Parking Wi-fi
Notes: ⊕ FREE HOUSE ❏ ❏ ☺ 10

This 18th-century pub in the picturesque village of Ashprington stands in the shadow of a beautiful 16th-century church and has stunning views of the River Dart. The building was originally the counting house for the neighbouring 500-acre Sharpham Estate. Formerly known as The Ashprington Inn, the small bar is fitted out in a traditional style, with work by local artists on display alongside the horse brasses - the perfect place to enjoy local Sharpham Vineyard wines or local real ales and ciders. All dishes at The Durant are cooked to order, using locally sourced ingredients wherever possible. Typical dishes from the daily-changing blackboard menu include pub favourites such as home-cooked ham, eggs and chips, pan-fried lambs' liver with onions and shepherd's pie with cheese topping. A more formal meal might begin with Brie and spinach tart, or sautéed scallops and black pudding with wholegrain mustard sauce. Follow on, perhaps, with Creedy Carver duck breast with plum sauce; fillet of venison with red berry sauce; or sea bass fillet with roasted cherry tomatoes and spring onion. Leave space for desserts such as blackberry and apple pie, and crème brûlée. The little courtyard to the rear provides a cosy spot to linger over a summer meal.

Recommended in the area

Sharpham Vineyard & Cheese Dairy; Elizabethan town of Totnes; River Dart

The White Hart

Address: Dartington Hall, TOTNES, TQ9 6EL
Tel: 01803 847111
Email: bookings@dartingtonhall.com
Website: www.dartingtonhall.com
Map ref: 2 SX86
Directions: A38 onto A384 towards Totnes.
Turn at Dartington church into Dartington Hall
Estate
Open: all day all wk Mon-Sat 10am-11pm, (Sun
10am-10.30pm) 🛏 †⊙† Booking required **L** all wk
12-2.30 **D** all wk 6-9
Facilities: Garden Parking
Notes: ⊕ FREE HOUSE †† ♟ 14

The White Hart is tucked away in the courtyard of 14th-century Dartington Hall, now famed for its association with the arts. The gardens in the surrounding 1200-acre estate are among the finest in the country, and contain several sculptural features, including a reclining figure by Henry Moore. The restaurant, originally the hall's kitchen, retains its historic architecture, original tapestry and huge open fireplace, although a recent makeover now provides a more contemporary, yet still atmospheric, environment. The decor complements the chunky beams, roughcast walls, flagstone floor, limed-oak settles and log fire of the informal bar. The same menu serves both areas, relying heavily on locally sourced and seasonal produce, such as cured ham, single-suckled beef, grass-reared lamb, additive-free and free-range chickens and eggs, fish selected daily at the local fish market, and interesting speciality cheeses. Typical main dishes include mussels marinière with french fries; chargrilled pork loin with wholegrain mustard, butter beans, roast squash and port reduction; and root vegetable, courgette and cannellini bean stew, gremolata and herb dumplings. At weekends food is served between noon and 9pm. Enjoy the range of West Country real ales, and choose wine from a list that classifies bottles by taste.

Recommended in the area

Buckfast Abbey; Dart Valley Railway; Dartington shops

Cridford Inn

Address: TRUSHAM, Newton Abbot, TQ13 0NR
Tel: 01626 853694
Email: reservations@vanillapod-cridfordinn.com
Website: www.vanillapod-cridfordinn.com
Map ref: 2 SX88
Directions: From A38 exit at junct for Teign Valley,
right, follow Trusham signs for 4m
Open: all wk 11-3 6.15-11 (Sat 11am-11pm Sun
noon-10.30) ⓪ **L** all wk 12-2.30 **D** all wk 7-9.30
⓪ **L** Sun 12-1 **D** Tue-Sat 7-9.30
Facilities: Garden Parking
Notes: ⊕ FREE HOUSE ⅋ ♟ 10

Heritage enthusiasts will be in seventh heaven here.
Researchers have pieced together a remarkable
history dating back over a thousand years, putting a
9th-century longhouse on the site before a rebuild
in the 13th century. A mosaic floor in the restaurant
and probably the oldest surviving window frame in
Britain add immense warmth and character, as do
the rough stone walls and old fireplaces. The only
chill in the air may be from the ghosts of a nun or
a cavalier. This picturesque thatched inn crouches
like an owl below towering trees near a brook;
the pretty terrace is an ideal summertime spot
to mull over the alfresco lunchtime dishes with a
pint of local bitter. Quite apart from the destination
fine dining of the chic Vanilla Pod restaurant,
the regularly changing bar menu boasts dishes
prepared from the finest Devonshire ingredients
– chargrilled 8oz prime Ivybridge rump steak with
Teignworthy real ale battered onion rings, and
slow-roasted Beadon Farm pork belly on black
garlic mash. In the Vanilla Pod, start with avocado,
Brixham crab and prawn cocktail, followed by pan-
fried haunch of Teign Valley venison, braised red
cabbage with red wine and thyme jus, or pan-fried
sea bass with fennel chips and tomato relish.

Recommended in the area

Canonteign Falls; Belvedere Castle; Haldon Forest
& Go Ape

Rose & Crown

Address: Market St, YEALMPTON, PL8 2EB
Tel: 01752 880223
Email: info@theroseandcrown.co.uk
Website: www.theroseandcrown.co.uk
Map ref: 1 SX55
Directions: Telephone for directions
Open: all wk Mon-Sat 12-2.30 6-11 (Sun all day)
📖 🍴 **L** all wk 12-2.30 **D** all wk 6.30-9.30
Facilities: Garden Parking Wi-fi
Notes: ⊕ ENTERPRISE INNS 🍴 🐾 🍷 10

Just a ten-minute drive from Plymouth city centre is this very stylish village pub for eating and drinking. The decor includes an attractive mix of tables and old dining chairs, with some good quality sofas, and a large fire place. The absence of curtains and other soft furnishings mean the acoustics are generally lively. This pub has a sensibly thought through balance between the contemporary and the traditional. The terraced garden, with a charming fountain, is a lovely spot in the warmer months. There is a good range of wines, but real ales are taken seriously too. The food on offer is a smart mix of modern pub food with restaurant presentation and quality. The regular-changing carte menu tends to include fish, game, meat and vegetarian dishes – all sourced as locally as possible. Typical are Creedy Carver duck terrine with apple chutney; or breaded fishcake to start, followed by West Country rump steak with triple cooked chips; or Plymouth hake fillet with basil mash, poached egg and mussel beurre blanc. A 2-course set lunch for £10 (3 courses for £13) is always popular. There is a private dining and a function room opposite – suitable for wedding receptions, other celebrations, meetings etc.

Recommended in the area

Kitley Caves; South West Coast Path; Dartmoor National Park

Dorset

The quay at Poole

Gaggle of Geese

Address: BUCKLAND NEWTON, Nr Dorchester,
DT2 7BS
Tel: 01300 345249
Email: goose@thegaggle.co.uk
Website: www.thegaggle.co.uk
Map ref: 2 ST60
Directions: On B3143, N of Dorchester
Open: all wk 10-3 6-11.30 (Sat-Sun all day in
summer) 🛏 🍽 Booking required **L** Mon-Sat
12-2, Sun 12-3 **D** Mon-Sat 7-9, Sun 6.30-8.30
Facilities: Garden Parking Wi-fi
Notes: ⊕ FREE HOUSE ♦♦ 🐾 🍷 10

An extraordinary village inn with a heart of gold,
the Gaggle harks back to times past when many
villages could claim such a retreat. Now as rare as
hen's teeth (there's a twice-yearly poultry auction
here, so who knows…); step from the lane into the
large front parlour, complete with sofas, wingbacks
in front of the welcoming fire, bookshelves,
matchboarding and scrubbed tables. A glance at the
bar reveals well lubricated handpumps dispensing
beers from Hop Back and Otter breweries,
farmhouse ciders and a perry from the local Bridge
Farm. The treats continue with a skittles alley, whilst
the grounds host a cricket pitch, croquet lawn and
orchard. Just like the Tardis, the inside expands to
reveal a sizeable, well appointed restaurant, where
top-notch meals include many sourced from the
home farm of landlord Mark Hammick. Be tempted
by a starter of Pecker's pan-fried pigeon breast with
poached egg, lardons and pan juices, but do leave
room for pan-fried loin and fillet of Cheselbourne
venison with miniature venison cottage pie, braised
red cabbage and fondant potato; or crispy skinned
sea bass with green Thai butternut squash broth,
completing with mulled wine poached pear with
Blue Vinny ice cream.

Recommended in the area

Minterne Gardens, Minterne Magna; Sherborne
Castle, Sherborne; Hardy's Cottage (NT), Dorchester

The Cock & Bottle

Address: EAST MORDEN, Wareham, BH20 7DL
Tel: 01929 459238
Map ref: 2 SY99
Directions: From A35 W of Poole right onto B3075,
pub 0.5m on left
Open: all wk 11.30-2.30 6-11 (Sun noon-3 7-10.30)
🍴 ⚫ **L** all wk 12-2 **D** Mon-Sat 6-9 (Sun 7-9)
Facilities: Garden Parking
Notes: ⊕ HALL & WOODHOUSE 🚶 🐕

Cob, the material which was originally used to build this 400-year-old Dorset longhouse, is a mixture of clay, sand, straw and earth. Although durable, it doesn't last forever, which is probably why the pub was given a new brick skin a couple of hundred years ago. Inside, it is still comfortably rustic, with low beams and lots of nooks and crannies warmed by the log fires. In Happy Chatters Bar a large curved wooden settle typifies the 'keep it simple' approach to furnishing, which, particularly when locals are playing darts and dominoes, makes you realise the traditional village local is far from dead. On the hand pumps are real ales from the Hall & Woodhouse brewery in nearby Blandford Forum, and two real ciders. An always-changing menu makes good use of fresh game and fish, including sea bass, haddock, salmon and skate. Meat dishes include lamb shank, steak and kidney pudding, pigeon pie and chef's own-recipe chicken curry. Among the homemade desserts are apple and rhubarb pie, and there is a selection of Dorset cheeses. Light lunches, bar meals and Sunday roasts are also available. The newly extended restaurant now has an outdoor eating area under a pergola. Well-behaved dogs are welcome.

Recommended in the area

Corfe Castle; Tank Museum, Bovington; Hardy's Cottage (NT)

The Acorn Inn

★★★★ ⊕ INN

Address: EVERSHOT, Dorchester, DT2 0JW
Tel: 01935 83228
Email: stay@acorn-inn.co.uk
Website: www.acorn-inn.co.uk
Map ref: 2 ST50
Directions: From A37 between Yeovil & Dorchester, follow Evershot & Holywell signs, 0.5m to inn
Open: all day all wk 11am-11.30pm ⓑ ⓘ **L** all wk 12-2 **D** all wk 7-9
Rooms: 10 en suite **S** £79-£109 **D** £99-£194
Facilities: Garden Parking Wi-fi
Notes: ⊕ FREE HOUSE ⓘ ⓘ ⓘ 11 ⓘ

Thomas Hardy immortalised this 16th-century, stone-built coaching inn as the 'Sow and Acorn' in *Tess of the d'Urbervilles*, and in later years notorious 'hanging' Judge Jeffreys is thought to have used the main hall to hold court. The inn is set in the pretty village of Evershot (Hardy's Evershead) in a designated Area of Outstanding Natural Beauty. The bar, warmed by a blazing fire, is the perfect place to enjoy local real ales, ciders and over 50 single malt whiskies. Meals and drinks can be taken in the bar, restaurant, outside on the patio or in the garden. Three of the bedrooms feature four-poster beds, and two are suitable for families. All rooms have en suite bathrooms and are equipped with flat-screen TV, Wi-fi and facilities for making hot drinks. All food is sourced locally whenever possible from sustainable sources and responsible suppliers, allowing the inn to take full advantage of the fantastic seafood, game and vegetables on their doorstep. The varied carte menu in the award-winning restaurant changes frequently according to the seasonally available ingredients, and the bar menu offers hearty wholesome dishes to accompany the real ales and ciders; there's also the daily-changing special board.

Recommended in the area

Mapperton House & Gardens; Jurassic Coast World Heritage Site; Dorchester

The Kings Arms

★★★★★ 🛏 INN

Address: North Rd, Charlton Horethorne,
SHERBORNE, DT9 4NL
Tel: 01963 220281
Email: admin@thekingsarms.co.uk
Website: www.thekingsarms.co.uk
Map ref: 2 ST61 **Directions:** On A3145, N of
Sherborne. Pub in village centre
Open: all day all wk 🛏 🍴 Booking required
L all wk 12-2.30 **D** Mon-Thu 7-9.30, Fri-Sat 7-10,
Sun 7-9 **Rooms:** 10 en suite **D** £110-£125
Facilities: Garden Parking Wi-fi
Notes: ⊕ FREE HOUSE 🚶 🐕 ♟ 13

A beautiful Edwardian building, with an imposing façade, totally renovated and restored by owners Tony and Sarah Lethbridge a couple of years ago, and now a country pub, with a modern restaurant and boutique accommodation. The bar, whose chic soft furnishings and pretty fabrics blend with natural slate and oak, has become one of Dorset's more fashionable meeting places. A wide walkway leads past a theatre-style kitchen and a display of local artwork to the Georgian-mirrored dining room, from which doors open on to an extensive terrace overlooking a croquet lawn and the countryside. Classically trained chefs use locally sourced, seasonal ingredients to prepare traditional and modern British dishes, such as starters of smoked salmon risotto; potted brisket of beef; or goats' cheese and beetroot salad. Main dishes might be rump of lamb, ratatouille suet pudding and rosemary jus; Mediterranean stuffed chicken breast, niçoise and couscous salad, new potatoes; or confit of duck leg, smashed carrot and swede, baby spinach. Finish a meal with stem ginger parfait, lime sorbet, caramelised pears; or warm chocolate tart with cinnamon doughnuts. There are stylish, individually designed bedrooms, each with a marble wet room and powerful rain shower.

Recommended in the area

Sherborne Castle & Sherborne Museum; Minterne Gardens; Montacute House

Rose & Crown Trent

Address: TRENT, Sherborne, DT9 4SL
Tel: 01935 850776
Email: dine@roseandcrowntrent.co.uk
Website: www.roseandcrowntrent.co.uk
Map ref: 2 ST51
Directions: Just off A30 between Sherborne & Yeovil
Open: noon-3 6-11 (Sat-Sun noon-11)
♿ ⦿ Booking required **L** Tue-Sun 12-3 **D** Tue-Sat 6-9
Closed: Mon
Facilities: Garden Parking
Notes: ⊕ WADWORTH ⫟ ⫟ ⚲ 8

This thatched inn is situated in a conservation village at the heart of the Ernest Cook Trust Estate. Here in 1651, at Trent House, Charles II hid for several days while making his bid to escape to France. The original inn dates from the 14th century, built for workers erecting the spire of the church opposite, although the structure as it is now is 18th century. The interior still speaks eloquently of its past, especially in the Trent Barrow Room, which has a massive open fire, plenty of seating, old bottles, books and walls that must resonate with whatever a former landlord called Buff Biggins got up to that made him 'infamous'. Generations of farmers have beaten a path here for a pint, these days brewed by Wadworth in Devizes. The chef creates some very tempting dishes from locally sourced produce. The menu might feature seared lamb tongue and sweetbread salad, cauliflower purée with broad beans; or crispy rabbit stuffed with mozzarella, prune purée and celeriac remoulade. Simpler dishes feature at lunchtime - ploughman's, sandwiches and village eggs and chips perhaps. Apart from the restaurant, which has wonderful views, you can eat alfresco in warmer weather.

Recommended in the area

Fleet Air Arm Museum, Yeovilton; Montacute House; (NT); Tintinhull House & Garden (NT)

County Durham

Upper Weardale

Rose & Crown

★ ★ ◉◉ HOTEL

Address: ROMALDKIRK, Barnard Castle, DL12 9EB
Tel: 01833 650213
Email: hotel@rose-and-crown.co.uk
Website: www.rose-and-crown.co.uk
Map ref: 11 NY92
Directions: 6m NW from Barnard Castle on B6277
Open: all day all wk 11-11 ⓑ **L** all wk 12-1.30
D all wk 6.30-9.30 †◉❙ **L** Sun 12-1.30 **D** all wk 7.30-8.45
Closed: 23-27 Dec
Rooms: 12 (5 GF) **S** £95-£125 **D** £135-£210
Facilities: Parking Wi-fi
Notes: ⊕ FREE HOUSE ♦♦ ♒ ♟ 14

This is a three-storey creeper-clad Georgian inn, stone-built like the adjoining cottages, and across the green from the ancient Saxon church christened the Cathedral of the Dale. Step inside and you'll see fresh flowers, varnished oak panelling, old beams, gleaming copper and brass artefacts. Enter the quirky little bar, all oak settles and a fire crackling in the vast grate, timeless brasses, carriage lamps and rural artefacts, or retire to the secluded lounge behind, lulled by the ticking of a grandfather clock or maybe a glass of Allendale Ale whilst relaxing in the wing-back chairs. The more formal panelled, two AA Rosette restaurant is another option in this wonderful warren. The luck of Teesdale is its thriving farming community which produces some of the best food in England, local sporting estates and the proximity of small fishing harbours. Making the most of this largesse, the chefs create a thoughtful range of dishes, starting perhaps with seared mackerel fillet, roasted fennel and walnut salad, before a main of roast pink rump of lamb, confit of shoulder, fondant potato, purple sprouting broccoli, mushrooms and red wine jus. Desserts might be crème brûlee or warm chocolate brownie and vanilla ice cream. Comfortable bedrooms and contemporary suites are available.

Recommended in the area

Yorkshire Dales National Park; Cauldron Snout Waterfall; Hamsterley Forest

Essex

Parish church, Saffron Walden

Axe & Compasses

Address: High St, ARKESDEN, CB11 4EX
Tel: 01799 550272
Map ref: 4 TL43
Directions: From Buntingford take B1038 towards
Newport, left for Arkesden
Open: all wk noon-2.30 6-11 (Sun noon-3,
7-10.30) ⬛ ⑩ **L** all wk 12-2 **D** all wk 6.45-9.30
Facilities: Garden Parking
Notes: ⬤ GREENE KING ♟ 14

Picture postcard perfect, this inn is in the narrow main street of a beautiful village. A stream called Wicken Water runs alongside, criss-crossed by footbridges leading to white, cream and pink colour-washed thatched cottages. The thatched section of the inn dates from 1650, but the building has since been extended to utilise the old stable block which accommodated horses until the 1920s, and a 19th-century addition that now houses the public bar. The beamed interior is full of character and includes the welcoming public bar, a softly lit restaurant, and a cosy lounge furnished with antiques, horse brasses and old agricultural implements. During winter there might be a warming fire blazing and in summer there is seating outside on the patio. Beer lovers will enjoy the real ales on tap which include, Greene King IPA, Olde Trip and Old Speckled Hen. For those who prefer the juice of the vine, there is a wine list that's split almost evenly between France and the rest of the world. The restaurant offers a full à la carte, while an extensive blackboard menu is available. Dishes include medallions of beef fillet and rösti potato with soft green peppercorns, brandy and cream; homemade moussaka with Greek salad and garlic bread; and sirloin steak cooked with a Drambuie, horseradish and mushroom sauce.

Recommended in the area

Audley End House & Gardens; Imperial War Museum Duxford; Mountfitchet Castle

The Cricketers

Address: CLAVERING, Saffron Walden, CB11 4QT
Tel: 01799 550442
Email: info@thecricketers.co.uk
Website: www.thecricketers.co.uk
Map ref: 4 TL43
Directions: M11 junct 10, A505 E, A1301, B1383.
At Newport take B1038
Open: all day all wk 🍴 L all wk 12-2 **D** all wk
6.30-9.30
Closed: 25-26 Dec
Facilities: Garden Parking Wi-fi
Notes: 🍺 FREE HOUSE 🍴 🍷 17

The Cricketers has served the local community for nigh-on 500 years and has been under the same ownership for over 30; there's beams, rural artefacts, brasses, cosy winter log fires, and outside a wisteria around the door and tables in the rose-fringed garden. This is a relaxing destination dining pub where head chef, Justin Greig, demonstrates his passion for using quality local ingredients, and develops his Italian-inspired, seasonally changing menus. Jamie Oliver, son of the owners Trevor and Sally Oliver, supplies the pub with wonderful seasonal vegetables, herbs and salads from his certified organic garden nearby, perfectly complementing the fresh, organic produce which are at the heart of the memorable fare on offer here.

Open the batting with breast of local pigeon, cooked pink with a light pea purée topped with watercress salad before scoring with medallions of Priors Hall Farm pork, sautéed in garlic butter with potato rösti, black pudding and rosemary jus; spicy venison meatballs with curly pappardelle; or home-made potato gnocchi with crushed butternut squash and goats' cheese. With a choice of 17 wines by the glass, and beers from East Anglia, time passes easily here. Children are particularly welcomed, and have their own small, dedicated menu.

Recommended in the area

Audley End House; Imperial War Museum Duxford; Cambridge

The Swan at Felsted

Address: Station Rd, FELSTED, Dunmow, CM6 3DG
Tel: 01371 820245
Email: info@theswanatfelsted.co.uk
Website: www.thegreatpubcompany.co.uk
Map ref: 4 TL62
Directions: M11 junct 8, A120 signed Felsted.
Pub in village centre
Open: all wk 11.30-3 5-11 (Sun 11.30-6)
🍴🍽️ **L** Mon-Sat 12-2.30, Sun 12-4 **D** Mon-Thu
5.30-9.30, Fri-Sat 5.30-9.45
Facilities: Garden Parking
Notes: 🍺 GREENE KING 👬 🐾 🍷 14

Ideally situated for exploring the stunning north Essex countryside, and only a short drive from Stansted Airport, The Swan is an imposing building and was for many years the village bank. It was rebuilt after a disastrous fire in the early 20th century, and the interior decoration has a fresh, contemporary feel. A pretty courtyard garden to the rear provides a tranquil, sheltered eating area overlooked by the village church, and during winter a roaring log fire greets guests as they cross the threshold. The kitchen has a great commitment to quality local produce, with dishes ranging from pork sausages, creamy mash and red onion gravy, or Swan bacon and cheese burger, to slow roasted lamb neck in a port, mushroom and baby onion sauce with dauphinoise potatoes or oven roasted cod, olive oil mash, local asparagus and nut brown butter. Fine wines, including a good selection by the glass, and well-kept cask ales also help to achieve a fine balance between the traditional English pub and a high quality restaurant. A stylish function room with its own entrance and bespoke menus is available for private parties of up to 18 people.

Recommended in the area
Hatfield Forest National Nature Reserve;
Mountfitchet Castle Experience;
Paycocke's House (NT)

The Compasses at Pattiswick

Address: Compasses Rd, PATTISWICK, CM77 8BG
Tel: 01376 561322
Email: info@thecompassesatpattiswick.co.uk
Website: www.thegreatpubcompany.co.uk
Map ref: 4 TL82
Directions: A120 from Braintree towards
Colchester. After Bradwell 1st left to Pattiswick
Open: all wk 11-3 5.30-11 (Sat 5.30-mdnt, Sun noon-
4 5.30-9) 🛏 **L** all wk 12-3 **D** Mon-Thu 5.30-9.30, Fri-
Sat 5.30-9.45, Sun 5.30-9 🍽 **L** Mon-Sat 12-3
D Mon-Thu 5.30-9.30, Fri-Sat 5.30-9.45, Sun 5.30-9
Facilities: Garden Parking Wi-fi
Notes: 🍺 FREE HOUSE 👬 🐾 🍷 13

Tucked away in delightful countryside, this
renovated gastro-pub offers a contemporary take
on country style, with a flagstone floor in the bar,
an open fire and rustic furniture. The menu of light
bar meals and à la carte dishes is packed with
quality produce, including a rich selection of game
from the surrounding woods. Dishes range from
traditional pub classics, such as beer battered fish
and chips, to leg of lamb steak with creamy roasted
garlic mash and red wine jus, along with daily
specials. Similarly, the children's menu concentrates
on simple classics popular with younger guests.
The balance between bar, restaurant and private
dining room enables The Compasses to cater for
any occasion, and it is popular with locals, walkers
and cyclists as well as those willing to travel in
search of quality. Outside, extensive patios offer
separate areas allowing families a clear view of
the children's play area, while locals can enjoy the
glorious Pattiswick sunsets with a well-kept pint of
Woodforde's Wherry, from Norfolk, or one of a range
of local ales from Nethergate Brewery.

Recommended in the area

Paycocke's House (NT); Beth Chatto Gardens;
Colchester Zoo

Canal lock at Beeleigh Falls, Maldon

Gloucestershire

Mill Street, Tewkesbury

The Old Passage Inn

★ ★ ★ ★ ◎ ◎ 🍴 RESTAURANT WITH ROOMS

Address: Passage Rd, ARLINGHAM, GL2 7JR
Tel: 01452 740547
Email: oldpassage@btconnect.com
Website: www.theoldpassage.com
Map ref: 2 SO71 **Directions:** A38 onto B4071
through Arlingham to river **Open:** 10-3 7-finish
🍴 **L** Tue-Sat 12-2, Sun 12-3 **D** Tue-Sat 7-9 🍽 **L** Tue-Sat
12-2, Sun 12-3 **D** Tue-Sat 7-9 Booking required in bar &
restaurant **Closed:** 25 Dec, Jan-Feb Tue & Wed eve, Sun
eve & Mon **Rooms:** 3 en suite
S £60-£130 **D** £80-£130 **Facilities:** Garden Parking
Wi-fi **Notes:** ⊕ FREE HOUSE ♥ ♥ ♥ 12

The 'old passage' in the name refers to the ford and
later ferry service that crossed the River Severn
here. The rich harvest of salmon and elvers that
once came from the river is now sadly depleted,
but chef Mark Redwood's seafood menu features
local, sustainable ingredients, such as freshwater
crayfish, whenever possible. Fresh lobster from
Pembrokeshire (sometimes from Cornwall) is
always available from the tank, and freshly shucked
oysters and fruits de mer are specialities. The simple
but innovative menus often change daily to reflect
what is available, but might include such dishes as
roast tranche of turbot served with parsley new
potatoes and hollandaise. The large dining room
has a fresh and airy appeal, and in summer you can

eat out on the garden terrace, with views across a
bend in the river towards Newnham-on-Severn and
the distant Forest of Dean. The three stunning en
suite bedrooms enjoy the same views and enable
guests to enjoy not only an exceptional breakfast,
but also take full advantage of the excellent wine
list at dinner, which includes plenty of half bottles
and wines by the glass, and features wines from the
Three Choirs Vineyard at Newent.

Recommended in the area

Wildfowl & Wetlands Trust, Slimbridge; Owlpen
Manor; Berkeley Castle

Eight Bells

Address: Church St, CHIPPING CAMPDEN, GL55 6JG
Tel: 01386 840371
Email: neilhargreaves@bellinn.fsnet.co.uk
Website: www.eightbellsinn.co.uk
Map ref: 3 SP13
Directions: In town centre
Open: all day all wk noon-11 (Sun noon-10.30)
🍴 ⛽ **L** Mon-Thu 12-2, Fri-Sun 12-2.30 **D** Mon-Thu
6.30-9, Fri-Sat 6.30-9.30, Sun 6.30-8.45
Closed: 25 Dec
Facilities: Garden Wi-fi
Notes: ⊕ FREE HOUSE 🚻 🐕 ♟ 8

Originally built in the 14th-century to house the stonemasons that built the nearby church, this lovely, flower decked inn was later used to store the peel of eight bells that were hung in the church tower. Just off the bustling high street of this showpiece Cotswold town, the Eight Bells was rebuilt in the 17th-century using the rough-hewn stones and timbers you see today. The way in is through a cobbled entranceway leading into two atmospheric beamed bars with open fireplaces and, in the floor of one, a surviving priest's hole; outside is an enclosed courtyard and terraced garden. The owners have gone to great lengths to avoid the Eight Bells turning into a gastro-pub. Although food is served, it's also a place to enjoy the Hook Norton and Purity real ales. Freshly prepared, locally sourced dishes are offered, such as lunchtime ciabatta sandwiches, home-made soup and fish pie. From a main menu come mature Cheddar cheese and spring onion fritters, followed by home-made, deep-filled chicken and leek shortcrust pastry pie; and seared lamb's liver with bubble and squeak, bacon and shallot jus. Coffee crème brûlée, and white chocolate cheesecake with winter fruit compôte are typical desserts. Children will be tempted by their own menu.

Recommended in the area

The Cotswold Way; Hidcote Manor (NT); Stratford-upon-Avon

Seagrave Arms

★ ★ ★ ★ ⑳ INN

Address: Friday St, Weston Subedge,
CHIPPING CAMPDEN, GL55 6QH
Tel: 01386 840192
Email: info@seagravearms.co.uk
Website: www.seagravearms.co.uk
Map ref: 3 SP13 **Directions:** A44 onto B4081
signed Chipping Campden. At junct with High St left
into Dyers Ln. 0.5m to Weston Subedge. Pub on left
Open: all day ⑩ **L** Tue-Sun 12-3 **D** Tue-Sun 6-9.15
Closed: Mon **Rooms:** 5 en suite (1 GF) **D** £95-£115
Facilities: Garden Parking
Notes: ⊕ FREE HOUSE ⁙ ⌁

This restored Georgian stone country inn and
restaurant is midway between the picturesque
Cotswolds honeypot villages of Broadway and
Chipping Campden, while Stratford-upon-Avon
and Cheltenham are only 20 minutes away by car.
Winter means open log fires and on sunny days
there's a much appreciated sheltered courtyard for
drinking and dining. The bar stocks real ales from
local breweries Hook Norton, Goffs of Winchcombe
and Purity of Great Alne, Hogan's cider from
Alcester, and even British lagers, from the Cotswold
Brewing Company. Most wines are offered by the
glass. As for the beers, diligent local sourcing keeps
food miles low and quality and sustainability high.
An extensive bar snacks menu lists sharing boards
of cheeses, such as Blue Brie from Stow, and home-
cured chorizo, while in the AA Rosette restaurant
the seasonal menus may offer starters of partridge
and polenta terrine; and crisp fried tiger prawns
with sweet chilli sauce, and mains of braised
rabbit with Dijon mustard, leeks and turnips; whole
grilled Cornish lemon sole with parsley butter; and
vine tomato and Parmesan risotto with roasted,
marinated vegetables. Luxury en suite bedrooms
are provided with king-size beds, flat-screen TVs
and complimentary toiletries.

Recommended in the area
Hidecote Manor Gardens (NT); Cotswold Falconry
Centre; Bourton-on-the-Water

The Tunnel House Inn

Address: Tarlton Rd, COATES, Cirencester, GL7 6PW
Tel: 01285 770280
Email: info@tunnelhouse.com
Website: www.tunnelhouse.com
Map ref: 2 SO90
Directions: A433 from Cirencester towards
Tetbury, 2m, right towards Coates, follow brown
inn signs
Open: all day all wk noon-late ⮕ **L** noon-9.30
D noon-9.30
Facilities: Garden Parking Wi-fi
Notes: ⊕ FREE HOUSE ⋔ ⋔ ♈ 9 ◧

In a glorious rural location down a very bumpy
track, this old Cotswolds pub by Sapperton Tunnel
once provided accommodation for the navvies
building the Thames and Severn Canal. The
enjoyably cluttered bar is festooned with pictures,
prints, posters and advertising signs, so there's
plenty to read over a pint, or head outside to the
garden and enjoy the views across the fields. Log
fires provide comfort when it's cold. Open all day
for food, the menu alters monthly according to
seasonal changes in local produce. Eat lightly with
a tomato, mozzarella and pesto sandwich or a
ploughman's, or choose something more filling such
as 8oz English rump or rib-eye steaks with beurre
Café de Paris, chips, mixed leaves and peppercorn
sauce; monkfish wrapped in prosciutto on a lentil
cassoulet; or cannelloni filled with roasted chunky
ratatouille topped with three-cheese sauce. There
are pub classics too, including Wiltshire honey-roast
ham and eggs, and beer-battered cod and chips.
For dessert, check out the individual blackberry
cheesecake, or profiteroles topped with rich
coffee, chocolate and hazelnut sauce. Children
will probably opt for their usual favourites to eat,
following which they can let off steam in their own
play area.

Recommended in the area
Westonbirt Arboretum; Cotswold Water Park;
Cirencester

The Green Dragon Inn

★★★★ 🛏 INN

Address: Cockleford, COWLEY, Cheltenham,
GL53 9NW
Tel: 01242 870271
Email: green-dragon@buccaneer.co.uk
Website: www.green-dragon-inn.co.uk
Map ref: 2 SO91
Directions: Telephone for directions
Open: all day all wk 🛏 🍴 **L** Mon-Fri 12-2.30, Sat
12-3, Sun 12-3.30 **D** all wk 6-10
Rooms: 9 en suite (4 GF)
Facilities: Garden Parking Wi-fi
Notes: ⊕ BUCCANEER 👬 🐕

A handsome stone-built inn dating from the 17th century, the Green Dragon is located in the hamlet of Cockleford at the heart of the picturesque Cotswolds. It is a popular retreat for those who appreciate good food, fine wine and real ales. The fittings and furniture are the work of Robert Thompson, the Mouse Man of Kilburn (so-called for his trademark mouse) who lends his name to the Mouse Bar, with its stone-flagged floors, beamed ceilings and crackling log fires. Nine cottage-style, en suite bedrooms are available, including a suite. All rooms are equipped with direct dial telephones and TVs, and breakfast is included, along with the newspaper of your choice. The menu takes in lunchtime sandwiches, children's favourites, and starters/light meals such as baked field mushroom with spinach, Cerney goats' cheese and cranberry relish, warm Thai chicken noodle salad and Caesar salad. The daily specials board might offer grilled brill fillet with an orange, watercress and fennel salad or roasted pork loin steak with pear and leek stuffing and cider gravy. The choice of real ales includes Battledown Premium, Directors and Butcombe. Additional features are the heated dining terrace and the function room/skittle alley.

Recommended in the area
Holst Birthplace Museum; Gloucester Cathedral;
Witcombe Roman Villa

The Inn at Fossebridge

★★★★ 🍽 INN

Address: Stow Rd, FOSSEBRIDGE, GL54 3JS
Tel: 01285 720721
Email: info@fossebridgeinn.co.uk
Website: www.fossebridgeinn.co.uk
Map ref: 3 SP01 **Directions:** M4 junct 15, A419
towards Cirencester, A429 towards Stow. Pub approx
6m on left **Open:** all day all wk (Sun noon-11.30)
🛏 🍽 **L** Mon-Fri 12-2.30, Sat 12-3, Sun 12-3.30
D all wk 6-9.30/10 Apr-Sep, all wk 6-9 Oct-Mar
Rooms: 9 en suite **D** £110-£165
Facilities: Garden Parking Wi-fi
Notes: 🛢 FREE HOUSE 👭 🏹

Although now a family-run Cotswolds dining pub
and country hotel, this attractive 17th-century
free house has a rich history as a former coaching
inn. Standing on the ancient Fosse Way and
surrounded by extensive grounds, it was once the
Lord Chedworth's Arms, his lordship a one-time
landowner whose name is commemorated by
the wonderful old bar. Here, and in the integral
restaurant, you'll find exposed beams, stone walls,
polished flagstone floors and open log fires at every
turn. The creative menus and daily specials board
offer tempting snacks and meals made from fresh,
local and seasonal produce - sandwiches, light
lunches, Fossebridge Classics (home-made burger)
as well as hearty main courses. Thus lunch or dinner
might begin with Cornish potted crab with toasted
malted bread, or chicken liver parfait with red onion
marmalade, and continue with the house signature
dish of saddle of Cotswold lamb, grilled lemon sole
or garden pea, asparagus and Parmesan risotto.
Warm chocolate fondant with Cotswold vanilla bean
ice cream or raspberry crème brûlée with white
chocolate shortbread would then still slip down a
treat. The bedrooms have all been sumptuously
appointed in Georgian style.

Recommended in the area

Chedworth Roman Villa (NT); Keith Harding's World
of Mechanical Music; Bibury Trout Farm

The Weighbridge Inn

Address: MINCHINHAMPTON, GL6 9AL
Tel: 01453 832520
Email: enquiries@2in1pub.co.uk
Website: www.2in1pub.co.uk
Map ref: 2 SO80
Directions: On B4014 between Nailsworth & Avening
Open: all day all wk noon-11 (Sun noon-10.30)
🍴 **L** all wk 12-9.30 **D** all wk 12-9.30 🍽 **L** all wk 12-9.30 **D** all wk 12-9.30 **Closed:** 25 Dec
Facilities: Garden Parking Wi-fi
Notes: ⊕ FREE HOUSE 👬 🐕 🍷 15

By the side of the old packhorse road to Bristol, now a footpath and bridleway, stands this part-17th century classic Cotswold inn. The weighbridge that once was here used to serve the local woollen mills, weighing the raw materials on arrival, and again when the finished cloth left for markets in Bristol, Bath and London. An illustration on the cover of the restaurant menu shows how it looked when the horsedrawn vehicles lined up to have their cargoes weighed, while memorabilia from the mills themselves and rural artefacts from the area are displayed around the pub. In the bar and restaurant you'll find a good choice of real ales, wines and traditional home-prepared hearty fare, including the inn's 'famous 2-in-1' pies. First produced here more than 30 years ago, these double delights contain a filling of your choice, such as salmon in a creamy sauce, or steak and kidney, in one half, while the other can be packed with cauliflower cheese, broccoli mornay or root vegetables to give a variety of combinations. Other main courses include lamb shank, seafood bake, chicken Maryland, and spinach and mushroom lasagne. Outside, the patios and sheltered landscaped gardens offer good views of the Cotswolds.

Recommended in the area

Westonbirt Arboretum; Woodchester Mansion; Chavenage House

The Feathered Nest Inn

★ ★ ★ ★ ★ ◎◎ ☺ INN

Address: NETHER WESTCOTE, OX7 6SD
Tel: 01993 833030
Email: info@thefeatherednestinn.co.uk
Website: www.thefeatherednestinn.co.uk
Map ref: 3 SP22 **Directions:** A424 between
Burford & Stow-on-the-Wold, follow signs
Open: all day ☕ ◎ **L** Tue-Sun 12-2.30 **D** Tue-Sun
6.30-9.30
Closed: 25 Dec, Mon
Rooms: 4 en suite
Facilities: Garden Parking Wi-fi
Notes: ⊕ FREE HOUSE ♦♦ ♠ ♀ 19

Thoughtfully updated and refurbished, this former malthouse now provides everything you'd expect from a traditional country inn. At its core is the pub itself, whose welcoming log-fired bar does brisk trade in cask-conditioned ales from Brakspear, Wychwood and other local breweries, and more than 19 Old and New World wines by the glass from a bin list that tops 200. Modern British cooking depends to a great extent on locally produced ingredients - indeed, many of the herbs and vegetables come from no further afield than the kitchen garden. The restaurant, which proudly holds two AA Rosettes, offers reasonably priced, daily changing lunch and dinner menus typically offering pan-fried hake with pak choi, cèpes and girolles; English Rose veal loin with potato terrine, carrots and elderberry dressing; and agnolotti, pasta parcels stuffed with squash and sage, and served with pickled red onions and cob-nuts. For a tasty bar snack try crispy chicken wings with chorizo mayonnaise, or a Lancashire Bomb cheese, tomato, onion and rocket sandwich. Take it outside to the garden terrace and sit in the shade of a sycamore tree. Individually decorated bedrooms are furnished with antiques and all the usual facilities, including Wi-fi. AA Pub of the Year for England 2011-12.

Recommended in the area

Birdland; Cotswold Farm Park; Snowshill Manor & Gardens (NT)

The Ostrich Inn

Address: NEWLAND, nr Coleford, GL16 8NP
Tel: 01594 833260
Email: kathryn@theostrichinn.com
Website: www.theostrichinn.com
Map ref: 2 SO50
Directions: Follow Monmouth signs from
Chepstow (A466), Newland signed from Redbrook
Open: all wk noon-3 (Mon-Fri 6.30-11.30, Sat
6-11.30, Sun 6.30-10.30) ⏚ ⚲ **L** all wk 12-2.30
D Sun-Fri 6.30-9.30, Sat 6-9.30
Facilities: Garden
Notes: ⊕ FREE HOUSE ⦙ 🐕

A 13th-century free house in a pretty village
close to two Areas of Outstanding Natural Beauty
- the Forest of Dean and the Wye Valley. It was
constructed for the workmen who built All Saints
Church opposite, known locally as the Cathedral of
the Forest. The pub's name probably came from the
ostrich emblem used by the Probyn family,
one-time local landowners. An unusual feature
is the priest hole, alongside the more predictable
wooden beams and log fire warming the large
lounge bar, where landlady Kathryn Horton serves
up to eight regular and guest real ales. You eat in
the small, intimate restaurant, the larger bar, the
walled garden or on the patio, choosing dishes
such as freshly prepared rack of Welsh lamb with
merguez sausage and smoked belly pork in rich
Madeira sauce; monkfish and tiger prawns in
rich chive butter cream sauce, Gruyère mashed
potato and dressed salad leaves; or creamy wild
mushroom and wilted rocket risotto, lemon and
white truffle oil and wild mushroom scented pepper.
In the bar expect 'fulfilling' soup, pastas, sizzling
ribs, and three cheese 'certainly not a quiche' tart.
With a reference to an affordable wine list, The
Ostrich can rest its case.

Recommended in the area

Clearwell Caves; Dick Whittington Family Leisure
Park; National Diving & Activity Centre, Chepstow

The Bell at Sapperton

Address: SAPPERTON, Cirencester, GL7 6LE
Tel: 01285 760298
Email: thebell@sapperton66.freeserve.co.uk
Website: www.foodatthebell.co.uk
Map ref: 2 SO90
Directions: From A419 between Cirencester &
Stroud follow Sapperton signs
Open: 11-2.30 6.30-11 (Sun 12-10.30)
🍴 **L** all wk 12-2.15 **D** all wk 7-9.15 booking required
Closed: 25 Dec, Sun eve in winter
Facilities: Garden Parking
Notes: ⊕ FREE HOUSE ♥ ♟ 20

Regular diners come to this restored Cotswold pub, located in an idyllic and historic village close to the source of the River Thames, for Paul Davidson and Pat LeJeune's regularly-changing menus. These are based on produce from an impressive line up of West Country and Welsh Borders suppliers. If you want just a drink, there are plenty of wines by the glass, while Paul's passion for real ales ensures his Uley Old Spot and Otter Bitter are always in tip-top condition. Although The Bell could hardly be further from the sea, it enjoys a reputation for the freshest fish and seafood, so check the chalkboards for the day's catch, which might include wild salmon, turbot, brill, and scallops (a wider selection is offered at weekends). The daily changing lunchtime menu features both light dishes, such as grilled sardines on red peppers with olive oil dressing, and more substantial ones, such as bacon chop with free-range fried egg and Butts Farm black pudding. Evening choices are home-cured salt cod croquette with pickled chicory, tomato and tarragon dressing; chargrilled Hereford rib-eye steak with roast tomato and mushrooms; and butternut and mascarpone risotto infused with truffle oil and salad leaves.

Recommended in the area

Cotswold Water Park; Westonbirt Arboretum; The Cotswolds

The Swan at Southrop

◎◎

Address: SOUTHROP, Nr Lechlade, GL7 3NU
Tel: 01367 850205
Email: info@theswanatsouthrop.co.uk
Website: www.theswanatsouthrop.co.uk
Map ref: 3 SP10
Directions: Off A361 between Lechlade & Burford
Open: all wk 12-3 6-11 ⚍ **L** all wk 12-3 **D** Mon-Sat
6-10 **Closed:** Dec 25
Facilities: Garden Wi-fi
Notes: ⊕ FREE HOUSE ⚭ ⚑

The early 17th-century, creeper-clad Swan sits almost smugly on the green in this trim Cotswolds village, as indeed it has every right to. Owned by Sebastian and Lana Snow, with the help of managers Dom and Joelle Abbott and sous chef Piotr Skcozen, this much-accoladed free house has fast gained an enviable reputation, and two AA Rosettes, for excellent, locally sourced 'turf to table' food and attentive, friendly service. The interior - bar, snug and restaurant - is surprisingly light for such an historic building, but homely too, especially with the open fires burning. Seasonal ingredients from the immediate area often feature on the menu, such as crayfish from the old gravel pits in Lechlade, partridge from the Hatherop Estate, and pork from Kelmscott (try slow-roasted pork belly with apples, cannellini beans and sage). Other possibilities are stuffed saddle of rabbit, prunes, spiced couscous and chickpeas; teriyaki of salmon, king prawns and oriental vegetable spaghetti; and wild mushroom risotto. As well as an extensive wine list are the beers - Swan Bitter, Hook Norton and a monthly local guest. An old-fashioned skittle alley doubles up as a delightful private room for larger parties. Accomodation is available in cottages on the Southrop Manor Estate. There is also a cookery school – Thyme at Southrop.

Recommended in the area

Bibury; Minster Lovell Hall; Buscot Park (NT)

The Farriers Arms

Address: Main St, TODENHAM, Moreton-in-Marsh,
GL56 9PF
Tel: 01608 650901
Email: info@farriersarms.com
Website: www.farriersarms.com
Map ref: 3 SP23
Directions: From Moreton-in-Marsh A429 N.
Right to Todenham
Open: all wk noon-3 6-11 (Sun 6.30-11)
🍴 L Mon-Sat 12-2, Sun 12-2.30 **D** Mon-Sat 6-9,
Sun 6.30-9 **Facilities:** Garden Parking
Notes: ⊕ FREE HOUSE ♦♦ ♣ ♟ 10

Leave Stratford-upon-Avon to the tourists for a
while and take a 15-minute drive to this picturesque
Cotswold village and its 17th-century pub. Find
a cosy seat in the bar, with its large inglenook
fireplace, polished flagstone floors, exposed stone
walls and hop hung beams. For a more formal
experience try the refurbished restaurant, or for
group bookings of up to 12, you can book the
secluded library surrounded by interesting old
books. In the summer months, the suntrap patio
garden provides a quiet spot with views of the
church. The menu in the bar and restaurant changes
regularly to offer a good range of freshly prepared
dishes using local produce, including Todenham-
reared beef, pork, lamb and game. So perhaps try

lamb rump with roast onion crushed potatoes and
minted gravy, or pan-fried pheasant breast with wild
mushrooms and chestnuts, Lyonnaise potatoes
and Madeira sauce. There's normally a fish option,
such as halibut wrapped in Parma ham, in a white
wine cream sauce; a vegetarian option might be
field mushroom topped with roasted vegetables
and apple and walnut risotto. Booking is essenial for
Sunday lunch when there's chalkboard choices, plus
roast beef and leg of pork. Cask Marque accredited
ales and premium Cotswold lager. are on offer.

Recommended in the area
Batsford Arboretum; Cotswold Farm Park;
Blenheim Palace

Kiftsgate Court Gardens

Greater Manchester

Dobcross

The Victoria

Address: Stamford St, ALTRINCHAM, WA14 1EX
Tel: 0161 613 1855
Email: the.victoria@yahoo.co.uk
Map ref: 6 SJ78
Directions: From rail station cross main road, right. 2nd left into Stamford St
Open: all day all wk noon-11 (Sun noon-6) 🥂 **L** Mon-Sat 12-3 **D** Mon-Sat 5.30-9 ⏺️ **L** Mon-Sat 12-3, Sun 12-4 **D** Mon-Sat 5.30-9
Closed: 26 Dec & 1 Jan
Notes: 🛢️ FREE HOUSE ❦ ♟ 10

Situated in the Stamford quarter of Altrincham, tucked away behind the main shopping street, The Victoria has been carefully restored as a traditional food-led tavern. This small, one-roomed pub offers a wood-panelled dining area to one side, and a more casual bar area on the other. There's a light lunch as well as the main menu, which changes every six to eight weeks according to seasonal availability and majors on locally sourced ingredients. Starters might include Morecambe Bay brown shrimp and battered prawn cocktail; Bury black pudding Scotch egg topped with locally smoked bacon; or Blacksticks Blue cheese and broad bean rice pudding. Among the main courses may be naturally raised Cumbrian pink veal and mushroom steamed pudding; and

oven-roasted monkfish on a bed of pease pudding. On Sunday, a traditional roast is also available, usually including locally raised rib of beef. The wine list features over 30 carefully chosen bottles, while there are a range of handpulled cask ales, as well as many non-alcoholic drinks from the temperance bar, such as Dandelion and Burdock. The search is on for products rarely seen on menus, and future delights may include dishes such as tripe, smoked eel and pressed tongue.

Recommended in the area

Dunham Massey Hall Park & Garden (NT); Altrincham Market; Altrincham Ice Dome

Hampshire

View from Butser Hill

The Anchor Inn

★★★★ ◎◎ INN

Address: Lower Froyle, ALTON, GU34 4NA
Tel: 01420 23261
Email: info@anchorinnatlowerfroyle.co.uk
Website: www.anchorinnatlowerfroyle.co.uk
Map ref: 3 SU73
Directions: From A31 follow Bentley signs
Open: all day all wk 🍴 **L** all wk 12-2.30 **D** all wk
6.30-9.30 🍴 **L** Mon-Sat 12-2.30, Sun 12-4 **D** Mon-Fri
6.30-9.30, Sat 6.30-10, Sun 7-9
Rooms: 5 en suite **S** £110-£140 **D** £110-£140
Facilities: Garden Parking Wi-fi
Notes: ⊕ THE MILLERS COLLECTION 🕯 🐾 🏆 9

The Anchor belongs to Miller's Collection, a group of sensitively restored old inns that evoke the feel of a bygone England. The decor in this classically furnished dining pub is influenced by WWI and WWII with rooms named after war poets. Thus, you may have a pint of Hampshire-brewed real ale while enjoying a meal and listening to cricket on a Robert's radio. As much produce as possible is sourced within a tight radius, so at the bar you might meet the farmer who produces the beef, or the keen shot who supplied the pheasant. The principally traditional British menu with occasional European influences should therefore be no surprise, nor should the two AA Rosettes. Begin with hand-picked Portland crab mayonnaise, chilli and lime, avocado purée and brown crab pâté on toast. Mains are typified by roast pheasant breasts, pan haggerty, cabbage and bacon, Puy lentils; free-range chicken Kiev with sun-dried tomato salad; and fillet of wild turbot with sauté potatoes, spinach and beef shin sauce. Unashamedly supporting country sports, the inn can organise local fishing or shooting. Overnight guests enjoy luxurious, individually designed rooms. Every Armistice Day there's a fund-raising lunch for the Royal British Legion.

Recommended in the area

Jane Austen's House; Birdworld; North Downs Way

The Wellington Arms

◎◎

Address: Baughurst Rd, BAUGHURST, RG26 5LP
Tel: 0118 982 0110
Email: hello@thewellingtonarms.com
Website: www.thewellingtonarms.com
Map ref: 3 SU56
Directions: From A4, E of Newbury, through Aldermaston. At 2nd rdbt 2nd exit signed Baughurst, left at T-junct, pub 1m
Open: 12-3.30 6-11 ⌚ **L** all wk 12-2.30
D Mon-Sat 6-9.30 **Closed:** Sun eve
Facilities: Garden Parking Wi-fi
Notes: ⊕ FREE HOUSE ⬤ ⬤ ⬤ 11

Lost down a maze of lanes in peaceful countryside between Basingstoke and Newbury, the remodelled 'Welly', formerly a hunting lodge for the Duke of Wellington, draws discerning diners from miles around due to the combined efforts of Jason King and Simon Page, who have worked wonders with the place since taking over some six years ago. Jason's daily chalkboard menus offer plenty of interest and imagination and much of the produce is organic and sourced within a five-mile radius of the pub, with salad leaves, herbs and vegetables from the pub's own polytunnel and three raised vegetable beds, eggs from their 100 rare breed and rescue hens, plus five Jacob sheep, four Tamworth pigs and three beehives. This translates to gazpacho of tomatoes, cucumbers and peppers, home-reared rack of pork with apple sauce; or Baughurst House roe deer braised in red wine and with a flaky pastry lid, and elderflower cordial jelly with Persian fairy floss and pouring cream; or flourless dark chocolate cake and espresso ice cream. Booking ahead is advisable as there's only eight tables inside the tastefully decorated single bar-cum-dining room. The garden has become an extension for diners too, and if the weather's a little on the chilly side just ask for a wool rug to keep you warm.

Recommended in the area

The Vyne (NT); Basing House; Roman Silchester

The Sun Inn

Address: Sun Hill, BENTWORTH, Alton, GU34 5JT
Tel: 01420 562338
Email: info@thesuninnbentworth.co.uk
Website: www.thesuninnbentworth.co.uk
Map ref: 3 SU64
Directions: From A339 between Alton & Basingstoke follow Bentworth signs
Open: all wk 12-3 6-11 (Sun 12-10.30) 🍴 **L** all wk 12-2 **D** all wk 7-9.30
Facilities: Garden Parking
Notes: 🍺 FREE HOUSE 👬 🐕 🍷 12

This delightful, flower-adorned, 17th-century pub stands at one end of Bentworth, just after you think you've passed the last cottage in the village. Full of character, little has changed over the years. There are three interconnecting, beamed, brick- and wood-floored rooms, each with its own inglenook fireplace, scrubbed pine tables with candles, oak benches, sparkling brassware and old pictures. Adding to this heady atmosphere are fresh flowers and plants, daily newspapers and magazines, and helpful cheery staff. It's a big hit with beer drinkers - as a thriving free house, it offers eight hand-pumped real ales, among them Ringwood Best, Hogs Back TEA and Andwell Resolute, all Hampshire brewed. There's an extensive menu of tempting home-prepared food, examples being steak and ale pie; beef stew with dumplings; calves' liver and bacon; giant filled Yorkshire pudding; half shoulder of lamb; avocado and Stilton bake; crispy beer-battered cod; venison cooked in Guinness; and pheasant casserole. Popular desserts are banoffee pie, warm chocolate brownie and apple and raspberry crumble. Outside at the front (don't worry, there's little passing traffic) is a row of tables with umbrellas and there's a small, pretty garden.

Recommended in the area

Gilbert White's House & Oates Collection; Watercress Line; Basing House

The Red Lion

Address: Rope Hill, BOLDRE, Lymington, SO41 8NE
Tel: 01590 673177
Website: www.theredlionboldre.co.uk
Map ref: 3 SZ39
Directions: M27 junct 1, A337 through Lyndhurst &
Brockenhurst towards Lymington, follow Boldre signs
Open: all wk 11-3 5.30-11 (Winter Sun noon-4
6-10.30, Summer Sat 11-11 Sun noon-10.30)
🍴 **L** Mon-Sat 12-2.30, Sun 12-3.30 (Summer
Sat 12-9.30, Sun 12-9) **D** Mon-Sat 6-9.30, Sun 6-9
(Summer Sat 12-9.30, Sun 12-9)
Facilities: Garden Parking
Notes: ⊕ FREE HOUSE 👫 🐕 🍷 17

Is the Red Lion old? Well, yes, if a mention in the
Domesday Book counts for anything, although
today's building dates from the comparatively
recent 15th century, when it evolved from a stable
and two cottages. It remains the quintessential
dog- and horse-friendly New Forest pub, with a
rambling interior of cosy, beamed rooms packed
with rural memorabilia. Home-made dishes are
based on Hampshire's excellent bounty (the pub is a
member of The New Forest Marque for use of local
produce) such as wild venison, a by-product of the
Forest's deer management policy, and sustainable
fish from local catches. The seasonal menus are
so full of appealing possibilities that selection of
a few representative dishes isn't easy, but give
thought to these: the famous steak and Ringwood
Ale pie; home-cooked Hampshire ham with New
Forest free-range fried eggs; pan-fried crab and
spring onion fishcakes, with a hint of fresh chilli; and
home-made beef Wellington with home-made New
Forest venison pâté. Check the pub's website and
book early for the monthly 'Pie & Pudding' evenings.
Whenever you go, always drive slowly through
the New Forest because animals not only wander
across roads, they sometimes lie down on them!

Recommended in the area

Beaulieu National Motor Museum; Buckler's Hard
Village & Maritime Museum; Lymington

The East End Arms

Address: Main Rd, EAST END,
nr Lymington, SO41 5SY
Tel: 01590 626223
Email: manager@eastendarms.co.uk
Website: www.eastendarms.co.uk
Map ref: 3 SZ39
Directions: From Lymington towards Beaulieu
(past Isle of Wight ferry), 3m to East End
Open: all wk 11.30-3 6-11 (Fri-Sun 11.30am-11pm)
L Mon-Sat 12-2.30 **L** all wk 12-2.30
D Mon-Sat 7-9.30
Facilities: Garden Parking
Notes: ⊕ FREE HOUSE ♦♦ ✈

Close to Beaulieu and historic Buckler's Hard, this New Forest inn, owned by John Illsley, former bass player of Dire Straits, combines the authenticity of a proper local with a good reputation as a gastro-pub. Ringwood ales are drawn straight from the wood in the Foresters Bar, where stone floors and open fires create a homely, traditional feel. The atmospheric lounge bar, with its sofas and winter fires, is a comfortable setting for a meal from the daily-changing brasserie-style menu. Locally sourced fish and seafood make a strong showing in dishes such as roast cod, creamy Savoy cabbage, potato galette and smoked salmon gravad lax velouté. Other dishes might be seared calves' liver with crisp Parma ham, carpaccio of beetroot and creamed potatoes, or curried mussel and saffron tart with tomato, basil and lime crème fraîche. The pub is well worth the drive down country lanes, or a short diversion from the nearby Solent Way long distance footpath. In the warmer summer months there's a pretty courtyard garden to sit in, and the pub also has five en suite bedrooms.

Recommended in the area

Bucklers Hard; Hurst Castle; Beaulieu Motor Museum

The Chestnut Horse

Address: EASTON, Winchester, SO21 1EG
Tel: 01962 779257
Email: info@thechestnuthorse.com
Website: www.thechestnuthorse.com
Map ref: 3 SU53
Directions: M3 junct 9, A33 towards Basingstoke,
then B3047. 2nd right, 1st left
Open: all wk noon-3.30 5.30-11 (Sun eve closed
winter) ₺ **L** Mon-Sat 12-2.30, Sun 12-4 booking
required **D** Mon-Sat 6-9.30 ⑩ **L** Mon-Sat 12-2, Sun
12-4 **D** Mon-Sat 6-9.30
Facilities: Garden Parking Wi-fi
Notes: ⊕ HALL & WOODHOUSE ⧍ ⌀

This 16th-century dining pub has a well-earned local
reputation for the quality of its food. Enjoying an
abundance of old English heritage character and
atmosphere, it has old tankards hanging from the
low-beamed ceilings in the two bar areas, and a
large open fire that is the central focus through the
winter months. Award-winning English beers can
be enjoyed in the bar or the garden. The candlelit
restaurants are equally inviting: the light, panelled
Green Room, and the darker low-beamed Red Room
with a wood-burning stove. A great way to start a
meal is the platter for two of lamb kofta, tempura
squid, Scotch quail egg, and prunes in Parma ham;
or you might be tempted by confit duck and sesame
praline salad; followed this with perhaps Thai green
curry; beer battered cod fillet, chips and minted pea
purée; or Irish stew and Guinness bread. Private
functions can be catered for and one of the smaller
of the two restaurants is ideal for functions for up
to 20 people. Take your walking boots with you
and you can work off any excesses on one of the
enjoyable countryside trails that start at the front
door.

Recommended in the area

Watercress Steam Railway; River Itchen (walking,
fishing); Intech Science Museum

The Gamekeepers

Address: Tunworth Rd, MAPLEDURWELL, RG25 2LU
Tel: 01256 322038 & 07786 998994
Email: info@thegamekeepers.co.uk
Website: www.thegamekeepers.co.uk
Map ref: 3 SU65
Directions: M3 junct 6, A30 towards Hook. Right across dual carriageway after The Hatch pub. Pub signed
Open: all wk Mon-Fri 11-3 5.30-mdnt (Sat 11-mdnt Sun 11-11) Booking required **L** Mon-Fri 11-2.30, Sat-Sun 11-9.30 **D** Mon-Fri 5.30-9, Sat-Sun 11-9.30
Facilities: Garden Parking Wi-fi
Notes: FREE HOUSE 10

Joseph and Elizabeth Phillips lived here in the mid-1800s. Originally, Joseph had been a shoemaker, but by the time of the 1861 census had changed career and become an innkeeper, his house having been turned into what was then called the Queen's Head. When you go into the dining room, look for two bricks, one each side of the fireplace, marked with the couple's initials and the date 1854, which was probably when the building was granted its licence. Acquiring its current name in 1973, the pub interior still displays its 19th-century origins through its low beams, flagstone floors and a well; outside, a large garden overlooks the gentle north Hampshire countryside. On the daily changing menu a good range of homemade contemporary dishes includes, as a starter, game terrine wrapped in sausagemeat and bacon with toasted brioche and apple, fig and rosemary chutney, followed by chargrilled beef fillet, dauphinoise potatoes, wilted baby spinach, cherry tomatoes, shimeji mushrooms, blue cheese and pink peppercorns butter with red wine jus. Children are welcome and smaller portions of most dishes are available; there's homemade sausages and burgers on offer as well.

Recommended in the area

Basing House; The Vyne (NT); Milestones - Hampshire's Living History Museum

The Fox

Address: NORTH WALTHAM, Basingstoke, RG25 2BE
Tel: 01256 397288
Email: info@thefox.org
Website: www.thefox.org
Map ref: 3 SU54
Directions: M3 junct 7, A30 towards Winchester. North Waltham signed on right. Take 2nd signed road
Open: all day all wk 11-11 **L** all wk 12-2.30 **D** all wk 6-9.30
Facilities: Garden Parking
Notes: FREE HOUSE 14

It is well worth leaving the tedium of the M3 for this free house and restaurant in a country lane just off junction 7. It was three farm cottages, dating from the 17th century, as becomes evident when you see the exposed beams and open fires. In the restaurant the fresh flowers look lovely, while in the cosy Village Bar there are four real ales, at least ten bottled ciders, and 14 wines by the glass. Not for consumption, though, is the collection of miniatures - more than 1,100 so far and counting (further contributions are always welcome). The bar and monthly changing restaurant menus and daily blackboard specials make full use of local game and other produce, as well as daily deliveries of fresh fish from the coast. Specialities include a superb cheese soufflé and main courses of Shetland mussels steamed in white wine and garlic; pork tenderloin medallions; halibut fillet stuffed with salmon mousseline; and wild mushroom Stroganoff. Regular 'special menu' evenings – Burns Supper and St George's Day, for example – are always popular. Meals can be served in the large garden, which includes a children's play area.

Recommended in the area

The Vyne (NT); Winchester Cathedral; Stonehenge

The Woolpack Inn

★★★★ @@ INN

Address: Totford, NORTHINGTON, SO24 9TJ
Tel: 0845 293 8066
Email: info@thewoolpackinn.co.uk
Website: www.thewoolpackinn.co.uk
Map ref: 3 SU53
Directions: A339 From Basingstoke onto B3036 signed Candovers & Alresford
Open: all day all wk ▟ **L** all wk 12-3 **D** Mon-Sat 6-close, Sun 6-8.30 ⦿ **L** all wk 12-3 **D** Mon-Sat 6-close **Closed:** 25 Dec eve **Rooms:** 7 en suite (4 GF) **S** £85-£105 **D** £85-£105 **Facilities:** Garden Parking Wi-fi **Notes:** ⊕ FREE HOUSE ✚ ⊓ ⚲ 12

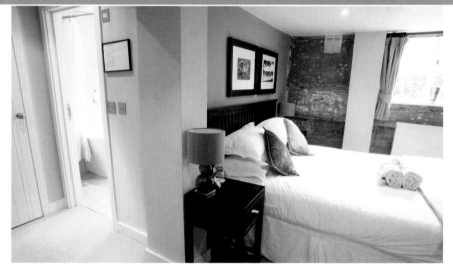

Its name recalling the days of the drovers who paused here while driving their sheep to market, Jarina and Brian Aherne's old flint-faced pub and restaurant stands almost alone in the peaceful Candover Valley. What a welcome sight it must have been to those old shepherds. Not far away is The Grange, once a stately home belonging to the Baring banking family, and now, the quite substantial bit that's left serves as a highly regarded opera venue. The inn's bar and restaurant areas must surely have featured in interior design magazines; it would be truly surprising if not, because they are very smart indeed. Local produce is used extensively for lunch, dinner and bar snacks and, in addition to the regularly changing, seasonal menu, there's always a traditional Sunday roast. Now, while the menu can not be called long, it manages to cover all main bases with, typically, Candover Park partridge breast; 42-day, dry-aged rib of Angus beef; pork fillet; lamb breast; crab and clam cake; market fish of the day; and open ravioli. The Ahernes and Berry Bros & Rudd choose the wines, which include several billed as 'exceptional value for money'. The en suite bedrooms are well appointed.

Recommended in the area

Avington Park; Watercress Line, New Alresford; Jane Austin's House Museum

The Bush

Address: OVINGTON, Alresford, SO24 0RE
Tel: 01962 732764
Email: thebushinn@wadworth.co.uk
Website: www.thebushinn@wadworth.co.uk
Map ref: 3 SU53
Directions: A31 from Winchester towards Alton & Farnham, approx 6m, left to Ovington. 0.5m to pub
Open: all day all wk ⅃ **L** all wk 12-2.30
D all wk 7-9
Facilities: Garden Parking Wi-fi
Notes: ⊕ WADWORTH ⅋ ⅃ ⅌ 19

A rose-covered vision of a bygone age, The Bush is as delightful as it is hard to find, tucked away just off a meandering lane and overhung by trees. Once a refreshment stop on the Pilgrim's Way linking Winchester and Canterbury, these days the pub is more likely to attract walkers exploring the Itchen Way. A gentle riverside stroll along the Itchen, which flows past the pretty garden, will certainly set you up for a leisurely drink or a lingering meal. The pub's interior is dark and atmospheric; there's a central wooden bar, high backed seats and pews, stuffed animals on the wall and a real fire. Ales on offer include Wadworth 6X, IPA and Malt & Hops, JCB, Horizon, Old Timer and guest beers. The regularly-changing menu makes good use of local produce.

Choices range from bar snacks, sandwiches and ploughman's lunches through to satisfying gastro-pub meals, taking in the likes of organic smoked trout mousse with warm toast, and slow-roasted belly pork on braised Savoy cabbage with organic cider jus. Finish with a traditional pudding such as Eton mess or rhubarb crumble. Not surprisingly, film crews love this location.

Recommended in the area

Avington Park; Winchester Cathedral; Mid-Hants Railway

The Rose & Thistle

Address: ROCKBOURNE, Fordingbridge, SP6 3NL
Tel: 01725 518236
Email: enquiries@roseandthistle.co.uk
Website: www.roseandthistle.co.uk
Map ref: 3 SU11
Directions: Follow Rockbourne signs from either
A354 (Salisbury to Blandford Forum road) or A338 at
Fordingbridge
Open: all wk 11-3 6-11 (Sat 11-11 Sun 12-8)
🔒 🍴 Booking required **L** all wk 12-2.30
D Mon-Sat 7-9.30
Facilities: Garden Parking Wi-fi
Notes: 🛢 FREE HOUSE 👬 🐕 🍷 12

Nestling in one of the most picturesque villages in the county, on the edge of the New Forest, this has everything you'd expect from the quintessential English pub: a tranquil setting, flowers around the door and a beautiful old building dating back to the 16th century. It has a welcoming low-ceilinged interior with oak beams and furniture, fresh flowers, magazines and an open fireplace. In summer, you can enjoy the delightful country garden. Well-kept real ales – Fuller's London Pride, Timothy Taylor Landlord and Palmers Copper Ale – are on offer, along with Scrumpy (cider), and a carefully selected wine list. Fresh seasonal food is cooked to order and includes fish such as skate, turbot and Cornish crab when available. The restaurant menu, available at lunch and dinner, offers perhaps venison steak with sloe gin and blackberries, pork belly with crab apple gravy, and tagliatelle with feta, spinach and sun blush tomatoes. Lighter lunch choices might be scrambled eggs with crispy proscuitto, locally-made pork and sausages with wholegrain mustard mash, and chickpea and butternut squash crumble; the Sunday lunch of rare roast sirloin of beef is also very popular. Desserts are all home made and an extensive local cheeseboard is delicious.

Recommended in the area

Rockbourne Roman Villa & Trout Fishery; Breamore House; Salisbury

The Plough Inn

Address: Woodman Ln, SPARSHOLT, Nr Winchester, SO21 2NW
Tel: 01962 776353
Map ref: 3 SU43
Directions: B3049 from Winchester towards Salisbury, left to Sparsholt, 1m
Open: all wk 11-3 6-11 (Sun 12-3 6-10.30)
🍴 ❖ Booking required **L** all wk 12-2 **D** Sun-Thu 6-9, Fri-Sat 6-9.30
Closed: 25 Dec
Facilities: Garden Parking
Notes: ⊕ WADWORTH ❖ ❖ ❖ 15

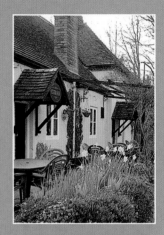

Set in beautiful countryside, just a stone's throw from Winchester, this inn is a great place to refresh yourself after a walk in the nearby Farley Mount Country Park. Owners Richard and Kathryn Crawford have a simple philosophy: to serve customers with good quality food and drink in a friendly atmosphere. The Plough was built about 200 years ago as a coach house for Sparsholt Manor, but within 50 years it had already become an alehouse. Since then it has been much extended, yet from the inside it all blends together very well, helped by the farmhouse-style furniture and the adornment with agricultural implements, stone jars and dried hops. The Wadworth brewery supplies all of the real ales, and there's a good wine selection.

The left-hand dining area is served by a blackboard menu offering such light dishes as feta and spinach filo parcels with a Thai pesto dressing or a beef, ale and mushroom pie with vegetables. To the right, a separate board offers meals that reflect a more serious approach – perhaps breast of chicken filled with mushrooms on a garlic and bacon sauce; lamb shank with braised red cabbage and rosemary jus; and several fish dishes. Booking is always advisable.

Recommended in the area

Winchester Cathedral; Mottisfont Abbey (NT);
Sir Harold Hillier Gardens & Arboretum

The Peat Spade

Address: Longstock, STOCKBRIDGE, SO20 6DR
Tel: 01264 810612
Email: info@peatspadeinn.co.uk
Website: www.peatspadeinn.co.uk
Map ref: 3 SU33
Directions: Telephone for directions
Open: all day all wk 11am-11pm (Sun 11am-10.30pm) 🍴 Booking required **L** all wk 12-2
D all wk 7-9
Closed: 25 Dec
Facilities: Garden Parking Wi-fi
Notes: ⊕ MILLER'S COLLECTION ♦ ♩ ☻ 10

The Peat Spade sits on the banks of the River Test in a corner of Hampshire countryside famed for being the fly-fishing capital of the world. Unusual paned windows overlook the peaceful village lane and idyllic heavily thatched cottages at this striking, redbrick and gabled Victorian pub. Located between Winchester and Salisbury, this classy country inn is a reminder of a bygone England and its country sport traditions. You will find a relaxed atmosphere in the cosy fishing and shooting themed bar and dining room, and a simple, constantly evolving menu listing classic English food. If you have been trying your luck on the river and have caught an elusive trout, the chef is more than happy to serve up the fruits of your labours for your dinner. Using locally-sourced produce, including allotment fruit and vegetables and game from the Leckford Estate, the choice may take in crisp pork belly, rocket, capers and lemon dressing for starters, with main dishes ranging from locally shot pheasant with pan-fried bread sauce and braised red cabbage to Test Valley trout and pan-roasted beetroot, watercress and horseradish cream. To drink, there's Ringwood Fortyniner on tap and ten wines by the glass. Accommodation is available.

Recommended in the area

Mottisfont Abbey (NT); Salisbury; Museum of Army Flying, Middle Wallop

Herefordshire

Ross-on-Wye

The Penny Farthing Inn

Address: ASTON CREWS, Ross-on-Wye, HR9 7LW
Tel: 01989 750366
Email: thepennyfarthinginn@hotmail.co.uk
Map ref: 2 SO62
Directions: 5m E of Ross-on-Wye
Open: all wk Mon 6-11, Tue-Thu noon-3 6-11, Fri noon-3 6-mdnt, Sat noon-mdnt, Sun noon-10.30
🍴 🍽 **L** Tue-Sun 12-2.30 **D** Tue-Sat 6-9
Facilities: Garden Parking Wi-fi
Notes: ⊕ PUBFOLIO 🧍‍♂️ 🐾

This whitewashed 17th-century blacksmith's shop and coaching inn is located high above the Wye Valley, with stunning views of the Malvern Hills, the Black Mountains and the Forest of Dean. From the beer garden, where dogs are welcome too, the views can really be appreciated. Inside are lots of nooks and crannies with oak beams, antiques, saddlery and warming log fires. The menu capitalises on the wealth of local vegetable and fruit growers' produce, and some of the best meat in the country. Begin with sauté king prawns in coriander batter with sweet chilli dip or creamy garlic mushrooms, then follow with home made Guinness and beef pie; whole lemon sole with garlic butter; slow roast belly pork with pan-fried black pudding and rich red wine jus; pan-fried guinea fowl supreme with thyme and bacon gravy, or one of the daily chalkboard specials, perhaps medallions of monkfish with king prawns in a saffron sauce. Leave enough room for one of the homemade desserts – especially one of the crumbles, crème brûlées or cheesecakes. For those who want to pack their walking boots, footpaths radiate from the front door.

Recommended in the area

International Centre for Birds of Prey; Goodrich Castle; Symonds Yat

The Saracens Head Inn

★★★★ ➡ INN

Address: SYMONDS YAT [EAST], HR9 6JL
Tel: 01600 890435
Email: contact@saracensheadinn.co.uk
Website: www.saracensheadinn.co.uk
Map ref: 2 SO51
Directions: Exit A40 at South Hereford Motor
Caravans signed Symonds Yat East, 2m
Open: all day all wk 🍽 †◎**L** all wk 12-2.30 **D** all wk
6.30-9 **Closed:** 25 Dec
Rooms: 8 en suite (1 GF) **S** £59-£70 **D** £94-£138
Facilities: Garden Parking Wi-fi
Notes: ⊕ FREE HOUSE 👬 🐾 🍷 10

For centuries this former cider mill has occupied its
spectacular position on the east bank of the River
Wye, where the river flows into a steep wooded
gorge. The inn's own ferry still operates by hand, just
as it has for the past 200 years. There's a relaxed
atmosphere throughout, from the flagstone bar to
the cosy lounge and stylish dining room, and you
can also eat on a sunny riverside terrace. Regularly
changing menus and daily specials offer both
the traditional: locally made faggots with mashed
potato, garden peas and onion gravy, for example;
and the modern: a sharing plate of charcuterie -
cecina de León, spicy chorizo, wild boar salami and
Milano salami, olives, balsamic onions and olive
ciabatta. A typical three course meal might start
with steamed River Teign mussels with local cider
and creamed leeks, followed by chargrilled Welsh
lamb chops with sautéed potatoes, Savoy cabbage
and rosemary jus. Complete your meal with one of
the desserts on the blackboard. The inn is situated
in an Area of Outstanding Natural Beauty on the
edge of the Royal Forest of Dean, so a stay in one of
the eight en suite bedrooms is a must if you intend
to explore the unspoiled local countryside.

Recommended in the area

Goodrich Castle; Tintern Abbey; Forest of Dean;
Monmouth

The Mill Race

Address: WALFORD, Ross-on-Wye, HR9 5QS
Tel: 01989 562891
Email: enquiries@millrace.info
Website: www.millrace.info
Map ref: 2 SO52
Directions: B4234 from Ross-on-Wye to Walford.
Pub 3m on right
Open: all wk 11-3 5-11 (Sat-Sun all day)
🍴 Booking required **L** Mon-Fri 12-2, Sat 12-2.30,
Sun all day **D** Mon-Sat 6-9.30, Sun 6-9
Facilities: Garden Parking Wi-fi
Notes: 🍺 FREE HOUSE ❤️ 🍷 14

In the beautiful Wye Valley, the award-winning Mill Race is a friendly village gastro-pub whose original stone floors and Welsh slate floor are well complemented by a modern interior. The blazing fire literally ensures a warm welcome, while the large terrace offers outdoor dining and views towards Goodrich Castle. The bar serves a selection of local ales and ciders, and the extensive wine list offers 14 by the glass. An environmentally responsible approach to local food sourcing, including from the pub's own farm two miles away and Bishopswood Shoot, lies behind a regularly changing menu of simple, well-prepared food. There's traditional pub classics such as venison burger with red cabbage pickle and chips; game pie with seasonal vegetables; and beer-battered pollack and chips, together with brasserie-style dishes such as spiced fig tart with goats' cheese; crayfish and avocado cocktail with lemon jelly; ricotta and squash rotollo with tomato and herb sauce; and seared duck breast with shallot Tatin. Suppliers Nights such as Chase Vodka Night and Wye Valley Ale Night promote the wonderful local produce. The pub makes a good base for local walks, including the one-mile Woodland Walk, which partly follows a disused railway line.

Recommended in the area

Symonds Yat; International Centre for Birds of Prey; Hereford Cathedral

Hertfordshire

Hoecroft Lane, near Little Hadnam

The Bricklayers Arms

Address: Hogpits Bottom, FLAUNDEN, HP3 0PH
Tel: 01442 833322
Email: goodfood@bricklayersarms.com
Website: www.bricklayersarms.com
Map ref: 3 TL00
Directions: M25 junct 18, A404 (Amersham road).
Right at Chenies for Flaunden
Open: all day all wk noon-11.30 (25 Dec 12-3)
Booking required **L** Mon-Sat 12-2.30, Sun
12-3.30 **D** Mon-Sat 6.30-9.30, Sun 6.30-8.30
Facilities: Garden Parking Wi-fi
Notes: FREE HOUSE 16

This picturesque, 18th-century listed country pub is an ivy-clad, flint building situated in a lovely village at the end of winding lanes that snake between Chipperfield and Latimer. The interior has low wooden beams, exposed brickwork and real log fires, and a warm welcome from Alvin and Sally Michaels is guaranteed. Over the past eight years, The Bricklayers Arms has gained an excellent reputation for its traditional English and French fusion menu created by the highly trained and award-winning chef, Claude Paillet. The same menu can be enjoyed throughout the restaurant and pub seven days a week, with dishes including the famous, home-smoked fish plate; home-made terrines; traditional Tring Ale battered cod;

21-day aged fillet steak, and fillet of locally reared Worcestershire Black Spot pork. There's always a choice of fresh fish dishes and vegetarian options on the menu plus tantalising specials of the day. A carefully selected wine list of over 140 varieties to suit all budgets and tastes is available, as well as beers and local ales on tap. If you're thinking of calling in for the ever popular Sunday lunch, be sure to book in advance.

Recommended in the area
Chenies Manor House; Berkhamsted Castle; Ashridge Estate (NT)

Alford Arms

Address: Frithsden, HEMEL HEMPSTEAD, HP1 3DD
Tel: 01442 864480
Email: info@alfordarmsfrithsden.co.uk
Website: www.alfordarmsfrithsden.co.uk
Map ref: 3 TL00
Directions: From Hemel Hempstead on A4146, 2nd left at Water End. 1m, left at T-junct, right in 0.75m. Pub 100yds on right
Open: all day all wk 11-11 (Sun 12-10.30)
🍴🍲 **L** Mon-Fri 12-2.30, Sat 12-3, Sun 12-4
D Mon-Thu 6.30-9.30, Fri-Sat 6.30-10, Sun 6.30-9.30
Closed: 26 Dec **Facilities:** Garden Parking Wi-fi
Notes: 🍺 SALISBURY PUBS LTD 👬 🐾 🍷22

An attractive Victorian pub in the unruffled hamlet of Frithsden, surrounded by National Trust woodland. The flower-filled garden overlooks the village green, and historic Ashridge Forest is nearby. Cross the threshold and in the dining room and bar you'll pick up on the warm and lively atmosphere, derived partly from the buzz of conversation, partly from the discreet background jazz, and partly from the rich colours and eclectic mixture of old furniture and pictures, mostly acquired from Tring salerooms. The seasonal menu and daily specials balance modern British with more traditional fare, mostly prepared from fresh, local produce. A good choice of 'small plates' ranges from rustic breads with roast garlic and olive oil, to oak-smoked bacon on bubble and squeak with hollandaise sauce and poached egg. Main meals with a similarly imaginative approach include Moroccan spiced lamb shank on sweet potato mash, pan juices and cumin yoghurt; Cornish fish stew with saffron potatoes, rouille and gruyère; and pumpkin gnocchi with roast beetroot, porcini, watercress and walnut pesto. Puddings are interestingly tweaked too, such as crispy banana and almond spring roll with lemongrass caramel.

Recommended in the area

Berkhamsted Castle; Walter Rothschild Zoological Museum; Whipsnade Wild Animal Park

Ashridge Park

Kent

Boating on the River Stour

Castle Inn

Address: CHIDDINGSTONE, TN8 7AH
Tel: 01892 870247
Email: info@castleinn-kent.co.uk
Website: www.castleinn-kent.co.uk
Map ref: 4 TQ54
Directions: 1.5m S of B2027 between Tonbridge & Edenbridge
Open: all day all wk 11-11 (Sun 12-10.30) 🍽 **L** all wk 12-4 **D** Mon-Sat 7-9.30 🍴 **L** Mon-Fri 12-2, Sat-Sun 12-4 **D** Mon-Sat 7-9.30
Facilities: Garden
Notes: ⊕ FREE HOUSE ♦ 🐾 ♟ 9

The building was first mentioned in 1420, although three more centuries elapsed before anyone sold ale here. Situated in a National Trust village, it forms part of a fine row of timber-framed houses, and has an interior full of original oak beams, mullioned windows and big fireplaces. As well as a public bar there is a saloon bar and private dining areas. Outside is the vine-hung courtyard and Garden Bar, while across a bridge lies a lawn and beautifully tended flowerbeds. Owner John McManus, previously of Le Gavroche, and head chef Adam Jaroszek share a passion for the highest standards and attention to detail. The bar menu offers snacks like home-made focaccia, as well as potato gnocchi; chicken Caesar salad; cottage pie; and braised Kentish lamb. In the evening you're more likely to find poached lemon sole; 42-day aged beef sirloin; poached and roasted leg of chicken; and pithiviers of provençale vegetables; with desserts such as treacle tart with almond and Chantilly cream, and Bramley apple crumble. There is a well chosen, modern wine list together with real ales, brewed in the village at the acclaimed Larkins Brewery, just 400 yards from the pub.

Recommended in the area

Hever Castle; Penshurst Place & Gardens; Chartwell (NT); Chiddingstone Castle

Griffins Head

Address: CHILLENDEN, Canterbury, CT3 1PS
Tel: 01304 840325
Map ref: 4 TR25
Directions: A2 from Canterbury towards Dover, then B2046. Village on right
Open: all wk 🍴 ❍ L all wk 12-2 **D** Mon-Sat 7-9.30
Closed: Sun pm
Facilities: Garden Parking
Notes: 🍺 SHEPHERD NEAME 🍷 10

Dating from 1286, the Griffins Head is an architectural gem of a building, a fine black-and-white half-timbered Wealden hall house, in a tiny farming hamlet amid rolling open countryside. Originally built as a farmhouse to serve the local estate, ale and cider were always brewed on the premises for the workers. The present Tudor structure is built around the original wattle and daub walls, remains of which can be viewed in one of the three delightfully unspoilt rooms, which also feature flagstone floors, exposed brick walls and beams and a tasteful mix of furnishings, from old scrubbed pine tables and chairs to church pews. Fine Shepherd Neame ales and home-made food have helped this old inn to make its mark with visitors as well as locals, among them Kent's cricketing fraternity. The constantly changing seasonal menu is typically English, and specialises in game from local estates, and locally caught fish where possible. Typical dishes might include lamb stew; braised steak, onions and mash; or sautéed prawns and squid; and traditional pub dishes like cottage pie and ham, egg and chips. Desserts include apple crumble, or home-made ice creams. The pretty garden is the setting for popular summer weekend barbecues.

Recommended in the area

Goodnestone Park Gardens; Howletts Wild Animal Park; Dover Castle

The Plough at Ivy Hatch

Address: High Cross Rd, IVY HATCH, TN15 0NL
Tel: 01732 810100
Email: info@theploughivyhatch.co.uk
Website: www.theploughivyhatch.co.uk
Map ref: 4 TQ55
Directions: Exit A25 between Borough Green &
Sevenoaks, follow Ightham Mote signs
Open: all wk noon-3 6-11 (Sat noon-11 Sun 10-6)
L Mon-Sat 12-2.45, Sun 12-6 **D** Mon-Sat 6-9.30
Closed: 1 Jan
Facilities: Garden Parking Wi-fi
Notes: FREE HOUSE 10

Deep in the countryside, this tile-hung village pub is a perfect spot for a lingering lunch or supper. The aim of Miles and Anna is to make it the centre of the community; their driving passion is to source the best locally produced farm products and present them as classic dishes on a British and European influenced menu that they update daily, all home made. Typical starters are beetroot-cured salmon with blinis and dill crème fraîche or chicken liver parfait. Main courses include pan-fried guinea fowl breast with roasted butternut squash and blackberry jus, or pan-fried fillet of grey mullet with herb-crushed new potatoes. For a lighter meal try local sausages or honey roast ham with hand-cut chips and their own free range eggs; there is also a sweet and savoury pancake menu. Desserts include seasonal fruit crumbles and tarts, treacle tart, plus local cheeses. Ales are mainly from Royal Tunbridge Wells Brewing Company, with guest ales from Larkins, Westerham and Hogs Back breweries. The back gardens are surrounded by cobnut trees and living amongst them is Maya and Ellie, the pet pigs who, with chickens, dog and cat, keep The Plough full of life and entertainment.

Recommended in the area

Ightham Mote (NT); Knole House & Park (NT); Oldbury Hill, Styants Wood & One Tree Hill (NT)

The Bottle House Inn

Address: Coldharbour Rd, PENSHURST,
Tonbridge, TN11 8ET
Tel: 01892 870306
Email: info@thebottlehouseinnpenshurst.co.uk
Website: www.thebottlehouseinnpenshurst.co.uk
Map ref: 4 TQ54
Directions: A264 W from Tunbridge Wells onto
B2188 N. After Fordcombe left towards Edenbridge &
Hever. Pub 500yds after staggered x-rds
Open: all day all wk 11-11 (Sun 11-10.30)
Closed: 25 Dec
Facilities: Garden Parking
Notes: ⊕ FREE HOUSE ♦♦ ♠ ♈ 11

A well-regarded dining pub, The Bottle House
was built as a farmhouse in 1492, and in 1806 a
licence was obtained to sell ales and ciders. It was
registered as an alehouse at each subsequent
change of hands, at a time when hop-growing was
the major local industry. The pub was reputedly
named after all the old bottles discovered during
a refurbishment in 1937, and is said to be the
originator of the ploughman's lunch, made with
bread from the old bakery next door and cheese
donated by Canadian soldiers billeted nearby. Today,
low beams and a copper-topped counter give the
bar a warm, welcoming atmosphere. Choose from
the range of Harveys and Larkins hand-pumped
beers and 11 wines by the glass.

The menu has something for everyone, starting with
ham hock, cornichon and parsley terrine or pan-
seared scallops with sautéed black pudding and
hot sweetcorn purée. Lighter meals and shares may
include garlic and chilli grilled crevettes with rustic
bread or home-made soup with half sandwich of
the day. For main courses enjoy slow-roasted belly
of pork with a light cider sauce and creamed Savoy
cabbage with bacon, or cornfed chicken breast with
tarragon cream sauce.

Recommended in the area

Hever Castle; Royal Tunbridge Wells; Penshurst
Place & Gardens

The Beacon

★★★★ 🍴 INN

Address: Tea Garden Ln, Rusthall,
nr ROYAL TUNBRIDGE WELLS, TN3 9JH
Tel: 01892 524252
Email: beaconhotel@btopenworld.com
Website: www.the-beacon.co.uk
Map ref: 4 TQ53 **Directions:** From Tunbridge
Wells take A264 towards East Grinstead. Pub 1m
on left **Open:** all day all wk 11-11 (Sun 12-10.30)
🛏 ⦿ **L** Mon-Thu 12-2.30, Fri-Sun 12-9.30 **D** Mon-Thu
6.30-9.30, Fri-Sun 12-9.30 **Rooms:** 3 en suite **S** £80
D £115 **Facilities:** Garden Parking
Notes: 🍺 FREE HOUSE ⦿ ♟ 12

High up on a sandstone outcrop just 1.5 miles
from Tunbridge Wells, The Beacon has one of the
best views in southeast England. Formerly a grand
country home, it retains impressive architectural
features, including stained glass, moulded
ceilings and an oak-panelled bar in which you
can select from a fine range of beers and wine to
complement the food. As members of Kentish Fare,
the proprietors are strongly committed to using
county-produced ingredients, and in the restaurant
you can choose from starters such home cured
smoked salmon on herb blinis with caviar flavoured
crème fraîche; or share charcuterie with home-
made pickles and Rusbridge bread. Your meal could
continue with locally caught sea bass with pak

choi and a light chorizo and potato salsa; or calves'
liver with creamed potatoes, spinach, pancetta
crisps and light mustard cream. Try to save room
for dessert, notably vanilla pod pannacotta or the
kickerbocker glory. Walk off your meal in the 17
acres of grounds, which include lakes, woodland
paths and a chalybeate spring. There's also a lovely
terrace and spacious, comfortable accommodation.

Recommended in the area

Royal Tunbridge Wells; Penshurst Place & Gardens;
Spa Valley Railway

The Coastguard

Address: ST MARGARET'S BAY, CT15 6DY
Tel: 01304 853176
Email: bookings@thecoastguard.co.uk
Website: www.thecoastguard.co.uk
Map ref: 4 TR34
Directions: A258 between Dover & Deal follow
St Margaret's at Cliffe signs. 2m, through village
towards sea
Open: all day all wk 11-11 (Sun 11-10.30)
⌂ ⊙ **L** all wk 12.30-2.45 **D** all wk 6.30-8.45
Facilities: Garden Parking Wi-fi
Notes: ⊕ FREE HOUSE ⚬ ⌂ ⌂

Sitting on the suntrap terrace here, the hazy smudge on the horizon is likely to be the French coast, shimmering beyond the silently passing ferries and freighters. Crane your neck upwards to see the White Cliffs of Dover behind this convivial waterside inn. The popular Heritage Coastal Path passes the door, whilst the watersport fans beach their kayaks here to indulge in a half of Gadd's of Ramsgate No. 5 bitter or a sip of Rough Old Wife cider. The food is renowned for its wonderful flavours, and all freshly made on the premises from local produce as far as possible. Many dishes have a story behind them: they might be based on an old Roman recipe, a reworked classic dish, or perhaps an original creation in response to something particularly outstanding that becomes available. The menus change twice daily, depending on the weather and what's available. Bar bites and starters feature local pork and cider pie; rabbit and mushroom parfait; or smoked haddock, spinach and Cheddar omelette, enough for nibblers. Those with heartier appetites may progress to hot devilled crab topped with mature Cheddar; smoked haddock roasted with a Shetland mussel and saffron cider cream, or gratin of Kentish broccoli with cider, mushrooms and leeks.

Recommended in the area

Dover Castle; Walmer Castle; South Foreland
Heritage Coast

Botany Bay

Lancashire

View towards Totridge, Forest of Bowland

Clog and Billycock

Address: Billinge End Rd, Pleasington, BLACKBURN,
BB2 6QB
Tel: 01254 201163
Email: enquiries@theclogandbillycock.com
Website: www.theclogandbillycock.com
Map ref: 6 SD62 **Directions:** M6 junct 29 to
M65 junct 3, follow Pleasington signs **Open:** all wk
noon-11 (Sun noon-10.30) ⊫ **L** Mon-Sat 12-2, Sun
& BHs 12-8 (afternoon bites Mon-Sat 2-6) **D** Mon-
Thu 5.30-8.30, Fri-Sat 5.30-9, Sun & BHs 12-8 ⦿ **L**
Mon-Sat 12-2, Sun & BHs 12-8 **D** Mon-Thu 5.30-8.30,
Fri-Sat 5.30-9 **Closed:** 25 Dec **Facilities:** Garden
Parking **Notes:** 🛢 FREE HOUSE ⅲ ⅲ

The Clog and Billycock has been part of
Pleasington's history for over 150 years. Its name
comes from the attire of an early landlord (a
billycock is black felt hat, a predecessor of the
bowler). Set in the quaint village of Pleasington, the
building has undergone an expensive renovation,
and the result is a warm and relaxing pub in which
to enjoy Thwaites ales, draught ciders, fine wines
and superb food. Winnie Swarbricks Goosnargh
cornfed chicken liver pâté makes an excellent light
lunch, while the ploughman's highlights the pub's
real food objectives, consisting of an impressive
plate of Garstang Blue, Leagrams Tasty Lancashire,
York hand-raised pork pie, pickled onion, pickled
white cabbage, piccalilli and bread. Hot options from
chef Nigel Haworth's locally sourced menu may
include heather-reared Lonk potpot with pickled red
cabbage; or scampi and squid in a bucket with chips
cooked in dripping. Simpson's Dairy rice pudding
could complete a meal to remember. Children
are welcomed with fun educational sheets and
competitions, as well as equally well thought-out
children's meals.

Recommended in the area

Pleasington Priory; Pleasington Old Hall Wood &
Wildlife Garden; Witton Country Park

The Millstone at Mellor

★★ 85% ◉◉ HOTEL

Address: Church Ln, Mellor, BLACKBURN, BB2 7JR
Tel: 01254 813333
Email: relax@millstonehotel.com
Website: www.millstonehotel.co.uk
Map ref: 6 SD62 **Directions:** M6 junct 31, A59
towards Clitheroe, past British Aerospace. Right at
rdbt signed Blackburn/Mellor. Next rdbt 2nd left.
Hotel at top of hill on right
Open: all day all wk ⬛ **L** Mon-Sat 12-9.30, Sun
12-9 **Rooms:** 23 (8 GF) **S** £56-£100 **D** £62-£120
Facilities: Parking Wi-fi
Notes: ◉ THWAITES INNS OF CHARACTER ♟ 10

If you're travelling through the beautiful Ribble
Valley, you're bound to come across this charming
old coaching inn. It's run by chef/patron Anson
Bolton and his wife, although it belongs to Blackburn
brewery Thwaites, which ensures a ready supply
of its real ales, as well as guests, lagers, ciders,
wines and speciality coffees. Anson has worked
tirelessly over the past ten years to maintain the
two AA Rosettes the restaurant has held since his
arrival, an achievement that relies on the sourcing
of fresh, in-season produce from only trusted local
and regional suppliers. In addition to what you might
perhaps expect from a Lancashire kitchen, such
as slow roast shank of Pendle lamb; and Bowland
steak, kidney and Wainwright's ale suet pudding,
there are specials to choose from a Best in Season
selection, such as monkfish and prawn Thermidor;
duck cottage pie with roast duck breast; and
chestnut, chick pea and butternut squash casserole.
For afters choose perhaps an ice cream sundae; or
vanilla crème brûlée with cinder toffee ice cream.
In the afternoon treat yourself to tea with mouth-
watering homemade biscuits and freshly baked
cakes. Upstairs are the bedrooms, all with fluffy
robes, lavender pouches in the wardrobe, luxury
Pecksniff toiletries and homemade biscuits.

Recommended in the area

Salmesbury Hall; Harris Museum & Art Gallery,
Preston; Gawthorpe Hall (NT)

The Highwayman

Address: BURROW, Nr Kirkby Lonsdale, LA6 2RJ
Tel: 01524 273338
Email: enquiries@highwaymaninn.co.uk
Website: www.highwaymaninn.co.uk
Map ref: 6 SD67
Directions: M6 junct 36, A65 to Kirkby Lonsdale.
A683 S. Burrow approx 2m
Open: Tue-Sat noon-11 (Sun noon-10.30)
L Tue-Sat 12-2, Sun & BHs 12-8 (afternoon bites
Tue-Sat 2-6) **D** Tue-Fri 6-9, Fri-Sat 5.30-9, Sun & BHs
12-8 **Closed:** Mon, 25 Dec
Facilities: Garden Parking
Notes: ⊕ RIBBLE VALLEY INNS 🐕 🏇

Starting life as a coaching inn during the 18th century, a legend surrounds this establishment regarding its use as a midnight haunt of notorious Lancashire highwaymen. The inn is set in a delightful country area close to the historic market town of Kirkby Lonsdale, popular for its pretty cottages, quaint streets and attractive shops and tea rooms. The Highwayman has a stone-floored interior with solid wood furniture and welcoming open fires. There is also a beautifully landscaped terraced garden. Thwaites cask ales, ciders and guest beers are served alongside a list of fine wines, and the menus are a tribute to regional specialities and local producers and suppliers. Typical dishes are Port of Lancaster Smokehouse kipper fillet, with boiled egg and watercress salad; Herdwick mutton pudding, capers, parsley mash and black peas; and Cartmel sticky toffee pudding with butterscotch sauce and vanilla ice cream. Don't miss the tri-counties cheeseboard, with the best from Lancashire, Yorkshire and Cumbria. The children's menu offers real food in smaller portions, and seasonal fun sheets are available to keep younger customers amused.

Recommended in the area
Sizergh Castle & Garden (NT); Levens Hall & Gardens; White Scar Caves

Penny Street Bridge

★★★ 74% TOWN HOUSE

Address: Penny St, LANCASTER, LA1 1XT
Tel: 01524 599900
Email: relax@pennystreetbridge.co.uk
Website: www.pennystreetbridge.co.uk
Map ref: 6 SD46
Directions: In town centre
Open: all day all wk
Rooms: 28 **S** £79–£105 **D** £85–£125
Facilities: Parking Wi-fi
Notes: ⊕ THWAITES INNS OF CHARACTER ↟ ♟ 9

When Preston's old Corporation Toll House was demolished in 1901, it was replaced by this marvellous building, initially two separate pubs, the White Cross Hotel and the Corporation Arms. In 2007 Thwaites Brewery acquired the premises and turned them both into a smart townhouse hotel, bar and brasserie, carefully retaining the period high ceilings, staircases, stained-glass windows and servant bell hooks. The atmosphere is relaxed and informal, with wooden floors in the brasserie, tub chairs in the traditional bar and, upstairs, impeccably decorated, triple-glazed bedrooms. The day might start with a full Lancashire breakfast (like English, but better they say!), then progress towards morning coffee, lunch and finally dinner,

for which the seasonal menus rely very much on Lancashire produce. Starters include pea and ham soup; and crab cakes with brown shrimp and caper vinaigrette; main courses are represented by steak and ale pie; daube of beef with mustard mash; and confit duck leg with beans and Puy lentil cassoulet; and dessert, chocolate brioche bread-and-butter pudding with custard; or Lancashire curd tart with stewed blackberries. Children will undoubtedly enjoy one of the various handmade pizzas cooked in an authentic oven.

Recommended in the area

Lancaster Castle, City Museum & Lancaster Maritime Museum; Morecambe coast

The Cartford Inn

Address: LITTLE ECCLESTON, Preston, PR3 0YP
Tel: 01995 670166
Email: info@thecartfordinn.co.uk
Website: www.thecartfordinn.co.uk
Map ref: 6 SD44
Directions: Off A586
Open: all day ⊙⌑ **L** Tue-Sat 12-2, Sun 12-8.30
D Mon-Thu 5.30-9, Fri-Sat 5.30-10
Closed: 25 Dec, Mon **L**
Facilities: Garden Parking Wi-fi
Notes: ⊕ FREE HOUSE ⋔

A 17th-century farmhouse that after a couple of centuries became a coaching inn. Today, this pleasantly rambling, three-storey building stands sentinel by the toll bridge over the tidal River Wyre, a few miles from its estuary and the Irish Sea. Owners Patrick and Julie Beaume have successfully combined traditional and contemporary elements, with a log fire in the winter grate, and positively up-to-date polished wood floors and chunky dining furniture. Established for many years now as a welcoming, real ale pub, it maintains four cask beers, at the time of writing Theakston's Old Peculier, Pride of Pendle from Moorhouse, Lakeland Gold from Hawkshead and Bowland's Hen Harrier. The restaurant provides an extensive menu of creative dishes using fresh local produce. Starters might include venison sausage casserole with horseradish dumpling; skewer of tempura king prawns; wood platters of antipasti, Fleetwood-landed seafood or organic crudités; and main courses of papillote of fresh sea bass and salmon mousseline; roast Goosnargh duck breast; and field and wild mushroom Stroganoff. There's a beer garden for alfresco dining with river views and the Trough of Bowland as a backdrop, and live music some Friday nights. Accommodation is available.

Recommended in the area

Blackpool Tower; Samlesbury Hall; Martin Mere Wildfowl & Wetlands Trust

The Three Fishes

Address: Mitton Rd, Mitton, WHALLEY, BB7 9PQ
Tel: 01254 826888
Email: enquiries@thethreefishes.com
Website: www.thethreefishes.com
Map ref: 6 SD73 **Directions:** M6 junct 31, A59 to
Clitheroe. Follow Whalley signs, B6246, 2m
Open: all day all wk ⓑ **L** Mon-Sat 12-2, Sun & BHs
12-8 (afternoon bites Mon-Sat 2-6)
D Mon-Thu 5.30-8.30, Fri-Sat 5.30-9, Sun & BHs 12-8
Closed: 25 Dec
Facilities: Garden Parking
Notes: ⊕ FREE HOUSE ⅰ ⚘ ⚲ 13

The Three Fishes is over 400 years old and has been
a pub for most of that time, providing refreshment
to travellers on the old road from the 16th-century
bridge at Lower Hodder and the ferry at Mitton.
The place was supposedly named after the three
fishes pendant in the coat of arms of John Paslew,
last abbot of nearby Whalley Abbey (look above
the entrance to see them carved in stone). The tiny
hamlet of Mitton is set on a limestone rise above
the River Ribble and is surrounded by beautiful
countryside. The pub prides itself on its genuine
Lancashire hospitality, real ales, and the best food
ever in its long history. The menu demonstrates
a passionate commitment to regional food, with
dishes such as Morecambe Bay shrimps, served
with blade mace butter and toasted muffin; heather
reared Lonk lamb Lancashire hotpot; and Lake
District farmers 10oz sirloin steak with proper
chips. You might finish your meal with Bramley
apple crumble with Simpsons double cream, or the
excellent Lancashire cheese board with biscuits and
fireside chutney. Photographs of local 'food hero'
producers and suppliers line the walls, in tribute
to their contribution to the success of The Three
Fishes.

Recommended in the area

Stonyhurst College; Clitheroe Castle; All Hallows
Medieval Church

The Inn at Whitewell

★★★★★ ⊛ INN

Address: Forest of Bowland, WHITEWELL,
Nr Clitheroe, BB7 3AT
Tel: 01200 448222
Email: reception@innatwhitewell.com
Website: www.innatwhitewell.com
Map ref: 6 SD64
Directions: From B6243 follow Whitewell signs
Open: all day all wk 10am-1am ■ L all wk
12-2 **D** all wk 7.30-9.30 ⭐ **D** all wk 7.30-9.30
Rooms: 23 en suite (2 GF) **S** £88-£187 **D** £120-£231
Facilities: Garden Parking Wi-fi
Notes: ⊕ FREE HOUSE ♦ ♩ ♟ 16

Despite its splendid isolation amid the wild beauty of the Forest of Bowland, there's much to enjoy at this ancient stone inn. The whole complex embraces a wine merchant, an art gallery, a shop selling home-made goodies, and 23 individually decorated bedrooms - not to mention seven miles of fishing rights. The somewhat eccentric interior is packed with a random collection of furnishings, including a vast assortment of old prints and paintings. The cooking takes a simple modern British approach: bar lunch dishes might include smoked salmon with lemon and granary bread; or spicy fried squid with soft noodles, carrot and sweet ginger salad. Bar suppers follow similar lines, or you can choose à la carte starters like home-cured gravad lax; or smoked Goosnargh chicken salad with beetroot and horseradish relish, followed by roast pork with pancetta and grain mustard mash; or fillet of beef accompanied by a little braised oxtail pie, baby onions, celeriac purée and red wine jus. There's a constantly changing selection of traditional puddings 'sometimes nursery-like' according to the menu, and home made ice creams complete the line up. There are stunning walks starting right from the front door.

Recommended in the area

Ribchester Roman Museum; Browsholme Hall;
Yorkshire Dales National Park

Leicestershire

Bradgate Country Park

The Queen's Head

★★★★ ◉ RESTAURANT WITH ROOMS

Address: 2 Long St, BELTON, LE12 9TP
Tel: 01530 222359
Email: enquiries@thequeenshead.org
Website: www.thequeenshead.org
Map ref: 7 SK42
Directions: On B5324 between Coalville &
Loughborough
Open: all day all wk ▐ ▌ﷳ **L** all wk 12-2.30 **D** all wk
6-9.30 **Closed:** 25-26 Dec
Rooms: 6 en suite **S** £70-£100 **D** £80-£150
Facilities: Garden Parking Wi-fi
Notes: ⊕ FREE HOUSE ▐ﬆ ﬅ ♈ 14

New owners Amanda Lockwood and business
partner Simon Nurse took over this pub, award-
winning restaurant and hotel in April 2011. Either
at the bar itself, or lounging in one of the leather
sofas, enjoy a pint of The Queen's Special, the
name always given to the guest real ale of the day,
often one suggested by a customer. In addition to
his managerial role, Simon is also the executive
chef and it falls to him and his head chef, David
Ferguson, to ensure that only the finest local
ingredients and produce end up on plates of diners.
Bar snacks include sausages with mustard mash
and onion gravy; fish pie; and croquet-monsieur.
Typical dishes on the restaurant menu might be fillet
of brill with mousseline, fennel and capers;
rare-breed Dexter beef and braised oxtail with
swede, potato millefeuille and red wine jus;
pot-roasted pheasant with celeriac, pancetta
and Brussel sprouts; and mushroom and
Stilton Wellington with hazelnut vinaigrette. The
Stilton, which comes from Colston Basset in
Nottinghamshire, is delicious with celery, crackers,
and grapes as a dessert, accompanied by a glass
of Cockburn's Ruby port, or you could choose
the pistachio soufflé with salt caramel ice cream.
The Queen's Head is licensed for civil wedding
ceremonies.

Recommended in the area

National Forest; Conkers; The Great Central Railway

London

Big Ben and the Houses of Parliament

North Pole Bar & Restaurant

Address: 131 Greenwich High Rd, Greenwich,
LONDON, SE10 8JA
Tel: 020 8853 3020
Email: info@northpolegreenwich.com
Website: www.northpolegreenwich.com
Map ref: 4 TQ38
Directions: Right from Greenwich rail station, pass
Novotel. Pub on right
Open: all day all wk noon-2am 🝢 **L** all wk 12-10
D all wk 12-10 🍴 **L** Sat-Sun 12-5 **D** all wk 6-10.30
Facilities: Garden Wi-fi
Notes: ⊕ FREE HOUSE ⁌⁌ 🏴 ♉ 9

With its name suggesting that here is the ideal place
to chill out, this transformed Victorian corner pub
can indeed provide everything you might want for
an evening on the town. Begin with an expertly
shaken cocktail in the bar before heading upstairs
for dinner in the grand green or the elegant red
room of the Piano Restaurant, then down to the
basement for dancing until late in the futuristic
South Pole DJ Club, with its bubble tanks, ultra-
violet lighting and chrome. But it's not just for night
owls. From midday bar meals and tapas are served
both inside and out, including in the garden Shisha
lounge. In the restaurant, where a pianist plays
on Thursday, Friday and Saturday nights, modern
European dishes might include chorizo risotto; roast
lamb chump, shallots, dauphinoise potatoes, thyme
sauce; Barbary duck breast on caramelised onion
with buttered pear, orange and red wine sauce;
pan-fried wild sea bass with shaved carrots, fennel,
beetroot and rocket salad, and balsamic and lime
vinaigrette; and ricotta and spinach cannelloni.
While you're in the restaurant, remember to look
up at the fish swimming around in the chandeliers.
On Sundays traditional roasts are added to the
repertoire, and children eat free.

Recommended in the area

National Maritime Museum; Royal Observatory
Greenwich; The Queens House

The Seven Stars

Address: 53 Carey St, LONDON, WC2A 2JB
Tel: 020 7242 8521
Email: roxy@roxybeaujolais.com
Map ref: 3 TQ38
Directions: From Temple N via The Strand & Bell Yard to Carey St. From Holborn SE via Lincoln's Inn Fields & Searle St to Carey St
Open: all day all wk 11-11 (Sat noon-11, Sun noon-10.30) ♿ **L** Mon-Fri noon-3, Sat-Sun noon-9
D Mon-Fri 5.30-9, Sat-Sun 12-9
Closed: 25-26 Dec, 1 Jan, Good Fri, Etr Sun
Facilities: Wi-fi
Notes: ⊕ FREE HOUSE

Built in 1602, this charming little pub at the back of the Royal Courts of Justice is presided over by the celebrated 'alewife' (as she calls herself) Roxy Beaujolais, cookbook author and TV food show presenter. Since she took it over it has had a subtle freshening and has expanded into the former legal wig shop next door—wigs are still displayed—to now provide 28 covers at green-chequered oilcloth-covered tables, in case you are diffident about sitting at the bar on Lloyd Loom stools. Roxy and her assistants cook simple dishes seven days a week that are, famously, slightly revisionist. A blackboard reveals what the market provides, which might include a meat, fowl or game pie; cockle bisque; paella with mixed sausages; linguine with chestnuts and truffle oil. Real ales from Adnams, Dark Star, Fullers and others are served, and a few good wines. The venerable pub cat Tom Paine wears a chorister's ruff, to the delight of customers - many of them barristers from across the road. The chalkboard outside lists frequently changing rules such as 'no querulousness', 'no apostrophe mistakes' and 'no dogs except Archie'. Even if you don't need the loo, try the narrow and ridiculously steep Elizabethan stairs.

Recommended in the area

The Soane Museum; The Hunterian Museum; Lincoln's Inn

Statue at the Royal Opera House, Covent Garden

Norfolk

Sunset at Cromer

The Hoste Arms

★★★ 88% ◉◉ HOTEL

Address: The Green, BURNHAM MARKET, PE31 8HD
Tel: 01328 738777
Email: reception@hostearms.co.uk
Website: www.hostearms.co.uk
Map ref: 8 TF84
Directions: Signed from B1155, 5m W of
Wells-next-the-Sea
Open: all day all wk ⓦ ⓞⓘ **L** all wk 12-2 **D** all wk 6-9
Rooms: 34 (7 GF) **S** £122-£241 **D** £149-£241
Facilities: Garden Parking Wi-fi
Notes: ⊕ FREE HOUSE ⋈ ♟ 16

Nelson's local, and one of Norfolk's most lauded and recognisable destination dining inns, with a magnificent combination of top-notch 2 AA Rosette food and distinctive accommodation, this old village manor house luxuriates in its location within the Norfolk Coast Area of Outstanding Natural Beauty, with the coastal path, marshlands, endless beaches and fascinating wildlife just a few minutes away. The bar of the 17th-century inn retains a traditional feel with its lively atmosphere, open log fire and East Anglian ales; there's also a pretty walled garden tucked behind the Moroccan-themed terrace, as well as a relaxed conservatory where you can chill out and read the papers over a cappuccino. The immense wine list is breathtaking, matching the notable surf and turf lunch menu available at the bar or in five restaurant areas, where the very finest Norfolk produce is gainfully employed in dishes such as Norfolk Coast assiette, just part of which includes soused mackerel, tempura oysters and Brancaster mussels, whilst home-made steak and kidney pud comes with honey-glazed parsnips and Chantenay carrots; there's a good clutch of vegetarian options too, completed by warm treacle tart and blackberry compôte. Dogs are very welcome to accompany you on your visit.

Recommended in the area

Titchwell Bird Reserve; Holkham Hall;
The Sandringham Estate

The Lord Nelson

Address: Walsingham Rd, BURNHAM THORPE,
King's Lynn, PE31 8HN
Tel: 01328 738241
Email: enquiries@nelsonslocal.co.uk
Website: www.nelsonslocal.co.uk
Map ref: 8 TF84 **Directions:** B1355 (Burnham
Market to Fakenham road), pub 9m from Fakenham
& 1.75m from Burnham Market. Pub near church
opposite playing fields
Open: all wk noon-3 6-11 (Jul-Aug noon-11pm)
🍴 L all wk 12-2.30 **D** all wk 6-9
Facilities: Garden Parking Wi-fi
Notes: ⊕ GREENE KING 👬 🐕 🍺 14

Opposite the delightful village cricket ground and
bowling green, this pub started life in 1637 as The
Plough. It was renamed The Lord Nelson in 1798,
to honour Horatio Nelson who was born in the
village. Visitors today can soak up an atmosphere
that has changed little over the past 370 years; you
can even sit on Nelson's high-backed settle. Drinks
are served from the taproom - specialities are cask
drawn Abbot Ale and Woodforde's Wherry, and
unique rum-based tipples such as Nelson's Blood,
described as 'Christmas pudding in a glass'. Belgian
chef, Peter de Groeve cooks dishes with balanced
flavours so that the quality of the ingredients
shines; look out for the locally sourced produce
on the menus - Sandringham Red Poll beef, and
Brancaster mussels and Cromer crab in season.
Typical dishes are farmhouse pâté with red onion
marmalade; and goats' cheese pannacotta with
grape must reduction; Gressingham duck breast
with Norfolk lavender sauce and gratin potatoes;
and lamb shank, carrot and coriander mash with
red wine sauce. There is a massive garden with
seating, a BBQ in summer and play equipment for
the children. Dirty wellies, and dogs straight from a
run on the beach are no problem here.

Recommended in the area
Holkham Hall; Titchwell Nature Reserve;
Sandringham House

The Pigs

Address: Norwich Rd, Edgefield, HOLT, NR24 2RL
Tel: 01263 587634
Email: info@thepigs.org.uk
Website: www.thepigs.org.uk
Map ref: 8 TG03
Directions: On B1149
Open: all wk Mon-Sat 11-2.30 6-11 (Sun & BHs 12-9)
Booking required **L** Mon-Sat 12-2.30, Sun &
BHs 12-9 **D** Mon-Sat 6-9
Facilities: Garden Parking
Notes: FREE HOUSE 17

Bags of character - how better to sum up this 17th-century pub? The building itself accounts for some of its appeal, of course, but the three locals who bought the freehold in 2006 deserve a mention in despatches for the major improvements they made. In the bar, Woodforde's, Adnams, and Edgefield Old Spot Abbot from Wolk Brewery are among the six real ales direct from the wood, and there's also in-house ginger beer. Influenced by what's locally available, the decidedly British food may well include dishes that trigger nostalgic thoughts and even unfamiliar cuts of meat. The Pigs' take on tapas, called 'iffits', includes crispy pig's ears with tartare sauce, and Cley smoked prawns. Porcine mains include the signature slow-cooked pork belly with smoky bacon, beans, black pudding and crackling, while from beyond the pig-sty come Cley smoked haddock plate pie; rare grilled skirt steak; and beetroot, pinenut and pearl barley stew. Sunday lunches are particularly popular, thanks to the Pudding Club. Children love the Piggleplay area, especially its zip wire, while indoor bar games and a Wednesday quiz amuse the adults. En suite bedrooms are available and one has an 8ft bed.

Recommended in the area

Felbrigg Hall (NT); North Norfolk Railway (The Poppy Line), Sheringham; RNLI Henry Blogg Museum, Cromer

Chequers Inn

Address: Griston Rd, THOMPSON, Thetford,
IP24 1PX
Tel: 01953 483360
Email: richard@thompsonchequers.co.uk
Website: www.thompsonchequers.co.uk
Map ref: 4 TL99
Directions: Between Watton & Thetford off A1075
Open: all wk 11.30-3 6.30-11 🍺 🍽 **L** all wk 12-2
D all wk 6.30-9
Facilities: Garden Parking Wi-fi
Notes: 🍺 FREE HOUSE 👬 🐾 🍷 8

With its low-slung thatched roof, and hidden among the trees in the heart of Breckland, this 17th-century free house was where manor courts, dealing with rents, land lettings and small crimes were once held. Original features include exposed beams and timbers and old farming implements hang from the walls. It's all very unpretentious, which means that there's something for everyone, including light bites in the bar, and a lunchtime menu (Monday–Friday) offering a 2 course set lunch for £7.25, as well as traditional fayre such as deep-fried breaded scampi, burgers and steak and kidney pudding. In the evening the menu stays along the traditional line, with old favourites like grilled rump, sirloin and gammon steaks. There is an extensive specials board where fresh fish dishes such as baked whole sea bream and freshly prepared game dishes (when in season) such as venison medallions and pigeon breast can be found. Dogs are welcome in the large rear beer garden, where there are also picnic tables. Purpose-built guest accommodation offers everything for the modern traveller. Nearby is the eight-mile Pingo Trail, host to glacially formed swamping depressions in the ground, and the Peddars Way footpath where uncommon and protected wildlife can be found.

Recommended in the area

Thompson Water; Peddars Way; Thetford Forest

The Orange Tree

Address: High St, THORNHAM, Hunstanton,
PE36 6LY
Tel: 01485 512213
Email: email@theorangetreethornham.co.uk
Website: www.theorangetreethornham.co.uk
Map ref: 8 TF74
Directions: Telephone for directions
Open: all day all wk 🍽 ▣ **L** all wk 12-3 **D** all wk
6-9.30
Facilities: Garden Parking Wi-fi
Notes: ⊕ PUNCH TAVERNS ♚ ♟ ♟ 21

Take a location by the green in a pretty coastal village, then add an interior brimming with charm and an award-winning (particularly for his seafood) executive chef, and you have the recipe for one of north Norfolk's most engaging pubs. Fish comes in fresh from local boats, and most of the meats are from the Royal estate at Sandringham a few miles away. Menus follow the seasons, with specials changing daily and new dishes appearing all the time. If you eat in the bar, you have plenty of choice as, for example, in pan-fried ox liver and bacon; Chiang Mai royal green lime leaf and coconut curry; or a just a sandwich, while from the longer restaurant menu you might start with Norfolk Coast fish soup (with Brancaster mussels as the headline act); follow with the pub's classic corn-fed chicken and wild mushroom pie; Portobello mushroom Wellington, sweet potato, smoked mozzarella, herb salad and red pepper dressing; or Moroccan spiced lamb rump, and finish with Orange Treeo, a neat pun of a dish featuring various preparations of said fruit. The children's menu admirably, if a little optimistically, lists crudités as a starter. Outside, the large garden is well provided with tables and benches.

Recommended in the area

Norfolk Lavender, Heacham; Hunstanton Sea Life Sanctuary; Sandringham House, Gardens & Museum

Wiveton Bell

Address: Blakeney Rd, WIVETON, Holt, NR25 7TL
Tel: 01263 740101
Email: enquiries@wivetonbell.co.uk
Website: www.wivetonbell.com
Map ref: 8 TG04
Directions: 1m from Blakeney. Wiveton Rd off A149
Open: all day all wk ⬛ ◉ Booking required **L** all wk
12-2.15 **D** all wk 6-9.15
Closed: 25 Dec
Facilities: Garden Parking Wi-fi
Notes: ⬛ FREE HOUSE ⚑ ♟ 17

This pretty, 17th-century inn overlooks the village green just a mile from Blakeney on Norfolk's beautiful north coast. Inside, an inglenook fireplace, settles, scrubbed wooden tables and oil paintings create a relaxed atmosphere where customers are just as likely to be walkers with muddy boots (and muddy dogs) as members of the area's business community. The award-winning restaurant is strong on local produce such as mussels, crabs, oysters and lobster, as well as game from the Holkham Hall Estate. Other dishes might include slow-roast Norfolk pork belly or braised oxtail with venison faggots. At lunchtime, lighter dishes are on offer, including chicken and bacon bruschetta, omelette Arnold Bennett, or a fine steak sandwich. Some of the Norfolk beers come from neighbouring brewery Yetmans, whose owner regards the Bell as his brewery taproom. In summer, the sheltered gardens, with their fine views of the village church and countryside, come into their own. Nice touches are the wind-up torches and umbrellas left in the bus shelter on the green for customers to use on the way to and from their cars. For those who wish to stay in the area, the Bell has four bedrooms and a restored fisherman's cottage.

Recommended in the area

Holkham Beach; seal-watching trips to Blakeney Point; Wells Beach

Cley next the Sea

Northamptonshire

Rushton Triangular Lodge

The Crown

Address: Helmdon Rd, WESTON, nr Towcester,
NN12 8PX
Tel: 01295 760310
Email: info@thecrownweston.co.uk
Website: www.thecrownweston.co.uk
Map ref: 3 SP54
Directions: Accessed from A43 or B4525
Open: all wk 6-11.30 (Fri-Sat noon-3.30 6-11.30 Sun
noon-3.30 7-11) 🍴 **L** Fri-Sun 12-2.30 **D** Tue-Sat 6-9.30
Closed: 25 Dec
Facilities: Garden Parking
Notes: 🌐 FREE HOUSE 🎿 🐾

This is a place that's oozing with history: a hostelry since the reign of Elizabeth I, the first documented evidence of The Crown pins the year down to 1593 and the first recorded owner was All Souls College, Oxford. Current owner Robert Grover has more recently completed a refurbishment of the building and brought renown to the pub for its excellent food, all prepared from fresh ingredients. A typical menu might start with goats' cheese and sun-dried tomato tart; chicken liver and pistachio terrine; or moules marinière and French bread. Mains range from the simple Charolais minute steak and caramelised onion baguette; or shepherd's pie with steamed vegetables; to lamb casserole with mint and apricots, vegetables and herb mash; wild mushroom risotto; chicken, leek and bacon pie with chips; or breast of duck with potato, Savoy cabbage, bacon rösti and kumquat sauce. Desserts take in a selection of ice creams and sorbets, as well as raspberry crème brûlée; lemon curd and ginger sponge pudding; and spiced apple pie with custard. A 45-bin wine list has been carefully selected to complement the food, and beer drinkers are rewarded with Greene King IPA, Hook Norton Best, Black Sheep, Landlord and other fine ales.

Recommended in the area

Sulgrave Manor; Silverstone; Canons Ashby House (NT)

Northumberland

Bamburgh Castle

The Pheasant Inn

★★★★ 🛏 INN

Address: Stannersburn, FALSTONE, NE48 1DD
Tel: 01434 240382
Email: stay@thepheasantinn.com
Website: www.thepheasantinn.com
Map ref: 11 NY78 **Directions:** A69, B6079, B6320,
follow signs for Kielder Water
Open: 12-3 6.30-11 🛏 **L** Mon-Sat noon-2.30
🍴 **L** Mon-Sat noon-2.30 **D** Mon-Sat 6.30-8.30
Closed: 25-27 Dec, Mon-Tue (Nov-Mar)
Rooms: 8 (5 GF) **S** £50-£60 **D** £90-£95
Facilities: Garden Parking
Notes: 🍺 FREE HOUSE 🛏 🐾

Set close by the magnificent Kielder Water, this classic country inn, built in 1624, has exposed stone walls, original beams, low ceilings, open fires and a display of old farm implements in the bar. Run by the welcoming Kershaw family since 1985, the inn was originally a farmhouse and has been appointed to a very high standard. The bright, modern en suite bedrooms, some with their own entrances, are all contained in stone buildings adjoining the inn and are set round a pretty courtyard. All the rooms, including one family room, are spotless, well equipped, and have tea- and coffee-making facilities, hairdryer, TV and radio alarm clock; all enjoy delightful country views. Delicious home-cooked breakfasts and evening meals are served in the bar or in the attractive dining room, or may be taken in the pretty garden courtyard if the weather permits. Irene and her son Robin are responsible for the traditional home cooking using local produce and featuring delights such as game pie and roast Northumbrian lamb, as well as imaginative vegetarian choices. Drying and laundry facilities are available and, for energetic guests, cycle hire can be arranged.

Recommended in the area

Hadrian's Wall; Scottish Borders; Northumbrian castles & stately homes

The Anglers Arms

Address: Weldon Bridge, LONGFRAMLINGTON, Morpeth, NE65 8AX
Tel: 01665 570271 & 570655
Email: johnyoung@anglersarms.fsnet.co.uk
Website: www.anglersarms.com
Map ref: 11 NU10
Directions: Take A697 N of Morpeth signed Wooler & Coldstream. 7m, left to Weldon Bridge
Open: all day all wk 11-11 (Sun noon-10.30) Morning coffee from 10am
🍴 **L & D** all wk noon-9.30 Booking required for restaurant **Facilities:** Garden Parking
Notes: ⊕ FREE HOUSE ♦♦

A 1760s coaching inn, now traditional pub and restaurant, overlooking the picturesque Weldon Bridge across the River Coquet. Your hosts here are John and Julie Young, who have created a bar that derives some of its warmth and friendliness from a collection of nice little touches - ornaments, antiques, quaint pieces of bric-a-brac, including some interesting hand-painted wall tiles, and fishing memorabilia. Meals in here are typified by mixed grill; home-made steak and ale pie; grilled salmon; oriental sizzling platter; and vegetable stew. As an unusual experience, dine in style in the Pullman railway carriage, where your choice might be a starter of garlic king prawns; scallop and bacon salad; or twice-cooked belly pork with honey-spiced apples, followed by a main course of tournedos Flodden, a prime fillet stuffed with Applewood cheese in bacon with garlic sauce; Borders rack of lamb; pan-fried breast of duck with honey-roasted parsnips, sweet potatoes and Cumberland glaze; or oven-baked peppers. Lighter meals include sandwiches and fresh garden leaf salads. The desserts board changes daily. Children will probably head outside for the playground.

Recommended in the area

Bamburgh Castle; Brinkburn Priory; Hadrian's Wall

Nottinghamshire

Newstead Abbey

The Martin's Arms

Address: School Ln, COLSTON BASSETT, NG12 3FD
Tel: 01949 81361
Email: martins_arms@hotmail.co.uk
Website: www.themartinsarms.co.uk
Map ref: 7 SK73
Directions: Off A46 between Leicester & Newark
Open: all wk noon-3.30 6-11
🍴 **L** Mon-Sat 12-2, Sun 12-5 **D** Mon-Sat 7-9.30
🍴 **L** all wk 12-2 **D** Mon-Sat 7-9.30
Closed: 25-26 Dec & 1 Jan eve
Facilities: Garden Parking
Notes: ⊕ FREE HOUSE 👫

So popular is this award-winning inn that it has made appearances on both regional and national television. It is a listed 18th-century building, set close to the old market cross in this stunning village in the Vale of Belvoir, an area that is renowned for its Stilton cheese. The interior has a real country house feel to it, with period furnishings, traditional hunting prints and seasonal fires in the Jacobean fireplace. Outside there is an acre of landscaped grounds, which includes a herb garden and well established lawns, backing on to National Trust land. The inn is a free house, serving a good range of real ales – Marston's Pedigree, Interbrew Bass, Greene King Abbot Ale, Timothy Taylor Landlord – from hand pumps. The wine list also offers seven wines by the glass. Good regional ingredients are a feature of the menu. Take, for example, the classic ploughman's lunch comprising Melton Mowbray pork pie, Colston Bassett Stilton or Cheddar, home-cured ham, pickles and bread. Alternatives in the bar include game pie, or fresh gnocchi with oven roasted tomatoes, peppers, spinach and parmesan cream. Typical restaurant dishes are cod fillet with lobster ravioli, potato rösti and creamed leek sauce; and bacon-wrapped rump of lamb with potato fondant and Puy lentils. Dogs are allowed in the garden only.

Recommended in the area

Belvoir Castle; Belton House (NT); National Water Sports Centre, Holme Pierrepoint

Oxfordshire

Punts on the River Cherwell near Magdalen College

The Vines

Address: Burford Rd, BLACK BOURTON, Black
Bourton, OX18 2PF
Tel: 01993 843559
Email: info@vineshotel.com
Website: www.vinesblackbourton.co.uk
Map ref: 3 SP20
Directions: A40 at Witney onto A4095 to Faringdon,
1st right after Bampton to Black Bourton
Open: all wk ⌂ ⓘ **L** Sat-Sun 12-2 **D** Mon-Sat 6-9,
Sun 7-9
Facilities: Garden Parking Wi-fi
Notes: ⊕ FREE HOUSE ⁑

A beautiful Cotswold village within easy reach of
Burford, Witney and the Thames Path is the setting
for The Vines, a traditional stone-built inn with an
elegant, contemporary feel and surrounded by
delightful gardens. The BBC's *Real Rooms* team
famously designed and transformed the restaurant
and bar, so expect a surprisingly stylish interior for
a Cotswold pub, with murals, wooden floors, big
plants in pots, and leather sofas fronting open log
fires. Relax with a pint of Hooky or linger over lunch
or dinner; the menus listing an imaginative choice
of modern British dishes with an international
twist, all freshly prepared using locally sourced
produce. Typical examples from the carte include
warm goats' cheese and caramelised red onion
tartlets; chargrilled Cajun chicken salad followed by
homemade puff pastry pie of the week; peppered
lamb cutlets with salsa verde; chicken breast
stuffed with asparagus spears, in Parma Ham with
creamy white wine sauce. Then choose one of the
straightforward sounding desserts such as Eton
Mess, apricot tart or chocolate mousse. There's
always a Sunday roast and a raft of Old and New
World wines by the glass. On sunny days, dine
alfresco on the sun-trap patio or play a nostalgic
game of Aunt Sally.

Recommended in the area

Cogges Manor Farm Museum; Cotswold Wildlife
Park; Blenheim Palace

The Inn for All Seasons

★★★ RESTAURANT WITH ROOMS

Address: The Barringtons, BURFORD, OX18 4TN
Tel: 01451 844324
Email: sharp@innforallseasons.com
Website: www.innforallseasons.com
Map ref: 3 SP21
Directions: 3m W of Burford on A40
Open: all day all wk Sun-Thu 11-2.30 6-11, Fri-Sat
11-11 🖳 †◎l **L** all wk 12-2.30 **D** all wk 6.30-9.30
Rooms: 10 en suite
Facilities: Garden Parking Wi-fi
Notes: ♦† ✓

The inn's humble beginnings were as two quarry cottages, where Cotswold stone was brought to the roadside destined for buildings such as Blenheim Palace and St Paul's Cathedral. As ale was probably dispensed to thirsty workers from the day the cottages were built, their transition to a coaching inn was inevitable. Within you will find a treasure trove of ancient oak beams, leather wing-back chairs and interesting memorabilia, giving it that true country pub feel. The well stocked bar offers draught ales from Devizes and Wiltshire plus guest beers. Matthew Sharp is a classically trained chef who selects seasonal local produce for his menus, including game from the Barrington Park Estate and local Gloucester pork and ham. The guaranteed daily supply of excellent fish makes the fresh fish board the best in the area. Look out for a whole cock crabs, fresh oysters, mussels, fish soup and other favourites. Meat lovers can enjoy grilled sirloin of Aberdeen Angus beef with fat chips, and roasted rump of Cornish lamb with dauphinoise potatoes. There is a more formal restaurant, as well as the bar area, to enjoy your meal plus a lovely beer garden. There are ten comfortable en suite bedrooms. Dogs are welcome.

Recommended in the area

Cotsworld Wildlife Park; Blenheim Palace; City of Oxford

The Red Lion Inn

Address: The High St, CHALGROVE, OX44 7SS
Tel: 01865 890625
Website: www.redlionchalgrove.co.uk
Map ref: 3 SU69
Directions: B480 from Oxford ring road, through
Stadhampton, left then right at mini-rdbt. At
Chalgrove Airfield right into village
Open: all wk 11.30-3 6-mdnt (Sat 11.30-3 6-1am Sun
all day) 🛏 🍽 **L** Mon-Sat 12-2, Sun 12-3
D Mon-Sat 6-9 **Closed:** 25 Dec
Facilities: Garden
Notes: ⊕ FREE HOUSE 👬 🐾

Since before the first known written record of 1637,
this old village pub has been owned by the parish
church. How fitting therefore that the surname of
the licensees, Raymond and Suzanne, is Sexton.
Local legend has it that, many moons ago, 'naughty'
church wardens would dine and carouse here,
a tradition of hospitality allegedly still much in
evidence today! There are several places in which
to put this to the test: gripping one of the five hand-
pulled real ales by the log fire in the main bar area;
in one of the cosy little nooks leading off the bar; in
the front garden, which leads down to duck-heaven
Chalgrove Brook; or in the large established garden
at the rear. There is also a choice of where to eat:
at one of the tables in the bar; in the separate
restaurant; or, again, outside. Depending on the
season, the à la carte menu might list fried saddle
and braised leg of hare with creamy mash; sliced
loin of venison with juniper and blackberry sauce;
breast of pheasant stuffed with leg meat, chestnuts
and tarragon in bacon; and pan-fried pavé of
organic salmon with crab and anise butter sauce.
There's a specials board too.

Recommended in the area

City of Oxford; Courthouse, Ridgeway Path; Long
Crendon (NT)

The Sir Charles Napier

◎◎

Address: Spriggs Alley, CHINNOR, OX39 4BX
Tel: 01494 483011
Website: www.sircharlesnapier.co.uk
Map ref: 3 SP70
Directions: M40 junct 6, B4009 to Chinnor. Right at
rdbt to Spriggs Alley
Open: noon-4 6-mdnt (Sun noon-6) ♿ **L** Tue-Fri
12-2.30 **D** Tue-Fri 6.30-9 ⚬| **L** Tue-Sat 12-2.30, Sun
12-3.30 **D** Tue-Sat 6.30-10
Closed: 25-26 Dec, Mon, Sun eve
Facilities: Garden Parking Wi-fi
Notes: ⊕ FREE HOUSE ♦ ♩ ♟ 12

High amidst the beech woods of the Chiltern Hills in
an Area of Outstanding Natural Beauty, elegant red
kites soar over this sublime flint-and-brick dining
inn, which is also just ten minutes from the M40.
Making the most of this secluded locale, seasonal
forays to the hedgerows and woods (customers can
join in) produce herbs, fungi and berries used in the
inventive menus, whilst the plump local game finds
its way into some of the extraordinary AA 2-Rosette
winning dishes here. Diners distribute themselves
amidst a most eclectically furnished suite of rooms,
with Michael Cooper's memorable sculptures, and
comfy sofas set near warming winter log fires.
Chef Chris Godfrey's menus offer so many exciting
choices - razor clams with chorizo, broad beans and
lemon; prosciutto with goats' curd, roast fig and
artichokes; or Cornish crab remoulade with avocado
and wild rocket, followed by Cornish haddock, petit
pois à la francais, mousseline potatoes and salsa
verde; blanquette of lamb with champ and summer
vegetables, or open lasagne of summer beans and
taleggio. All accompanied by a noteworthy wine
list of over 200 choices. Before, or after, dinner
time may be spent in the superb grounds – there's
really nowhere nicer on a lovely summer evening
especially with a glass of wine in hand.

Recommended in the area

The Chiltern Hills; West Wycombe Park; Garsington
Opera at Wormsley

The Trout at Tadpole Bridge

★★★★ INN

Address: Buckland Marsh, FARINGDON, SN7 8RF
Tel: 01367 870382
Email: info@troutinn.co.uk
Website: www.troutinn.co.uk
Map ref: 3 SU29 **Directions:** A420 onto A417 to Faringdon, take A4095 signed Bampton, pub 2m
Open: 11.30-3 6-11 Booking required **L** all wk 12-2 **D** all wk 7-9
Closed: 25-26 Dec, Sun eve (Nov-Apr)
Rooms: 3 en suite (4 GF)
Facilities: Garden Parking Wi-fi
Notes: FREE HOUSE 12

Once a riverside toll house, this 17th-century free house has a classic 'Wind in the Willows' name and setting on the banks of the Thames, just twenty minutes from Oxford. A previous winner of the AA Pub of the Year for England, the inn has log fires to welcome visitors and the locals who come in every night for the fine range of regional beers such as Ramsbury Bitter and White Horse, while in summer there is an extensive riverside garden to enjoy, especially if there's a jug of Pimms to hand. Owners Gareth and Helen Pugh have run several fine-dining restaurants and take food seriously. The chef Pascal makes good use of the best local ingredients – seasonal game, suckling pig, and even crayfish caught at the bottom of the garden, to name but a few. Typical menu and special board choices start with chicken liver and duck foie gras parfait with green fig chutney; and croustade of goats' cheese and rosemary, blackberry and cassis dressing. Follow on with roast partridge caramelised pears, straw potatoes and beetroot sauce; or breast of duck, parsnip and lavender purée and pickled walnuts. Six individually designed en suite bedrooms are available if you choose to stop over.

Recommended in the area

Kelmscott Manor; Badbury Hill; Kingston Lisle Park

The White Hart

◎◎

Address: Main Rd, FYFIELD, Nr Abingdon, OX13 5LW
Tel: 01865 390585
Email: info@whitehart-fyfield.com
Website: www.whitehart-fyfield.com
Map ref: 3 SU49
Directions: 7m S of Oxford, just off A420 (Oxford to Swindon road)
Open: 12-3 5.30-11 (Sat 12-11 Sun 12-10.30)
🍴 Booking required **L** Tue-Sat 12-2.30, Sun 12-3
D Tue-Sat 7-9.30 **Closed:** Mon ex BH
Facilities: Garden Parking Wi-fi
Notes: ⊕ FREE HOUSE 🍷 14

A 15th-century chantry house, the White Hart retains many original features, including a tunnel to Fyfield Manor which was an escape route for priests during the Dissolution of the Monasteries. The original soaring eaves and beams, huge stone-flanked windows and flagstones are overlooked by a minstrels' gallery, now the main restaurant. Owners, Mark and Kay Chandler, are self-confessed 'foodies' who are steadfast in their pursuit of seasonal food from trusted local suppliers and their own garden, which provides a regular supply of fruit, vegetables and herbs. Menus change daily depending on what is fresh and seasonal and everything is made in house, including bread, pasta and ice creams. Starters might be home-cured salmon gravad lax with marinated cucumber salad; or duck rillette, parsley, caper and shallot salad. For main courses, perhaps try the wild seabass fillet with samphire and crab bisque; or slow roasted pork belly with celeriac purée, crackling and cider jus. Puddings are just as tempting, especially hot chocolate fondant with salted caramel ice cream. With over 50 wines on the list, 14 of which are sold by the glass, there's something for everyone. A good range of cask-conditioned ales always includes something from Hook Norton.

Recommended in the area

Ashmolean Museum; Blenheim Palace; White Horse at Uffington

The Five Horseshoes

Address: Maidensgrove, HENLEY-ON-THAMES,
RG9 6EX
Tel: 01491 641282
Email: admin@thefivehorseshoes.co.uk
Website: www.thefivehorseshoes.co.uk
Map ref: 3 SU78
Directions: A4130 from Henley-on-Thames, 1m,
B480 signed Stonor. In Stonor left, through woods,
over common, pub on left
Open: all wk noon-3.30 6-11 (Sat noon-11 Sun
noon-6)
Facilities: Garden Parking
Notes: ⊕ BRAKSPEAR ⋔ ⋔

A favourite haunt of foodies and nature lovers for many years, the Five Horseshoes is a 16th-century pub in the Chilterns Area of Outstanding Natural Beauty. It exudes old world character with its wooden beams, brasses, wrought iron and welcoming open fires; there are two snug bar areas and a large conservatory restaurant with breathtaking views, plus two beer gardens. The chef specialises in taking traditional English dishes and giving them a modern twist to intensify the flavours and textures, and alongside pub favourites, local game and foraged food nearly always feature on the menu. Starters sure to tempt are croustillant of confit duck with red onion marmalade; or home-smoked salmon with soused vegetables. Then either stick to the inn's fish and chips; beef or venison burger; pork sausages or gammon steak, or choose a more complicated dish such as roast haunch of fallow venison, potato purée, sautéed spinach and sauce poivrade; or pan-fried black bream fillet, Palourde clams, seared scallops, tagliatelle, garlic and hazelnut butter. For a lighter appetites there's a wide choice of sandwiches too. Mountain bikers and hikers are welcome, but please leave those muddy boots at the door!

Recommended in the area

River & Rowing Museum; Mapledurham House & Watermill; Warburg Nature Reserve

The Kingham Plough

★★★★ ◎◎ ⓘ INN

Address: The Green, KINGHAM, OX7 6YD
Tel: 01608 658327
Email: book@thekinghamplough.co.uk
Website: www.thekinghamplough.co.uk
Map ref: 3 SP22
Directions: B4450 from Chipping Norton to Churchill. 2nd right to Kingham
Open: all day all wk 🍴 **L** & **D** 12-9 (Sun 12-8)
🍴 **L** Mon-Sat 12-2, Sun 12-2.30 **D** Mon-Thu 7-8.30; Fri-Sat 6.30-9 **Closed:** 25 Dec **Rooms:** 7 en suite
S £75-£105 **D** £90-£130 **Facilities:** Garden Parking Wi-fi **Notes:** ⊕ FREE HOUSE 👪 🐾

If there is a quintessential Cotswold pub, then maybe this is it. One of Kingham's many attractive, stone-built 17th- and 18th-century houses, it overlooks the woody village green, and its bar and two-AA Rosette restaurant draw customers from all over. Co-owner and executive chef Emily, and head chef Gareth change the short menu daily to make full use of supplies from local fruit farms, smallholdings and game estates, as well as the foraged fungi and sea vegetables that go into their modern British dishes. Typically, these might include salt cod and ham hock terrine; soft boiled Daylesford egg, salsify, broccoli and mushrooms on toast; haunch and faggot of Muntjac venison with beetroot tart; Evenlode lamb pudding with sprouting broccoli; and Cornish plaice with cuttlefish stew. Alongside the carte are bar snacks of homemade pork pie with pickle; Cotswold rarebit with sourdough soldiers; and scotched quail's eggs. At the end of an evening don't be surprised if the menu has moved on from the one you started with as dishes are replaced with even more seasonal produce! In the bar you'll find hessian-covered stools, locally produced real ales, scrumpy and fruit juices and a well-researched European wine list. The en suite bedrooms provide top quality and comfort.

Recommended in the area

Cotswold Wildlife Park; Blenheim Palace; Chastleton House (NT)

The Baskerville

★★★★ INN

Address: Station Rd, LOWER SHIPLAKE,
Henley-on-Thames, RG9 3NY
Tel: 0118 940 3332
Email: enquiries@thebaskerville.com
Website: www.thebaskerville.com
Map ref: 3 SU77 **Directions:** Just off A4155, 1.5m
from Henley **Open:** all day all wk 9.30am-11pm (Sun
noon-4.30 7-10) 🍴 🛏 Bkfst served Mon-Sat 9.30-12,
L Mon-Sat 12-6, Sun 12-2.30 **D** Mon-Thu 6-9.30, Fri-
Sat 6-10 **Closed:** 1 Jan **Rooms:** 4 en suite **S** £77.50
D £87.50 **Facilities:** Garden Parking Wi-fi
Notes: ⊕ ENTERPRISE INNS 👪 🐾 🍷 12

It's said that Arthur Conan Doyle was inspired
to write *The Hound of the Baskervilles* by the
menacing stone dogs' heads on the gates at nearby
Crowsley Park, where real Baskervilles once lived.
Be that as it may, there's nothing to disconcert
visitors to this welcoming gastro-pub 200 metres
from the River Thames. With a modern-rustic
interior, it also has an attractive 100-seat garden
where barbecues are held in summer. Seasonal,
well-balanced menus feature British cuisine with
European and Far-Eastern influences, a principle
that declares its hand through dishes such as crispy
baby squid with aromatic Asian salad and honey,
lemon and chilli dressing; hazelnut-crumbed French
goats' cheese with lemon and beetroot salad; salt
beef with horseradish mash, watercress cream
sauce, whisky- and honey-glazed carrots and curly
kale; rich chicken liver and Cointreau parfait with
toasted bread, kumquat chutney and dressed
leaves; and a Shiplake butcher's beef, pork and
chilli sausages with bubble and squeak cake. The
Regatta Room, a private dining area for up to 12, is
named for the Henley Regatta, a popular event that
makes booking a table and staying overnight in the
accommodation essential.

Recommended in the area
Cliveden (NT); Stonor Park; Henley-on-Thames

The Crown Inn

Address: PISHILL, Henley-on-Thames, RG9 6HH
Tel: 01491 638364
Email: enquiries@thecrowninnpishill.co.uk
Website: www.thecrowninnpishill.co.uk
Map ref: 3 SU78
Directions: A4130 from
Henley-on-Thames, right onto B480 to Pishill
Open: all wk 11.30-3 6-11 (Sun noon-3 7-10)
🛏 🍴 **L** all wk 12-2.30 **D** all wk 7-9.30
Closed: 25-26 Dec
Facilities: Garden Parking
Notes: 🌐 FREE HOUSE 🕴 🐎

A pretty 15th-century brick and flint former coaching inn, The Crown has enjoyed a colourful history. It began life in medieval times, serving ale to members of the thriving monastic community, then in later years, served as a refuge for Catholic priests escaping Henry VIII's draconian rule. It contains possibly the largest priest hole in the country, complete with a sad story about one Father Dominique, who met his end there. Moving forward to the swinging 60s, the thatched barn housed a nightclub hosting the likes of George Harrison and Dusty Springfield. Nowadays, the barn is licenced for civil ceremonies as well as serving as a function room. In the pub itself, the bar is supplied by mostly local breweries, including Marlow, and the menu changes frequently and features local produce cooked fresh to order. Lunch and dinner are served every day and can be enjoyed inside the pub with its three log fires or in the picturesque garden overlooking the valley, depending on the season. Bed and breakfast accommodation is available. The name of the village is often a subject of conversation, some say it was to do with wagon horses relieving themselves once they had got to the top the hill or maybe simply because peas used to be grown around here!

Recommended in the area

Stonor Park; Greys Court, (NT); River & Rowing Museum

The Royal Oak

Address: High St, RAMSDEN, OX7 3AU
Tel: 01993 868213
Website: www.royaloakramsden.com
Map ref: 3 SP31
Directions: B4022 from Witney towards Charlbury, right before Hailey, through Poffley End
Open: all wk 11.30-3 6.30-11 (Sun 11.30-3 7-10.30)
🛏 🍽 **L** all wk 12-2 **D** Mon-Sat 7-9.45, Sun 7-9
Closed: 25 Dec
Facilities: Garden Parking
Notes: ⊕ FREE HOUSE 🚬 🍷 30

Once upon a time, stagecoaches between London and Hereford stopped at this 17th-century inn standing opposite the church in the pretty Cotswold village of Ramsden. These days it is popular with walkers exploring the lovely countryside, but whether you feel like walking or not, stop here for its old beams, warm fires, stone walls and, of course, refreshment. As a free house it offers beers for which real ale aficionados would willingly join the rambling fraternity, while the 200-bin wine list would particularly appeal to those appreciating their Bordeaux, with many of them available by the glass. The bar menu regularly features a pie of the week, and there are also favourites such as real Italian meatballs; home-made beef burgers; and wild mushroom pasta with shiitake and porcini mushrooms. The main menu features the very best of fresh, local, seasonal food, with regular fish deliveries. To start your meal, expect moules marinière (with Hebridean mussels); chicken liver parfait with cognac and raisins; and baked avocado, cheese and prawn gratin. Main courses include smoked haddock cooked with whisky, cream and cheese; confit of duck leg with quince sauce and Puy lentils; and pan-fried calves' liver with wild mushroom sauce.

Recommended in the area

Blenheim Palace; Minster Lovell Hall; Rollright Stones

The Crown Inn

Address: Sydenham Rd, SYDENHAM, OX39 4NB
Tel: 01844 351634
Website: www.crownsydenham.co.uk
Map ref: 3 SP70
Directions: M40 junct 6, B4009 towards Chinnor.
Left onto A40. At Postcombe right to Sydenham
Open: 12-3 5.30-11 (Sat noon-11 Sun noon-3)
🍴 🍽 **L** Tue-Sun 12-2.30 **D** Tue-Sat 7-9.30
Closed: 1 wk Jan, 1 wk Aug, Sun eve, Mon
Facilities: Garden
Notes: ⊕ THE SYDENHAM PUB CO 🎎 🐕

In a small village below the scarp slopes of the Chilterns, this pretty 16th-century inn shows how careful refurbishment can successfully incorporate both traditional and modern styles. Old photographs, for example, hang contentedly alongside contemporary paintings. The secluded garden is the just the place to enjoy and drink in the summer months but the cosy interior is no less tempting in cooler times with its blazing log fire. The menu is short – barely a dozen items are featured – but expect good things of those that are, such as plum tomato and thyme soup; or chicken liver and brandy pâté, toasted brioche and fig relish to start, then perhaps seared pepper crusted haunch of venison, baked potato mash and blackberry gravy;

un-dyed organic smoked haddock and spinach risotto; or goats' cheese and wild mushroom Wellington with beetroot relish to follow. Finish with apple and blackberry crumble with custard; white chocolate and raspberry cheesecake; or chocolate fondant and vanilla ice cream. In the bar, a pint of Brakspear would go well with a ploughman's, omelette, baguette or pizza. Treasure Hunts starting and finishing at The Crown take you through some of the prettiest villages in this part of Oxfordshire.

Recommended in the area

Hell Fire Caves; Stonor Park; City of Oxford

Bridge of Sighs, Oxford

Rutland

Oakham School

The Jackson Stops Country Inn

Address: Rookery Rd, STRETTON, LE15 7RA
Tel: 01780 410237
Website: www.thejacksonstops.com
Map ref: 7 SK91
Directions: From A1 follow Stretton signs
Open: 12-4, 6-11 🔒 🍴 **L** Tue-Sun 12-3 **D** Tue-Sat 6.30-9.30
Closed: Sun eve, Mon
Facilities: Garden Parking
Notes: 🛢 FREE HOUSE 👫 🐕 🍺

The long, low, stone-built partly thatched building actually dates from 1721, and has plenty of appeal: stone fireplaces with log fires, exposed stone and quarry tiled floors, scrubbed wood tables and no fewer than five intimate dining rooms. In the timeless and beamed snug bar, the choice of real ales lifts the heart, boding well for the excellent value to be had from the dishes on the menu, all freshly prepared and cooked by the kitchen staff. Children are well looked after too, as they can choose from their own menu or take smaller portions from the adult choice. So order a pint of Oakham and settle outside in the garden if it's a sunny day. Back inside you can play the ancient pub game of nurdling; the game's world championships are held here each June. And, if you were wondering about the pub's name: there can be few pubs in the country that have acquired their name by virtue of a 'For Sale' sign. One was planted outside the pub for so long during a previous change of ownership that the locals dispensed with the old name – the White Horse – in favour of the name of the estate agent on the board.

Recommended in the area

Oakham Castle; Lyddington Bede House; Rutland Country Museum & Visitor Centre

Somerset

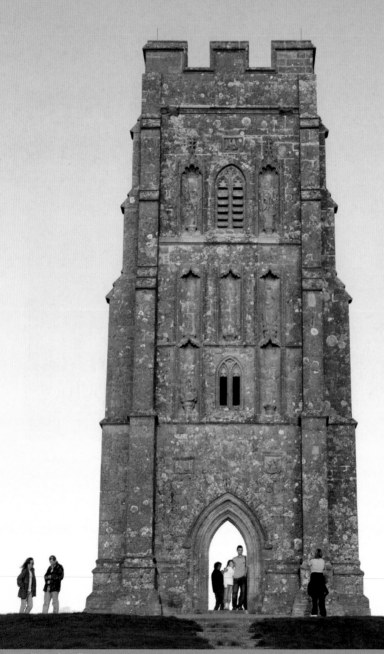

Glastonbury Tor

The Marlborough Tavern

Address: 35 Marlborough Buildings, BATH, BA1 2LY
Tel: 01225 423731
Email: info@marlborough-tavern.com
Website: www.marlborough-tavern.com
Map ref: 2 ST76
Directions: 200mtrs from W end of Royal Crescent
Open: all day all wk noon-11 (Fri-Sat noon-12.30am)
L Mon-Sat 12.30-2.30, Sun 12.30-4 **D** Mon-Sat
6-10, Sun 6-9 **Closed:** 25 Dec
Facilities: Garden Wi-fi
Notes: FREE HOUSE 16

This award-winning gastropub has provided food and drink since the 18th century, which probably means some of its earliest customers had just moved into the famous Royal Crescent, just around the corner. It successfully combines the atmosphere of a friendly local with the food quality of a top restaurant, thus you'll find a selection of well-kept local ales, a healthy mix of New and Old World wines, and on the menus freshly prepared, well presented British food that reflects not only the seasons, but local availability and quality. As head chef Richard Knighting says: 'It's more than lip service to a passing fad; it's driven by a simple desire to give customers what they want'. Although not strictly speaking locally sourced, the fish that comes up from Cornwall and Devon is traditionally caught, sustainable and fresh. Often available therefore are Cornish fillets of mackerel with salsa verde and fries; and Butcombe beer-battered haddock with mushy peas, caper mayonnaise and hand-cut chips. Other possibilities are marinated Charolais steak salad with horseradish cream and watercress; and mushroom, leek, truffle and pearl barley risotto. Or for a snack, a toasted Wiltshire ham and Cheddar cheese sandwich, or a belly pork and apple sauce ciabatta.

Recommended in the area

Thermae Bath Spa; Pulteney Bridge; Longleat House & Safari Park

The Hunters Rest

★ ★ ★ ★ INN

Address: King Ln, Clutton Hill, CLUTTON, BS39 5QL
Tel: 01761 452303
Email: info@huntersrest.co.uk
Website: www.huntersrest.co.uk
Map ref: 2 ST65
Directions: On A37 follow signs for Wells through
Pensford, at large rdbt left towards Bath, 100mtrs
right into country lane, pub 1m up hill
Open: all day all wk ⓑ ⑩ noon-9.45
Rooms: 5 en suite **S** £67.5-£77.5 **D** £95-£130
Facilities: Garden Parking Wi-fi
Notes: ⊕ FREE HOUSE ♦ ⌂ ☂ 10

Originally a hunting lodge that was built for the
Earl of Warwick in about 1750, the inn is situated
amid beautiful countryside high on Clutton Hill
overlooking the Cam Valley to the Mendips and the
Chew Valley to Bristol. Historic character, including
beams, exposed stonework and log fires, has been
complemented by modern amenities, creating
a cosy atmosphere inside. There's a landscaped
garden outside, complete with a miniature railway
to carry passengers around the grounds. The beers
served here include Otter Ale, Sharp's Own, Hidden
Quest and Butcombe, and there is a reasonably
priced wine list with a good choice by the glass.
Home-made dishes from the menu range through
bakehouse rolls and giant oggies (pasties) with a

variety of fillings, to grills and other popular pub
fare including Somerset faggots, with onion gravy;
hot and spicy chicken Madras; chilli burritos; and
lambs' liver and bacon. Desserts are worth saving
some room for too – tarte au citron with blackberry
ice cream; and maple and walnut cheesecake to
name but two. The inn offers accommodation in
individually designed bedrooms which include
four-poster suites, antique furniture, direct dial
telephones, LCD TVs and Wi-fi.

Recommended in the area
Bath; Cheddar Caves; Wells Cathedral

The Queens Arms

Address: CORTON DENHAM, Sherborne, DT9 4LR
Tel: 01963 220317
Email: relax@thequeensarms.com
Website: www.thequeensarms.com
Map ref: 2 ST62
Directions: From A303 follow Sutton Montis, South Cadbury & Corton Denham signs. Through South Cadbury, 0.25m, left, up hill signed Corton Denham. Left at hill top to village. Approx 1m, pub on right
Open: all wk 🍴 🍽 **L** all wk 12-3 **D** Mon-Sat 6-10, Sun 6-9.30
Facilities: Garden Parking Wi-fi
Notes: ⊕ FREE HOUSE 👬 🐕 🍷 23

Tucked away in the ancient village of Corton Denham, on the Somerset-Dorset border, The Queens Arms, a previous winner of AA Pub of the Year for England, offers real drink, real food and real comfort. Food is simple but good, sourced mainly from the surrounding countryside, as well as from home-reared pork and chickens. In the bar you might want to order a pint of local beer or cider, or a bottled beer from the wide international selection, and maybe ask for a pork pie at the same time. There are also eight local apple juices on offer along with a well chosen wine and whisky list. Or, having booked a lunch table in the bustling dining room, try the crispy pork belly, poached apple and roast beetroot salad; or chargriled pigeon breast with sweet pickled vegetable salad. The dinner menu typically offers dishes such as Corton Denham lamb cutlets, dauphinoise potatoes, roast swede with a tarragon and shallot reduction; or oven-baked John Dory, new potatoes with garlic, caper and chorizo butter. Stay over in one of the eight individually-styled bedrooms.

Recommended in the area

Fleet Air Arm Museum; Montacute House (NT); Haynes International Motor Museum

The Helyar Arms

★★★★ ☺ INN

Address: Moor Ln, EAST COKER, BA22 9JR
Tel: 01935 862332
Email: info@helyar-arms.co.uk
Website: www.helyar-arms.co.uk
Map ref: 2 ST51
Directions: 3m from Yeovil. Take A57 or A30, follow East Coker signs
Open: all wk 11-3 6-11 🍽️ ⊙ **L** all wk 12-2.30 **D** all wk 6.30-9.30
Rooms: 6 en suite
Facilities: Garden Parking Wi-fi
Notes: ⊕ PUNCH TAVERNS 👫 🐾

This Grade II listed building dates back in part to 1468 and reputedly takes its name from Archdeacon Helyar, a chaplain to Queen Elizabeth I. Log fires warm the charming old world bar, where Butcombe, Black Sheep and Hobgoblin ales are backed by Stowford Press and Taunton Traditional ciders. There's a skittle alley, comfortable accommodation and a separate restaurant occupying an original apple loft. The kitchen makes full use of local produce, including wood pigeon, rabbit, venison, pheasant and fish from the south Devon coast, to create the seasonally changing menus and the blackboard specials. There's plenty of choice, from sandwiches and lighter bites (maybe salmon, pea and mint farfelle with lemon cream) to starters such as cream spinach, pinenut and blue cheese tartlet, or ham hock and leek terrine with Coker apple and sage chutney; then main courses of roast pork tenderloin with apricot mousse, sage potatoes and cardamom jus; or home-baked honey-glazed ham with two free-range fried eggs and chips. Succulent steaks can be cut to order and grilled, plus their steak sandwich is award winning. All the puddings here are home made - perhaps try banana and butterscotch crème brûlée with lavender shortbread - and coffees and teas come with home-made petits fours.

Recommended in the area

Glastonbury Tor; Barrington Court; Somerset Levels

George Inn

Address: High St, NORTON ST PHILIP, BA2 7LH
Tel: 01373 834224
Email: georgeinn@wadworth.co.uk
Website: www.georgeinnnsp.co.uk
Map ref: 2 ST75
Directions: A36 from Bath to Warminster, 6m, right onto A366 to Radstock, village 1m
Open: all day all wk 🍽️ ⓣ❍ Mon-Sat 11.30-9 (Sun 12-9)
Facilities: Garden Parking Wi-fi
Notes: ⊕ WADWORTH ♦♦ 🐾

With more than 700 years under its belt, this Grade I listed building is one of the country's oldest continuously licensed inns. Just over a decade ago, the Wadworth brewery meticulously restored it, and during the process uncovered medieval wall paintings, now preserved. Other noteworthy features are the stone-slated roof, massive doorway, cobbled courtyard and impressive timbered galleries. The owners strive to source all the ingredients for their two menus locally, so expect the bar menu to feature steak, ale and mushroom pie, or Asian marinated lamb and pepper kebabs. In the beamed restaurant, choose from a starter of duck and orange terrine; or wine marinated figs with blue cheese and walnuts; then follow with perhaps an individual local venison wellington; pan-fried garlic and coriander chicken with noodles; or pear and feta filo strudel. Save room for a delicious home-made dessert – lime and tequila pannacotta; fresh fruit crumble with custard or clotted cream; or just choose from a very tempting and unusually flavoured award-winning ice creams and sorbets. Outside you can eat in the ancient and atmospheric courtyard and from the beer garden watch cricket on the Mead.

Recommended in the area
Bath & Roman Baths; Longleat; Cheddar Gorge

The Carpenters Arms

Address: STANTON WICK, Nr Pensford, BS39 4BX
Tel: 01761 490202
Email: carpenters@buccaneer.co.uk
Website: www.the-carpenters-arms.co.uk
Map ref: 2 ST66
Directions: From A37 at Chelwood rdbt take A368 signed Bishop Sutton. Turn right to Stanton Wick
Open: all day all wk 11-11 (Sun 12-10.30)
🛏 🍽 Booking required **L** Mon-Sat 12-2.30, Sun 12-9
D Mon-Thu 6-9.30, Fri-Sat 6-10, Sun 12-9
Closed: 25-26 Dec
Facilities: Garden Parking
Notes: 🍺 FREE HOUSE 🍴 🍷 10

Just 20 minutes from either Bath or Bristol, this charming stone-built pub is set in the tranquil hamlet of Stanton Wick, overlooking the Chew Valley. It began life as a row of miners' cottages and retains its cottagey style, with a spacious terrace, perfect for summer drinks. Behind the pretty flower bedecked façade, you'll find a low-beamed bar with a convivial atmosphere and no intrusive music. A choice of real beers is served, including Butcombe, Sharp's Doom Bar, and an extensive wine list combining New and Old World favourites. The menu changes regularly to offer the best seasonal produce, including fish from Cornwall, West Country beef and local game in season. Typical dishes include a starter of steamed mussels, cider, leek and cream sauce; or potted duck with garlic ciabatta croutons, rocket salad with plum and apple chutney, and a main course of pan-roasted pork loin with apricot and sausagemeat stuffing, sauté potatoes, spinach and mushroom cream sauce; or risotto of peas, rocket, beetroot and feta cheese. For smaller appetites there's a range of sandwiches, and children have their own choices. A function room is available for use by groups of 20–36.

Recommended in the area

Cheddar Gorge; Longleat; Wookey Hole Caves

The Blue Ball

Address: TRISCOMBE, Bishops Lydeard, TA4 3HE
Tel: 01984 618242
Email: enq@blueballinn.info
Website: www.blueballinn.info
Map ref: 2 ST13 **Directions:** From Taunton take
A358 past Bishops Lydeard towards Minehead
Open: noon-3 6-11 (Fri-Sat 12-11 Sun 12-7)
🍽 **L** Tue-Sat 12-2, Sun 12-3 **D** Tue-Sat 7-9
🍴 **L** Tue-Sat 12-2, Sun 12-3 **D** Tue-Sun 7-9
Closed: 25 Dec, 26 Dec eve, 1 Jan eve, Mon, Sun eve
(winter only)
Facilities: Garden Parking
Notes: ⊕ FREE HOUSE 🍺 🏴 🍷 11

For the original artist in 1608, the brief for the inn sign must have been straightforward – just paint a blue ball. To drovers and other travellers over the ensuing centuries, this simple sign has meant food, drink and lodging. Today it means it more than ever. However, anyone who last visited before 2001 might be a little confused as the pub bit has switched from one side of the road to the other and now occupies the former stables, while the accommodation is in what used to be the pub. Open fires warm the thatched bar, where three local hand-pulled real ales, a scrumpy cider and Thatcher's Gold vie for attention. Food is locally sourced and as organic as possible, not because it's trendy, but because the chefs believe it tastes better in dishes such as pressed gammon terrine, pineapple chutney, freid quails egg; or white onion soup with (or without) smoked eel for starters; then oxtail cottage pie; scallops with pea and ham risotto; steamed Quantock game suet pudding; stone bass with lobster; roast Exmoor partridge with spiced plum compôte; and wine-candied pear and shortbread. The Quantock Hills rise up steeply behind from the village, so there are plenty of scenic walks and terrific views to enjoy.

Recommended in the area

Hestercombe Gardens; Cleeve Abbey; Exmoor National Park

Staffordshire

View from Wolf Edge

The Yorkshireman

Address: Colton Rd, COLTON, WS15 3HB
Tel: 01889 583977
Email: theyorkshireman@btconnect.com
Website: www.wine-dine.co.uk
Map ref: 6 SK02
Directions: From A51 rdbt in Rugeley follow rail
station signs, under rail bridge, to pub
Open: all wk 12-2.30 5.30-11 (Sat 12-11 Sun 12-6)
L Mon-Sat 12-2.30, Sun 12-6 **D** Mon-Fri 6-9.30,
Sat 6-11 **L** Mon-Sat 12-2.30, Sun 12-6 **D** Mon-Sat
6-9.30
Facilities: Garden Parking Wi-fi
Notes: ⊕ FREE HOUSE 👬 🛪 ♟ 10

The heritage of this Victorian edge-of-town pub opposite Rugeley's Trent Valley railway station is lost in the mists of time, but it had a boisterous period as 'Wilf and Rosa's Tavern' and as a meeting place for farmers and soldiers when there was just sawdust and straw on the floor. Today it is a panelled, wood-floored dining pub specialising in dishes using the best of Staffordshire produce and offering beers from a local micro-brewery including, unusually, a lager. The eclectic furnishings are part of the charm, and the Stubbs' paintings attract much comment. Just as much part of the furnishings is the pub's greyhound, Dahl, who seems happy to welcome other well-behaved dogs into his domain. The menu is updated regularly,

as season and supply allow, but a good range covering all the bases is assured. Starters may be mushroom and spinach parcel with Shropshire Blue cheese sauce; or pan-fried pigeon breast, black pudding and caramelised apple salad. Mains such as Staffordshire asparagus risotto topped with roast peppers and mozzarella, or saffron-marinated cod, roasted vine tomato with courgette and watercress salad. Staffordshire-reared steaks are a speciality, as are dishes featuring Gloucester Old Spot pork. The Yorkshire Deli has a special Sunday menu.

Recommended in the area

Shugborough Hall (NT); Cannock Chase; Lichfield Cathedral

The Holly Bush Inn

Address: Salt, STAFFORD, ST18 0BX
Tel: 01889 508234
Email: geoff@hollybushinn.co.uk
Website: www.hollybushinn.co.uk
Map ref: 6 SJ92
Directions: Telephone for directions
Open: all day all wk noon-11 (Sun noon-10.30)
🍴 Mon-Sat 12-9.30, Sun 12-9
Facilities: Garden Parking
Notes: ⊕ FREE HOUSE ♦♦ ♛ 12

In an area cut through by several major roads, it's good to find such a peaceful spot, and then take time to discover the glorious Staffordshire countryside that lies hidden away from the highways. The Holly Bush Inn was licensed during the reign of Charles II although the building itself dates from around 1190, and heavy carved beams, open fires and cosy alcoves still characterise the comfortably old-fashioned interior. Like most other landlords, owner Geoff Holland aims to serve good quality real ales and wines. What helps to differentiate Geoff, though, is his insistence on providing non-processed, mostly organic, fully traceable food, and on minimising his hostelry's impact on the environment by setting up a worm farm. Traditional British dishes include grilled pork chops with a honey and whole-grain mustard glaze; braised lamb and apples flavoured with nutmeg and allspice; and breaded wholetail scampi. Daily specials might be butternut squash and goats' cheese lasagne; fillet of beef Wellington and chargrilled red snapper with Jamaican spiced chutney. The Holly Bush mixed grill is a favourite plateful. At lunchtime tripledecker sandwiches, jacket potatoes and toasties are available. Beers include Adnams, Pedigree and guest ales.

Recommended in the area

Shugborough Hall (NT); Weston Park; Cannock Chase; Trentham Gardens; Alton Towers

Lichfield Cathedral

Suffolk

Boats moored on the River Stour, Dedham

The Queen's Head

Address: The Street, Bramfield, HALESWORTH, IP19 9HT
Tel: 01986 784214
Email: qhbfield@aol.com
Website: www.queensheadbramfield.co.uk
Map ref: 4 TM37
Directions: 2m from A12 on A144 towards Halesworth
Open: all wk 10.30-2.30 6.30-11 (Sun noon-3 7-10.30) ⅃ **L** all wk 12-2 **D** Mon-Fri 6.30-9.15, Sat 6.30-10, Sun 7-9 **Closed:** 25 Dec
Facilities: Garden Parking Wi-fi
Notes: ⊕ADNAMS ⅋ ⍆ ⏃8

A lovely old building in the centre of Bramfield on the edge of the Suffolk Heritage Coast near historic Southwold. The enclosed garden, ideal for children, is overlooked by the thatched village church which has an unusual separate round bell tower. The pub's interior welcomes with scrubbed pine tables, exposed beams, a vaulted ceiling in the bar and enormous fireplaces. In the same capable hands for over 14 years, the landlord enthusiastically supports the 'local and organic' movement – reflected by a menu which proudly names the farms and suppliers from which the carefully chosen ingredients are sourced. There is nonetheless a definite cosmopolitan twist in dishes such as grilled dates wrapped in bacon on mild mustard sauce; or grilled goats' cheese with smoked duck breast, mustard marinated beetroot and walnut salad to begin with, then 'Emmerdale Farm' Darsham steak, kidney and Adnams Ale pie; fillet of pollock with garlic and crispy cheese crust; or a vegetarian choice of peppered mushroom and Stilton pie. Children are treated to Suffolk Red Poll beef burgers or Moat Farm sausages. Amanda's home-made desserts are tempting, as is the platter of three local cheeses with celery – Lincolnshire Poacher, Suffolk Blue and Norfolk White Lady.

Recommended in the area

Suffolk Heritage Coast; RSPB Minsmere Nature Reserve; Snape Maltings

Sibton White Horse Inn

★★★★ ◎ INN

Address: Halesworth Rd, SIBTON, IP17 2JJ
Tel: 01728 660337
Email: info@sibtonwhitehorseinn.co.uk
Website: www.sibtonwhitehorseinn.co.uk
Map ref: 4 TM36 **Directions:** A12 at Yoxford
onto A1120, 3m to Peasenhall. Right opposite
butchers, inn 600mtrs **Open:** all wk 12-2.30 6.30-11
(winter) 6-11 (summer) Sun 12-3.30 🍴❤ Booking
required **L** Mon-Sat 12-2, Sun 12-2.30 **D** all wk 7-9
Closed: 26-27 Dec **Rooms:** (3 GF) **S** £60-£75
D £65-£90 **Facilities:** Garden Parking Wi-fi
Notes: ⊕ FREE HOUSE ♩ ♟ 9

In the heart of the Suffolk countryside, yet five
minutes from the A12, this rustic 16th-century inn
is off the beaten track. It retains much Tudor charm
with stone floors, exposed brickwork and ships'
timbers. A genuine free house, the bar is the place
to enjoy pints of Adnams Bitter or Woodforde's
Wherry, with a choice of dining areas to sample the
award-winning food. Owners Neil and Gill Mason are
committed to producing high quality food from fresh
local ingredients - and, to prove it, they grow many
vegetables in the raised beds behind the pub. In the
buzzy restaurant, you can order old favourites like
smoked haddock fish cake, salad Niçoise and hard-
boiled egg; ox liver with bacon, creamed potato and
broccoli. For those diners in search of something a
little more special, there's pan-seared Suffolk wood
pigeon with confit shallot, fine beans, dried cherry
tomato and redcurrant jus; wild River Dee salmon
fillet with black olive potato cake; or Henham Estate
venison loin, dauphinoise potatoes, braised red
cabbage and redcurrent jus. Finish, perhaps, with
Earl Grey pannacotta, or plum tart Tatin, pistachio
cream and caramel sauce. A secluded courtyard has
a Mediterranean feel when the sun comes out, and
bedrooms in an adjacent annexe are available.

Recommended in the area

RSPB Nature Reserve Minsmere; Saxtead Green
Post Mill; Framlingham Castle

The Crown Inn

Address: Bridge Rd, SNAPE,
nr Saxmundham, IP17 1SL
Tel: 01728 688324
Email: snapecrown@tiscali.co.uk
Website: www.snape-crown.co.uk
Map ref: 4 TM35
Directions: A12 from Ipswich towards Lowestoft,
right onto A1094 towards Aldeburgh. In Snape right
at x-rds by church, pub at bottom of hill
Open: all wk 🍴🍽 Booking required **L** all wk 12-2.30
D all wk 6-9.30
Facilities: Garden Parking
Notes: ⊕ADNAMS 👫 🐕 🍷 12

First-time visitors to this 15th-century former smugglers' inn are often astonished by the adjoining smallholding where a veritable menagerie of livestock is lovingly reared by Teresa and Garry Cook. It pays not to become too attached however, as these are destined for the table at this marvellously atmospheric pub (no gaming machines or background music here), with abundant old beams, log fire, brick floors and, around the large inglenook, a very fine double Suffolk settle. The strong British menus, and daily specials, feature allotment produce, foraged seasonal wild ingredients, fish from Orford fishermen and locally raised beef. The menus are forever changing but expect dishes such as Brancaster mussels with shallots, white wine and garlic; or beetroot cured salmon with crème fraiche and quail's eggs to kick things off, followed by home-reared rare breed pork sausages with mash, beans and shallot gravy; or Crag farm minced beef cottage pie might appear, all helped along with Adnams beers or a choice from 12 wines by the glass. There is a spacious garden for summer dining, and being just a five-minute walk to Snape Maltings Concert Hall, pre- and post-concert dining is also available.

Recommended in the area

Suffolk Coast National Nature Reserve; RSPB Mismere & Orford Ness reserves; Framlingham Castle

The Anchor

Address: Main St, WALBERSWICK, Southwold,
IP18 6UA
Tel: 01502 722112
Email: info@anchoratwalberswick.com
Website: www.anchoratwalberswick.com
Map ref: 4 TM47
Directions: A12 onto B1387, follow Walberswick
signs
Open: all day all wk 🏨 🍴 Booking required **L** all wk
12-3 **D** all wk 6-9
Facilities: Garden Parking Wi-fi
Notes: ⊕ ADNAMS 👬 🐕 ♟ 22 🍺

Sophie Dorber's long-standing connections with the Suffolk coast, include running the food franchise at Aldeburgh yacht club, while in London, husband Mark ran an award-winning pub. Then one day in 2004, breakfasting with friends on a golden Walberswick beach, they decided to buy The Anchor's lease and create a family-friendly village local. And that's what they've done. They stock a good range of character real ales, 20 world-class bottled beers and 150 wines from some highly inspired winemakers, choosing to offer: "Only (what) we would actively seek to drink if the flood waters were to surround Walberswick and we became an island". Their approach to food is robust, following the seasons with produce from their own garden and villagers' allotments. Starter examples would be West Mersea oysters with red onion vinaigrette; main courses of mushroom and Stilton risotto; roast cod with brioche herb crust; and Suffolk rib-eye steak with horseradish and caper butters; and for dessert, Jamaican ginger bread with clotted cream ice cream. Curry nights are every second Friday. 2011 has seen the renovation of the dining room, a corridor becoming a bar, and the creation of a meadow at the end of the garden to make a delightful and peaceful place to relax.

Recommended in the area

Suffolk Heritage Coast; Snape Maltings; RSPB Minsmere Nature Reserve

Little Hall, Lavenham

Surrey

Leith Hill

The Stephan Langton

Address: Friday St, ABINGER COMMON,
Dorking, RH5 6JR
Tel: 01306 730775 & 737129
Email: info@stephanlangtonpub.co.uk
Website: www.stephanlangtonpub.co.uk
Map ref: 3 TQ14
Directions: Exit A25 between Dorking & Guildford
at Hollow Ln. 1.5m, left into Friday St
Open: all wk 11-3 5-10.30 (Sat 11-11 Sun 12-9)
🔒 🍽 Booking required **L** Tue-Sat 12-2.30, Sun 12-4
D Tue-Sat 6.30-9.30
Facilities: Garden Parking Wi-fi
Notes: ⊕ FREE HOUSE ♦♦ 🐾

Undulating mixed woodland surrounds this secluded hamlet at the base of Leith Hill, which is nothing more than a tranquil hammer pond and a handful of stone and timber cottages. This is prime Surrey walking country and a popular pit-stop is The Stephan Langton, a 1930s building named after the first archbishop of Canterbury, who was supposedly born in Friday Street. He helped draw up the Magna Carta and a copy of the document is pinned to a wall in the rustic, bare-boarded bar. Equally unpretentious is the adjoining dining room, with its open fires. Having conquered Leith Hill, the highest summit in south-east England, relax on the sun-trap patio and savour a thirst-quenching pint of locally-brewed Hog's Back TEA or Shere Drop. Peruse the short, inviting menu that hits the spot with lunchtime sandwiches and starters like smoked chicken and leek risotto. Typical hearty main dishes take in grilled cod with Tuscan bean broth; beef slow-braised in beer with root vegetables, bashed neeps and tatties; seared venison with roasted beetroot, local watercress and crème de cassis jus. Changing daily specials make the most of local produce, much of it sourced from the surrounding Wooton Estate.

Recommended in the area

RHS Garden Wisley; Clandon Park (NT); Hannah Peschar Sculpture Garden

The Bat & Ball Freehouse

Address: 15 Bat & Ball Ln, Boundstone,
FARNHAM, GU10 4SA
Tel: 01252 792108
Email: info@thebatandball.co.uk
Website: www.thebatandball.co.uk
Map ref: 3 SU84
Directions: A31 onto A325 (signed Birdworld).
Left at Bengal Lounge. At T-junct, 1st right, left into
Sandrock Hill Rd. 0.25m, left into Upper Bourne Ln
Open: all day all wk 11-11 (Sun noon-10.30)
Booking possible **L** Mon-Sat 12-2.15, Sun 12-3
D Mon-Sat 7-9.30, Sun 6-8.30 **Facilities:** Garden
Parking Wi-fi **Notes:** ⊕ FREE HOUSE ♦♦ ⋔ ♀ 8 ◖

Tucked down a lane in a wooded valley south of
Farnham, this 150-year-old inn is well worth seeking
out. Hops for the local breweries in Farnham and
Alton were once grown in the valley, and originally
the hop pickers were paid in the building that
eventually became the pub. An enterprising tenant
began to provide the pickers with ale, relieving
them of some of their hard earned cash! Very much
a community pub, the interior features terracotta
floors, oak beams, a roaring fire on colder days,
and plenty of cricketing memorabilia. The lovely
garden has a terrace with vine-topped pergola and
a children's play fort. Expect six regularly changing
cask-conditioned ales, a range of quaffable wines,
and home-cooked food at reasonable prices.

Starters and light meals might include homemade
hot Scotch egg with piccalilli; or a plate of various
cured herring fillets and sardine fillet marinated in
basil oil. Slow braised creamy rabbit, cider and grain
mustard stew with mashed potato; and chorizo and
belly pork stew (haricot beans, tomato, red wine and
smoked paprika) with crusty bread are typical of
the flavoursome dishes on offer. There's live music
on the last Thursday of the month, and a beer, cider
and music festival is held every second week in
June.

Recommended in the area

Birdworld; Frensham Ponds; Alice Holt Forest
& Go Ape

Hare and Hounds

Address: Common Rd, LINGFIELD, RH7 6BZ
Tel: 01342 832351
Email: info@hareandhoundspublichouse.co.uk
Website: www.hareandhoundspublichouse.co.uk
Map ref: 4 TQ34
Directions: From A22 follow Lingfield Racecourse signs into Common Rd
Open: all day †◎¶ **L** Mon-Sat 12-2.30, Sun 12-3
D Mon-Sat 7-9.30
Closed: 1-5 Jan, Sun eve
Facilities: Garden Parking
Notes: ⊕ PUNCH TAVERNS †† ⌁

Just a short drive from Lingfield Park racecourse, this charming 18th-century country pub has a welcoming atmosphere for propping up the bar with a pint of real ale or cider or a glass of wine from the carefully considered list, sitting by the fire, or relaxing in the candlelit snug. The pub has a good name for its modern and classic food; the owners have worked in the UK and France and have developed some great seasonal recipes. Using local produce whenever possible, the menu may start with chilled foie gras and duck tart, red grape jelly and pickles with biscotti; or young squid tempura, chorizo, horseradish cream and chickpea salad, followed by whole roast mackerel, cured ham, borlotti beans and prawn bisque; or roast stuffed breast of free range chicken with black truffle, crushed swede and gratin dauphinois (for two). Desserts might include lemon curd and raspberry 'Faberge Egg', sticky toffee pudding with crème fraîche ice cream; and warm banana cake with liquorice ice cream and honeycomb. On a sunny day, enjoy the split-level decked garden and the new enclosed turfed area, both fantastic spots for a quiet drink or a light lunch.

Recommended in the area

Lingfield Park Racecourse; Hever Castle; Tilgate Park

Bryce's at
The Old School House

Address: OCKLEY, Dorking, RH5 5TH
Tel: 01306 627430
Email: fish@bryces.co.uk
Website: www.bryces.co.uk
Map ref: 3 TQ14
Directions: 8m S of Dorking on A29
Open: noon-3 6-11 ☕ **L** all wk 12-2.30 **D** all wk 6-9.30 ✦ **L** all wk 12-2.30 **D** all wk 7-9.30
Closed: 25-26 Dec, 1 Jan, (Sun pm Nov, Jan-Feb)
Facilities: Parking **Notes:** ⊕ FREE HOUSE ✦ ♦ ♟ 15

Formerly a boarding school, this Grade II listed building dates from 1750 and has been established for 19 years as Bryce's. The village is set amid lovely countryside offering some great downland walking. Its distance from the sea may come as a surprise, as Bill Bryce is passionate about fresh fish and offers seven starters and main courses of exclusively fish dishes in the restaurant, with non-fish daily specials and a vegetarian selection. The chefs base their dishes on what is the freshest produce on the market. Perhaps start with the glazed seafood Thermidor crêpe; a trio of Arbroath Smokie; or carpaccio of Yellow Fin Tuna with herb salad. The main courses might include fillets of south coast grey mullet, bubble and squeak with sweet and sour salsa; Moroccan spiced cod fillet with fruit rice; or an assiette of fish fillets with cardamom sauce and pea shoots. The home-made desserts shouldn't be overlooked, try the glazed lemon and lime tart with pineapple sorbet; or pannacotta, summer berry compôte with cinnamon shortbread. The bar has its own tempting menu, and there are excellent house wines to choose from.

Recommended in the area

Hannah Peschar Sculpture Garden; Leith Hill (NT); Denbies Wine Estate, Dorking

The Inn @ West End

Address: 42 Guildford Rd, WEST END, GU24 9PW
Tel: 01276 858652
Email: greatfood@the-inn.co.uk
Website: www.the-inn.co.uk
Map ref: 3 SU96
Directions: On A322 towards Guildford. 3m from M3 junct 3, just beyond Gordon Boys rdbt
Open: all wk noon-3 5-11 (Sat noon-11, Sun noon-10.30) 🍴 ❍ **L** all wk noon-2.30 **D** all wk 6-9.30
Facilities: Garden Parking Wi-fi
Notes: ⊕ ENTERPRISE INNS ♠ ♟ 15

The people of Surrey certainly know a good dining pub, but this doesn't preclude anyone from simply enjoying a pint of Timothy Taylor Landlord or Fuller's London Pride, or a fine evening on the terrace. Gerry and Ann Price have created an establishment that out-manoeuvres many a competitor with events like fish and game cooking presentations and wine/food-matching evenings. The modern interior is open plan, with wooden floors, crisp linen and an open fire. The kitchen makes good use of home-grown produce and other locally sourced ingredients, game shot by Gerry himself, and fresh fish collected in the pub's own van from whichever port it is freshest and best. While the accomplished kitchen team guarantees no shortage of ideas for new dishes, they make sure old favourites don't fall off the bottom of the seasonal menus, so expect typical mains of braised brisket of beef, caramelised onions and balsamic mushroom; pan-fried rib of English veal with brandy and stock cream; a selection of British fish served with tomato and dill risotto and poached duck egg; pan-roasted loin and slow-cooked haunch of wild hare with chocolate and juniper sauce; and poached egg on celeriac with mushroom hash and lightly spiced aubergine.

Recommended in the area

Claremont Landscape Garden; Painshill Park; Sandown Park Racecourse

East Sussex

Beachy Head, South Downs

The Bull

★★★★ INN

Address: 2 High St, DITCHLING, BN6 8TA
Tel: 01273 843147
Email: info@thebullditchling.com
Website: www.thebullditchling.com
Map ref: 4 TQ31
Directions: From Brighton on A27 take A23, follow
Pyecombe/Hassocks signs, then Ditchling signs, 3m
Open: all day all wk 11-11 (Sun 11-10.30) ⅃ **L** Mon-
Fri 12-2.30, Sat 12-9.30, Sun 12-9 **D** Mon-Sat 6-9.30,
Sun 12-9 **Rooms:** 4 en suite
Facilities: Garden Parking Wi-fi
Notes: ⊕ FREE HOUSE ¶¶ ⚲ ☕ 21

The Bull, a 16th-century former coaching inn, is
the place to head for following a day on the South
Downs. It's been restored with passion (and a
contemporary touch) by Dominic Worrall, yet still
exudes historic charm and character. In the bar
you'll find feature fireplaces with glowing log fires,
sagging ceiling timbers, bare boards and a mixture
of simple benches, carved settles and farmhouse
chairs at big scrubbed wooden tables. Quirky objets
d'art, modern art and vases of lilies on the bar add a
touch of class. There are four individually decorated
bedrooms, each named after their principle colour.
Ruby, for example, has bright red walls, white-
painted wall timbers, Thai silk curtains, a plasma
TV/DVD player, digital radio, a sleigh bed with
Egyptian cotton sheets and a claw-foot bath in the
tiled bathroom. Local is the watchword when it
comes to food and drink, with top notch ales from
Harvey's (Lewes) and Dark Star (Partridge Green)
breweries on hand pump and a quaffable fizz from
Ridge View Vineyard up the road. Menus change
daily and make good use of lamb from Foxhole
Farm on the edge of the village, seasonal game,
including venison from the Balcombe Estate and
fish caught off the south coast.

Recommended in the area

Booth Museum of Natural History; Royal Pavilion,
Brighton; Borde Hill Garden

The Tiger Inn

Address: The Green, EAST DEAN, BN20 0DA
Tel: 01323 423209
Email: tiger@beachyhead.org.uk
Website: www.beachyhead.org.uk
Map ref: 3 TV59
Directions: From A259 between Eastbourne & Seaford. Pub 0.5m
Open: all day all wk ⓑ **L** all wk 12-3 **D** all wk 6-9
Facilities: Garden Parking Wi-fi
Notes: ⊕ FREE HOUSE ♦♦ ⚲ ♀ 10

The village occupies a steep-sided dry valley just inland from Beachy Head, the highest chalk sea cliff in England. Facing the village green, pleasantly distant from the main coastal road, this whitewashed, low-slung 14th-century free house has entertained smuggling gangs, soldiers from the Napoleonic wars, World War II Spitfire pilots and, today, discerning readers of Britain's Best Pubs. Among them are walkers and cyclists, for the South Downs are tailor-made for such pursuits, so not for nothing does the local Gilbert Estate-owned Beachy Head micro-brewery call its strongest beer Legless Rambler, available with its stablemates in the bar here. Thirsts quenched, most visitors turn their attention to food, from a light lunch of sandwiches; crispy Sussex bacon with baked Brie and apple salad; or smoked salmon and prawns with mustard vinaigrette, to the more substantial grilled sea bass with basil-infused Greek salad; slow-roasted pork belly and Bramley apple dressing; seared duck, spring onion and cucumber salad with sesame, plum dressing; or vegetarian risotto. A bonus is that this old pub does not allow vehicles past its frontage, so you can walk from the bar directly on to the green with no fear of being mown down, your drinks tray intact. Five bedrooms are available.

Recommended in the area

Drusillas Park; South Downs Way; Paradise Park, Heritage Trail & Gardens

The Hatch Inn

Address: Coleman's Hatch, HARTFIELD, TN7 4EJ
Tel: 01342 822363
Email: nickad@bigfoot.com
Website: www.hatchinn.co.uk
Map ref: 4 TQ43
Directions: A22 at Forest Row rdbt, 3m to
Coleman's Hatch, right by church
Open: all wk 11.30-3 5.30-11 (Sat-Sun all day)
🍴⏺ **L** all wk 12-2.15 **D** booking required Mon-Thu
7-9.15, Fri-Sat 7-9.30
Closed: 25 Dec except for drinks
Facilities: Garden
Notes: 🍺 FREE HOUSE ⏹ 🐾 ♟ 10

Reputedly dating back to 1430, The Hatch Inn was converted from three cottages thought to have housed workers at the local water-driven hammer mill, and it may also have been a smugglers' haunt. The pub is well placed for country walking, as well as serving as a filming location for television dramas and advertisements. There are two large beer gardens for alfresco summer dining, one of which enjoys views out over the forest, and is only minutes away from the restored Poohsticks Bridge, immortalised in A.A. Milne's *Winnie the Pooh* stories. Owner Nicholas Drillsma and his partner, Sandra Barton, have collected many accolades over the last 15 years. Quality ingredients and imaginative techniques make for exciting menus created by head chef Gregory Palmer and his team. Evening appetisers might include a red onion marmalade and goats' cheese tart Tatin with roast beetroot salad, Roquefort and walnuts, followed by roast rump of lamb with dauphinoise potatoes and rosemary and port reduction. All desserts are homemade – highly recommended is the sticky toffee pudding, hot toffee sauce and locally made ice cream. No reservations are available at lunchtime but evening booking is essential.

Recommended in the area

Pooh Bridge; Ashdown Forest; Standen (NT); Royal Tunbridge Wells

The Middle House

Address: High St, MAYFIELD, TN20 6AB
Tel: 01435 872146
Email: kirsty@middle-house.com
Website: www.middlehousemayfield.co.uk
Map ref: 4 TQ52
Directions: E of A267, S of Tunbridge Wells
Open: all wk ♨ **L** Mon-Fri 12-2, Sat 12-2.30
D Mon-Sat 6.30-9.30, Sun all day ⏺**L** Tue-Sun 12-2
D Tue-Sat 6.30-9
Facilities: Garden Parking
Notes: ⊕ FREE HOUSE ⁑ ♟ 9

Built in 1575 for Sir Thomas Gresham, who was Elizabeth I's Keeper of the Privy Purse and founder of the London Stock Exchange, The Middle House is one of the finest timber-framed buildings in Sussex. Inside, the house retains many of its original features, including a Grinling Gibbons' fireplace and a splendid oak-panelled restaurant. This is a family-run business specialising in a very wide variety of food using all local, fresh produce. The ever-changing menus include a large fish selection and vegetarian options. Among the choices to be enjoyed in the cosy bar or the more formal restaurant are chicken breast filled with leeks and gruyère cheese wrapped in filo pastry with a parsley, cream and white wine sauce; seared tuna loin steak on pak choi with a sweet and sour sauce; pan-fried local venison steak with a rich bacon lardon, port and prune sauce. An extensive wine list offers wines and champagne by the glass, and the pub's bar offers real ales including Harveys, the local brew and several guest beers. This is a great high street pub whether you're nipping in for a pint or stopping a little longer to enjoy both the food and the atmosphere. Ample parking is available.

Recommended in the area

Bateman's (NT); Spa Valley Railway; Royal Tunbridge Wells

Mermaid Inn

★★★ 81% ◉ HOTEL

Address: Mermaid St, RYE, TN31 7EY
Tel: 01797 223065
Email: info@mermaidinn.com
Website: www.mermaidinn.com
Map ref: 4 TQ92
Directions: A259, follow signs to town centre, into Mermaid St
Open: all wk noon-11 ⓑ **L** all wk 12-2.30 **D** all wk 6-9 ⓘⓞⓘ **L** all wk 12-2.30 **D** all wk 7-9.30
Rooms: 31 **S** £90-£110 **D** £180-£260
Facilities: Garden Parking Wi-fi
Notes: ⊕ FREE HOUSE ⓘ♀ 15

Step into this timbered, foliage-covered old building from Mermaid Street's ancient cobbles and nearly 600 years of history hit you smack between the eyes. Dating from 1156, the inn was rebuilt in 1420 from ships' timbers and baulks of Sussex oak, with fireplaces carved from French stone ballast rescued from the harbour. Hidden in the chimney breast of the fireplace in the Lounge Bar is a priest's hole, used when it was a crime to be caught harbouring a Roman Catholic. Another relic is the secret stairway leading from behind a bookcase in Dr Syn's Bedchamber to the bar, once the haunt of the infamous band of smugglers known as the Hawkhurst Gang. Artwork by students at the Slade School of Art decorates the linenfold-panelled restaurant, awarded an AA Rosette, and where the British and French cooking includes slow-cooked potted duck; pan-fried Rye Bay sea bass; traditional steak and kidney pudding; braised Canterbury pork belly; and fricassée of woodland mushrooms. The Norman cellars, as you might imagine, hold a large selection of wine. Stay overnight and you may have unexpected company – ghosts have been seen in several bedrooms, so remember, don't leave clothes on the chair in the James Room.

Recommended in the area

Great Dixter; Sissinghurst; Romney, Hythe & Dymchurch Railway

The Ypres Castle Inn

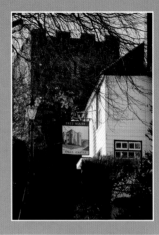

Address: Gun Garden, RYE, TN31 7HH
Tel: 01797 223248
Email: info@yprescastleinn.co.uk
Website: www.yprescastleinn.co.uk
Map ref: 4 TQ92
Directions: Behind church & adjacent to Ypres Tower
Open: all day all wk ⓑ ⓞ **L** all wk 12-3
D Mon-Sat 6-9
Facilities: Garden Wi-fi
Notes: ⓦ FREE HOUSE ⁑ ⓨ 12

'The Wipers', as locals call it, was once the haunt of smugglers. Built in 1640 in weather-boarded style, and added to by the Victorians, it's the only pub in the citadel area of the old Cinque Port of Rye with a garden. The garden, with roses, shrubs and views of the 13th-century Ypres Tower, once defensive which then became a prison before becoming a museum, and of the River Rother with its working fishing fleet. Colourful art and furnishings help make the interior warm and friendly. The seasonally changing menu is largely sourced locally, providing a good range of lunchtime snacks, including ploughman's, and sandwiches, backed by half a dozen daily specials. The evening menu may propose moules marinière, cracked Dungeness crab, grilled Rye Bay plaice and turbot, and meaty options of grilled rack of Romney salt marsh lamb, organic Winchelsea beef and pork, and home-made prime beefburger. There are usually four cask-conditioned ales and an extensive wine list. On Friday nights the atmosphere hots up with live jazz, rock and blues. The pub has no accommodation facilities, but there are plenty of possibilities nearby.

Recommended in the area

Smallhythe Place (NT); Romney, Hythe & Dymchurch Railway; Port Lympne Wild Animal Park

BRIGHTON PIER

West Sussex

Beach at West Wittering

The Fox Goes Free

★ ★ ★ ★ INN

Address: CHARLTON, nr Goodwood, PO18 0HU
Tel: 01243 811461
Email: enquiries@thefoxgoesfree.com
Website: www.thefoxgoesfree.com
Map ref: 3 SU81 **Directions:** A286, 6m from
Chichester towards Midhurst
Open: all day all wk 11-11 (Sun noon-11) ⓑ **L** Mon-
Fri 12-2.30, Sat-Sun 12-10 booking required **D** Mon-
Fri 6.30-10, Sat-Sun 12-10 ⓘ **L** all wk 12-2.30 **D** all
wk 6.30-10 **Closed:** 25 Dec eve **Rooms:** 5 en suite
S £65-£120 **D** £90-£120 **Facilities:** Garden Parking
Wi-fi **Notes:** ⊕ FREE HOUSE ⓘ ⓘ

King William III loved this beautiful old brick and
flint building, often bringing his royal cronies down
from London to enjoy the hunting. Today the
surrounding countryside, part of the Goodwood
Estate, remains unspoilt, while the pub itself is full
of period charm, with low-beamed ceilings, brick
floors, two huge fireplaces and a bread oven. The
friendly, welcoming bar offers a good selection of
local real ales, including one named after the pub,
and well-chosen wines. Delicious, locally sourced
West Sussex produce is offered in a choice of seven
different seating areas, so that in winter you may
enjoy the warmth from open fires, and on summer
days the charming, apple-tree-filled garden, aka
'the best room in the house', the South Downs in

view all around. Bar favourites include home-made
steak and kidney pie, and beer-battered cod and
chips, while the main, daily changing menu offers
crispy leg of Gressingham duck confit with Savoy
cabbage, bacon and plum sauce; belly of pork with
Chinese five-spice and stir-fried vegetables; whole
Brixham lemon sole with garlic and herb butter; and
roasted pepper stuffed with couscous, olives and
caramelised onions with red pepper coulis. Five en
suite bedrooms are available.

Recommended in the area

Weald & Downland Open Air Museum; Goodwood
House; West Dean Gardens

Royal Oak Inn

★★★★★ 🛏 🏵 INN

Address: Pook Ln, East Lavant, CHICHESTER,
PO18 0AX
Tel: 01243 527434
Email: info@royaloakeastlavant.co.uk
Website: www.royaloakeastlavant.co.uk
Map ref: 3 SU80 **Directions:** 2m N of Chichester.
Exit A286 to East Lavant centre
Open: all day all wk 7am-11.30pm 🍴 **L** Mon-
Sat 12-5.30 **D** all wk 6-9.30 🍽 **L** all wk 12-2.30
Closed: 25 Dec **Rooms:** 8 en suite
S £95-£160 **D** £105-£295 **Facilities:** Garden Parking
Notes: 🍺 FREE HOUSE 🚻 🐕 🍷 16

In a quiet village two miles north of Chichester
stands this archetypal country pub and restaurant,
offering stylish en suite rooms and two self-catering
cottages. The interior is characterised by beams,
bare brick walls, fireplaces and an intimate bar
area with highly slumpworthy sofas and armchairs.
The restaurant itself is furnished with pine tables
and tall, modern leather chairs, and serves French,
Mediterranean and New English cuisine backed
by daily blackboard specials, all crying out to be
accompanied by one of the many world-sourced
wines. Extensively used local ingredients include
crab and scallops from the English Channel. Try a
starter of tian of smoked salmon, fresh salmon and
salmon roe; beetroot and Pinot Noir risotto; or West
Sussex pork and rabbit terrine with fig chutney,
warm toast and salad leaves. Main courses might
include duck, duck and duck (breast, ballantine and
Charlotte), pan-fried bream with a seafood paella; or
smoked garlic polenta cake, chargrilled haloumi and
harissa-spiced aubergine provençale. Among the
inviting desserts are spiced plum and oat crumble
with home-made custard; orange curd trifle infused
with Grand Marnier; and glazed lemon tart with a
hedgerow compôte and mascarpone.

Recommended in the area
Chichester Cathedral; Goodwood House;
South Downs Way

The Anglesey Arms at Halnaker

Address: HALNAKER, Chichester, PO18 0NQ
Tel: 01243 773474
Email: info@angleseyarms.co.uk
Website: www.angleseyarms.co.uk
Map ref: 3 SU90
Directions: From centre of Chichester 4m E on A285 (Petworth road)
Open: all wk 11-3 5.30-11 (Sat-Sun 11am-11pm)
L Mon-Sat 12-2.30, Sun 12-3 **D** Mon-Sat 6.30-9.30
Facilities: Garden Parking Wi-fi
Notes: PUNCH TAVERNS 14

Whether you pop in for a quick drink or a full meal, you'll find a warm welcome at this charmingly old-fashioned Georgian inn, which stands in two acres of landscaped grounds on the Goodwood Estate, famous for horse racing, especially Glorious Goodwood in July, and motor racing events - The Festival of Speed and the Goodwood Revival. Step inside to find a wood-floored bar where hand-pulled ales such as Bowman Swift One are on offer or choose from the extensive list of unusual wines from small vineyards. Hand-cut sandwiches, ploughman's, local sausages, and other traditional pub favourites will fill the odd corner, or you could sample something from the carte. The kitchen team makes skilful use of meat from fully traceable and organically raised animals, as well as locally caught fish from sustainable stocks. The Anglesey has built a special reputation for its steaks, cut from British beef and hung for at least 21 days. Dinner might begin with wild mushrooms on toasted ciabatta; or home-made Selsey crab pâté, followed by confit of duck, plum sauce with bubble and squeak; or Thai-style red king prawn or vegetable curry. Home-made pudding round things off nicely. The garden, with its many wooden bench tables, is just the spot in warmer weather to enjoy a drink and a meal.

Recommended in the area

Goodwood events; Boxgrove; Chichester

The Grove Inn

Address: Grove Ln, PETWORTH, GU28 0HY
Tel: 01798 343659
Email: steveandvaleria@tiscali.co.uk
Website: www.groveinnpetworth.co.uk
Map ref: 3 SU92
Directions: Outskirts of village, just off A283
Open: Tue-Sat 12-3 6-11 (Sun 12-3) 🍴 🍽 **L** Tue-Sun
12-2.30 **D** Tue-Sat 6-9.15
Closed: Sun eve & Mon (ex BH)
Facilities: Garden Parking
Notes: ⊕ FREE HOUSE 👥 🎯

The Grove Inn is a 17th-century free house in the heart of the South Downs. It sits on the outskirts of historic Petworth, a town much visited for its many and varied antique shops. Inside, the inn provides a cosy bar with oak-beamed ceilings and a large stone inglenook fireplace, as well as the Conservatory Restaurant, where diners can look out over the garden and enjoy good views of the South Downs. There is also a patio area with a pergola. Dishes are chosen from a seasonal menu, which is completely rewritten every six to eight weeks, with some daily changes for good measure. Typical starters include smoked salmon, chive and cream cheese roulade; home-made parsnip soup; and duck liver and mushroom terrine. Among the main courses are natural smoked haddock topped with Welsh rarebit; well-matured chargrilled fillet steak with truffle mash and cracked black peppercorn sauce; and wild mushroom risotto with parmesan and truffle oil. To follow there could be banana pancake with honey rum toffee sauce or lemon posset, as well as a choice of cheeseboards. Three whites, three reds and a rosé are available by the glass, with many more choices available on the main wine list.

Recommended in the area

Cowdray Park; Lurgashall Winery; Petworth House & Park (NT)

Royal Oak

Address: The Street, POYNINGS, BN45 7AQ
Tel: 01273 857389
Email: ropoynings@aol.com
Website: www.royaloakpoynings.biz
Map ref: 3 TQ21
Directions: From A23 onto A281 signed Henfield
& Poynings
Open: all day all wk 11-11 (Sun noon-10.30)
Facilities: Garden Parking Wi-fi
Notes: ⊕ FREE HOUSE ♦ ♦ ♟ 14

Here since the 1880s, the award-winning Royal
Oak clearly remains a popular village pub. Indeed,
should you chance by and look in through the
windows, particularly at night when the lights
are on, you might expect to be seduced by its
contemporary decor, comfy sofas, solid oak floors
and old beams hung with hop bines. You will find
a bar serving Lewes-brewed Harveys real ales and
globally sourced wines from Enotria, a leading wine
importer. In the restaurant you can choose from a
constantly evolving regular menu that may list confit
leg and pan-roasted breast of Sussex pheasant
with game faggot, buttered cavalo nero, shallot and
sherry vinegar jus; spiced lamb kofta with a rich
tomato sauce, carrot and coriander couscous and
tzatziki; fish pie with free-range egg, Cheddar-glazed
creamed potato and dressed mixed leaves; and
asparagus and red pepper risotto with parmesan
shavings, and balsamic syrup. Then again, some of
the dishes are good old pub favourites like handmade Henfield sausages with creamed potato, rich
gravy and red onion jam. The chalkboard specials
menu changes daily, and there are also tapas-size
portions from the grazing menu, sandwiches and
ciabattas. The barbecue menu proves popular
during the summer months.

Recommended in the area
Devil's Dyke; Newtimber Place; Brighton Pavilion

The Countryman Inn

Address: Countryman Ln, SHIPLEY, RH13 8PZ
Tel: 01403 741383
Email: countrymaninn@btinternet.com
Website: www.countrymanshipley.co.uk
Map ref: 3 TQ12
Directions: A272 at Coolham into Smithers Hill Ln.
1m, left at T-junct
Open: all wk 10-4 6-11 🕩🍴 **L** all wk 11.30-3.30
D all wk 6-10
Facilities: Garden Parking
Notes: ⊕ FREE HOUSE 🐾 ♟18

A rural hostelry in the traditional style, The Countryman is set in open countryside close to the small village of Shipley, surrounded by 3,500 acres of farmland owned by the Knepp Castle Estate. The area is in the process of being turned back to a more natural state, with the introduction of fallow deer, free-roaming Tamworth pigs, Exmoor ponies and English Longhorn cattle. Many wild birds have also been encouraged to return to the area, as the new growth of wild grasses and plant life provide a welcoming habitat. You can even do a bit of bird watching from the inn's garden in fine weather. Inside you'll find Harvey's and organic Horsham ales, over 30 wines from around the world and in the winter, warming log fires. Free-range meat and vegetables from local farms make their appearance on the restaurant menu alongside fresh fish from Shoreham and Newhaven and local game in season. Menus change frequently, and as well as the carte there is also a range of ploughman's lunches, bar snacks, daily specials and Sunday roasts. Shipley's historic eight-sided smock mill (so-called because of its likeness to a traditional farm labourer's smock) is worth a visit.

Recommended in the area

Leonardslee Lakes & Gardens; Parham House & Gardens; Amberley Working Museum

Arundel Cathedral

Warwickshire

Chesterton Windmill

The Bell

Address: ALDERMINSTER, Stratford-upon-Avon,
CV37 8NY
Tel: 01789 450414
Email: info@thebellald.co.uk
Website: www.thebellald.co.uk
Map ref: 3 SP24 **Directions:** On A3400, 3.5m S of
Stratford-upon-Avon
Open: Mon-Thu 9.30-3 6-11, Fri-Sat 9.30-11, Sun
9.30-5 🍽 Booking required **L** Mon-Fri 12-2, Sat
12-2.30, Sun 12-3 **D** Mon-Thu 7-9, Fri-Sat 6-9
Closed: Mon Jan-Mar
Facilities: Garden Parking Wi-fi
Notes: ⊕ FREE HOUSE ♦♦ ♦ ♀ 14

The interior of this award-winning, 18th-century coaching inn successfully combines traditional and modern to create a truly eclectic mix. The warm and welcoming traditional bar has flagstone floors, low beams, open fires and candlelit tables, while the more contemporary restaurant and conservatory, overlooking the landscaped courtyard garden, has a vibrant and buzzing atmosphere. Here the individual areas lend themselves to private dining, meetings and parties. The well-stocked bar offers a host of traditional ales, including The Bell's own Alscot Ale, wines, spirits and cocktails, and the great food is prepared from fresh seasonal produce sourced almost entirely from local suppliers; much of the game and lamb comes from the estate itself, along with vegetables grown in Alscot Park's kitchen garden. Kick off with perhaps the Dolcelatte, fig and red onion chutney tartlet or pan-fried pigeon breast marinated in port, spicy couscous with pear and sage chutney. Then continue with oven-roasted Gressingham duck breast, Savoy cabbage, dauphinoise potatoes and blackberry jus; lemon and garlic baked pave of salmon with prawn risotto; or slow-roasted shoulder of Alscot lamb, herb mash and redcurrant jus. The friendly staff and a relaxed atmosphere make this a very popular venue.

Recommended in the area

Stratford-upon-Avon; Anne Hathaway's Cottage;
Hidcote Manor (NT)

The Golden Cross

Address: Wixford Rd, ARDENS GRAFTON, B50 4LG
Tel: 01789 772420
Email: info@thegoldencross.net
Website: www.thegoldencross.net
Map ref: 3 SP15
Directions: Telephone for directions
Open: all wk 🍴🍽️ **L** all wk 12-2.30 **D** all wk 5-9
Facilities: Garden Parking Wi-fi
Notes: 🌐 CHARLES WELLS 🚻

Guarding a crossroads on the edge of the village, this 18th-century pub always seems to have something going on, from meetings of the local MG owners club to Songs 'n' Steak on Thursdays. Flagstone floors, a wood-burner, lots of low beams and local photographs around the walls give the bar a traditional look and feel, and you can expect a good real ale line-up too. Behind the scenes, the talented chefs prepare fresh food from local suppliers to appear on seasonal menus and specials boards for consumption in the bar, dining room, on the patio or in the garden. Always popular are pavé of ham with bubble and squeak; Thai green chicken curry; grilled fillet of sea bass; and spinach pancakes. Faggots made to an old pub recipe are served every day with mash and mushy peas. Moreover, there's always a steak option and a choice of interesting fish from Devon, such as monkfish tail curry (fish comes in daily, except Mondays, as the fishermen have Sundays off), while typical specials include seared pigeon breast; slow-braised blade of beef; and slow-cooked shank of lamb. One of two options for sharing is a oven baked boxed Camembert with garlic and thyme, onion marmalade, pear chutney and toasted farmhouse bread.

Recommended in the area

Stratford-upon-Avon; Ragley Hall; Anne Hathaway's Cottage

The Bulls Head

Address: Stratford Rd, WOOTTON WAWEN, B95 6BD
Tel: 01564 792511
Email: info@thebullsheadwoottonwawen.co.uk
Website: www.thebullsheadwoottonwawen.co.uk
Map ref: 3 SP16
Directions: On B3400, 4m N of
Stratford-upon-Avon, 1m S of Henley-in-Arden
Open: all day all wk ⏹ **L** Mon-Sat 12-2.30, Sun 12-5
D all wk 6-9.30
Facilities: Garden Parking Wi-fi
Notes: ⊕ BILLESLEY PUB COMPANY ⅰ ⌀ ⍾ 8

A smart, black-and-white timber-framed pub, just one of the notable old buildings in Wootton Wawen, just a mile or so from picturesque Henley-in-Arden and ideally placed for touring and exploring Warwickshire and the Cotswolds. Originally two separate cottages, it displays a stone with the date 1317, and the bar and snug areas feature rug-strewn flagstone floors, low, gnarled oak beams, old church pews, and leather sofas fronting log fires. Ale drinkers will find Marston's Pedigree, Banks Original and Hobgoblin ales on tap in the bar, while the food offering here takes in ham, egg and chips, classic fish and chips, and the hearty Bull's Head club sandwich filled with bacon, chicken, lettuce, tomato and egg mayonnaise. The same tone and style are maintained in the magnificent 'great hall' restaurant, with its vaulted ceiling and yet more exposed beams. Here you can tuck into smoked salmon roulade with chive scented cream cheese; or classic Caesar salad, followed by braised lamb shank with caramelised onion gravy; or roast salmon with watercress sauce; lambs' liver, mash, bacon and onion jus; or Thai green chicken curry with fragrant jasmine rice, followed by sticky toffee pudding; or warm chocolate fondant with banana ice cream.

Recommended in the area

Warwick Castle; Coughton Court (NT); Ragley Hall, Park & Gardens

West Midlands

Old cathedral ruins, Coventry

The Malt Shovel at Barston

Address: Barston Ln, BARSTON, Solihull, B92 0JP
Tel: 01675 443223
Website: www.themaltshovelatbarston.com
Map ref: 3 SP27
Directions: M42 junct 5, A4141 towards Knowle.
Left into Jacobean Ln, right at T-junct (Hampton Ln).
Left into Barston Ln, 0.5m
Open: all day all wk ⬛ Booking required **L**
Mon-Sat 12-2.30, Sun 12-4 **D** Mon-Sat 6-9.30
⭐ Booking required **L** Sun 12-4 **D** Mon-Sat 7-9.30
Facilities: Garden Parking
Notes: ⬤ FREE HOUSE

A neat village pub, seemingly in the middle of nowhere, but just a short hop from Birmingham, The Malt Shovel is a bustling, award-winning free house with modern soft furnishings and interesting artefacts.. Natural wood and pastel colours characterise the interiors of this stylishly converted early 20th-century mill building. The bar is cosy and relaxed with winter log fires, and the restaurant is housed in an adjacent converted barn. The imaginative, modern British dishes make the best of seasonal ingredients, and fresh fish is delivered daily. The menu includes starters of seared Scottish scallops on pea purée with Colnakilty black pudding and crisp bacon; mildly spiced king prawns, passionfruit and chilli sauce; grilled line-caught mackerel, free-range slow roast pork belly and buttered Savoy cabbage. These may be followed by grilled plaice, roast sweet potato, crab and black Tuscan olive oil dressing; Cornish wild turbot with shelled mussels, crayfish, samphire and saffron broth; or lamb noisette on hazelnut and merlot risotto, rosemary and mint gremolata. Save a little room for one of the temping desserts - Madagascan vanilla pannacotta, warm rhubarb and pecan shortbread; or raspberry Eton mess. There's a super garden for summer alfresco dining.

Recommended in the area

National Motor Museum; Hackwood House (NT);
Baddesley Common (NT)

Isle of Wight

Coastal Footpath BB30
Sandown 2.

Coastal path towards Sandown

The Seaview Hotel & Restaurant

Address: High St, SEAVIEW, PO34 5EX
Tel: 01983 612711
Email: reception@seaviewhotel.co.uk
Website: www.seaviewhotel.co.uk
Map ref: 3 SZ69
Directions: B3330 from Ryde, left signed Puckpool, along seafront, hotel on left
Open: all wk
Notes: ⊕ FREE HOUSE ♦♦ ♨

In a sailing-mad Victorian village, this smart, sea-facing hotel is crammed with nautical associations. There are ships' wheels, oars, model ships, and lots of polished wood and brass. The Front Bar & Lounge resembles a naval wardroom and is home to a collection of naval artefacts, while the Pump Bar at the back is like a traditional pub, with a fish-focused menu. You may also eat in the small Victorian dining room, or the Sunshine restaurant and conservatory, both of which share a modern European (with a hint of British) menu that offers the very best of the season, caught or grown around the island - fish straight from the sea; pork and beef from its lush grazing land; venison from the hotel's own farm; and tomatoes, garlic and herbs from its garden.

The menu might include spider crab risotto with fennel sauce as a starter; Wight lamb shepherd's pie, carrot purée and beef sauce; or lightly curried cod, spiced lentils, buttered spring greens and herb crème fraîche sauce as a main course; and pineapple parfait, black pepper ice cream, with sweet red pepper and chilli syrup for dessert.

Recommended in the area

Seaview Wildlife Encounter (Flamingo Park); Osborne House; Isle of Wight Steam Railway

The New Inn

Address: Mill Ln, SHALFLEET, PO30 4NS
Tel: 01983 531314
Email: info@thenew-inn.co.uk
Website: www.thenew-inn.co.uk
Map ref: 3 SZ48
Directions: 6m from Newport to Yarmouth on A3054
Open: all day all wk 🛥 ❦❷ **L** Booking required all wk 12-2.30 **D** all wk 6-9.30
Facilities: Garden Parking Wi-fi
Notes: ⊕ ENTERPRISE INNS ♦ ♠ ♟ 11

It was built as a vicarage in 1743, yet somehow within 50 years it had become a pub, for which its inglenook fireplaces, flagstone floors and low-beamed ceilings were surely always better suited. A seasoned award-winner, it stands at the foot of the Newtown River estuary, which encourages the sailing fraternity to eat and drink here and, since the 65-mile coastal path passes the door, there's always a fair sprinkling of walkers too. It certainly makes the most of its estuarine location by specialising in seafood like whole crab and lobster salads; smoked tuna with lime salsa; the house special of moules marinière; halibut steak with garlic prawns; and even fillet of conger eel with Bombay potatoes and curry oil. Sandwiches and baguettes come with a variety of fillings, and other confirmed favourites include gammon, eggs and chips; local handmade sausages and mash with onion gravy; breast of chicken with roasted red peppers and smoked cheese; and vegetarian and children's options. In addition to four well-kept real ales, the 60-bin wine selection is considered one of the most extensive on the Isle of Wight. Settle in the elevated decked garden and take advantage of the island's impressive sunshine record.

Recommended in the area

Carisbrooke Castle; Ventnor Botanic Garden; Osborne House

The Crown Inn

Address: Walkers Ln, SHORWELL,
nr Newport, PO30 3JZ
Tel: 01983 740293
Email: karen@crowninnshorwell.co.uk
Website: www.crowninnshorwell.co.uk
Map ref: 3 SZ48
Directions: Left at top of Carisbrooke High Street.
Shorwell approx 6m
Open: all day all wk ⮶ ⭐ Booking required **L** all day
12-9.30 **D** all day 12-9.30
Facilities: Garden Parking Wi-fi
Notes: ⊕ ENTERPRISE INNS ⭑ ⭑ ⚲ 12

Outdoor types have voted The Crown their favourite destination pub. While it must help that it is only five miles from the centre of the island, they clearly love its authentic country atmosphere, winter log fire and summer rear garden with an arum lily-decorated trout stream. Also exerting a strong pull, no doubt, are the six real ales, including an island brew. The building is part 17th century, and different floor levels attest to many alterations, but while the most recent rebuild has seen a large increase in floor area, the pub is still full of character. Certainly nothing has upset the resident female ghost who shows her disapproval of card playing by scattering cards on the bar floor overnight. Food consists of home-made favourites based on locally sourced lamb, beef, fish and seasonal game. Make sure you check out the specials board that usually lists ten choices, such as sea bass, salmon and roasted duck breast; or there are classic pub dishes like sausage and mash; wild mushroom risotto; Spanish chicken; and smoked salmon and prawn tagliatelle. Other dishes include sharing platters for two; dusted lemon and pepper plaice; luxury fisherman's pie and vegetarian choices such as mushroom, blue cheese and leek lasagne. A Wendy house, slide and swings keep youngsters amused.

Recommended in the area

Blackgang Chine; Needles Old Battery (NT);
Isle of Wight Steam Railway

Wiltshire

Castle Combe

The Three Crowns

Address: BRINKWORTH, Chippenham, SN15 5AF
Tel: 01666 510366
Website: www.threecrowns.co.uk
Map ref: 3 SU08
Directions: From Swindon take A3102 to Royal Wootton Bassett, take B4042, 5m to Brinkworth
Open: all day all wk 10am-mdnt ⓑ ſⓄl **L** Mon-Sat 12-2, Sun 12-9 **D** Mon-Sat 6-9.30, Sun 12-9
Closed: 25-26 Dec
Facilities: Garden Parking Wi-fi
Notes: ⊕ ENTERPRISE INNS ⅰ⅟ ⅿ ⅞ 27

The current licensees, Anthony and Allyson Windle, have been here over 20 years and are now well into researching this quiet little pub's history. They know that it opened with its current name in 1801, but suspect that in the 18th century it traded under a different name. In 1927 Kelly's directory lists it as a hotel, serving teas and light refreshments; today it is one of the area's most popular eating venues. Menus are written on large blackboards, which make it easy to keep up with the daily, market-driven changes. Everything is homemade using top quality ingredients, main dishes being typified by aged West Country beef, lamb and mint pie, supreme of halibut and vegetarian tagliatelle, all cooked to order and served with a generous selection of fresh vegetables. Lighter lunches range from Caesar salad to slow-roast belly pork and beef chilli. The bar stocks a wide range of well-kept cask ales, keg beers and lagers, and Anthony and his wine merchant have carefully chosen (and tasted, over a period, naturally!) an 80-bin wine list. In winter there is an open log fire, while in summer the doors are flung open to the peaceful patio and garden.

Recommended in the area

Westonbirt Arboretum; Cotswold Water Park; Lydiard House & Park

The Dove Inn

★★★ ◉ INN

Address: CORTON, Warminster, BA12 0SZ
Tel: 01985 850109
Email: info@thedove.co.uk
Website: www.thedove.co.uk
Map ref: 2 ST94
Directions: 5m SE of Warminster. Exit A36 to Corton
Open: all wk noon-3 6-11.30 ▨ ⊠ **L** all wk 12-2.30 **D** all wk 6.30-9
Rooms: 7 en suite (5 GF) **S** £60-£80 **D** £80-£120
Facilities: Garden Parking Wi-fi
Notes: ⊕ FREE HOUSE ⊪ ⊭

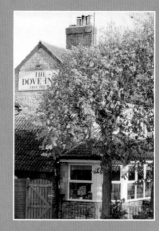

Little changed by the passage of time, The Dove is a 19th-century free house in a village in the Wylye Valley. Inside is a flagstone and oak-floored bar with a log-framed wood-burning stove, where locals enjoy a beer or two - several real ales are always on offer - and a bit of banter. The bar extends into a comfortable, relaxing restaurant and conservatory where diners can enjoy a sumptuous meal or light snack freshly prepared by the talented young chef and his creative team. There are grazing menus featuring cheese fondue, cured meats and smoked salmon; and starters of sautéed Sicilian-style courgette caponata with Somerset brie and toasted brioche; and steamed Shetland mussels with chorizo and Stowford Press cider sauce.

Mains might include grilled whole spatchcock baby chicken; wild mushroom and truffle with fresh potato gnocchi; Sharps Doom Bar-battered haddock fillet; and local wild rabbit, pancetta, wild mushroom and cider pie. Finally, there are the desserts - sticky date pudding with caramel sauce and double cream, and macadamia nut crème brûlée. Whatever you choose, the reason for the AA Rosette award will be apparent. Outside in the courtyard, cottage-style bedrooms overlook a pretty, apple tree-shaded beer garden.

Recommended in the area

Longleat House & Safari Park; Westbury White Horse; Stonehenge

The Fox and Hounds

Address: The Green, EAST KNOYLE, Salisbury,
SP3 6BN
Tel: 01747 830573
Email: pub@foxandhounds-eastknoyle.co.uk
Website: www.foxandhounds-eastknoyle.co.uk
Map ref: 2 ST83
Directions: From A303 follow Blandford/East
Knoyle signs onto A350, through Milton to
The Green
Open: all wk 11.30-3 5.30-11 ⓑ ⑴ **L** all wk 12-2.30
D all wk 6-9
Facilities: Garden Parking Wi-fi
Notes: ⊕ FREE HOUSE ⅰ⅛ ⅰ⅜ ⅞ 15

Surrounded by excellent walking and with stunning views of the Blackmore Vale, The Fox and Hounds is a picturesque 15th-century thatched free house that was built originally as three cottages. Here, guests can enjoy an imaginative menu and a range of traditional ales and ciders from West Country brewers as well as many wines by the glass. The village, which is situated on a greensand ridge, was once home to the family of Jane Seymour, Henry VIII's third wife, as well as Christopher Wren, whose father was the local vicar. Inside the pub, all is comfortable and cosy, with flagstone flooring, natural stone walls and sofas positioned next to wood-burning fires in winter. Diners can enjoy a meal in the light, airy conservatory or in the patio area. A varied menu, based on local produce, contains a range of snacks and main meals. These might include ploughman's or pizzas (from the clay oven), as well as lamb chump on mash, venison, 21-day-old fillet or sirloin steak with a choice of sauces, Thai green curry or Moroccan vegetable tagine. For those with room to spare, Pavlova with passion fruit coulis and warm chocolate fudge cake are among the desserts.

Recommended in the area

Stonehenge; Stourhead House & Gardens (NT); Longleat

The Beckford Arms

Address: FONTHILL GIFFORD, nr Tisbury, SP3 6PX
Tel: 01747 870385
Email: info@beckfordarms.com
Website: www.thebeckfordarms.co.uk
Map ref: 2 ST93
Directions: From A303 (E of Wincanton) follow
Fonthill Bishop sign. At T-junct in village right, 1st left
signed Fonthill Gifford & Tisbury. Through Fonthill
Estate arch to pub
Open: all day all wk ⬤ ⊙ **L** Mon-Sat 12-2.30, Sun
12-3 **D** all wk 6-9.30
Facilities: Garden Parking Wi-fi
Notes: ⊕ FREE HOUSE ⁍⁍ ⁍ ⁌ 12

Next time you're stuck in slow-moving traffic on the A303 between Mere and Stonehenge, turn off for this traditional, yet classy pub on the edge of the rolling parkland of Lord Margadale's 10,000-acre Fonthill Estate. The original house was built by William Beckford, a Lord Mayor of London in the mid-18th century; his son sold the estate in 1823. In the herringbone-patterned, parquet-floored bar the beers come from local breweries in Melksham and Berwick St Leonard and Butcombe in Somerset; there's also a local wine, Fonthill Glebe Seyval Blanc. Cocktails include the Beckford Bellini, using locally produced peach liqueur, and the Beckford Bloody Mary, using horseradish grown in the garden, while in winter a huge open fire warms the mulled wine.

The kitchen keeps the bar well stocked with pork pies and other snacks all day. Seasonally changing menus offer day-boat landed fish; locally caught trout; Creedy Carver duck breast; game pies; aged Wiltshire steaks; and even suckling pig spit-roasted on the open fire. Vegetarians might like Heritage tomatoes, deep-fried Laverstoke mozzarella, basil and aubergine purée, and linguini with roasted squash, sage, field mushrooms, parmesan and pumpkin seeds. After Sunday lunch, settle down to a classic movie in the sitting room.

Recommended in the area

Stourhead (NT); Stourton House Flower Garden;
Shaftesbury Abbey Museum & Garden

The Angel Coaching Inn

Address: High St, HEYTESBURY, BA12 0ED
Tel: 01985 840330
Email: admin@angelheytesbury.co.uk
Website: www.angelheytesbury.co.uk
Map ref: 2 ST94
Directions: A303 onto A36 towards Bath, 8m, Heytesbury on left
Open: all day all wk 🍴 **L** all wk 12-2.30 **D** all wk 6.30-9.30 🍴 **L** all wk 12-2.30 **D** all wk 6.30-9.30
Facilities: Garden Parking Wi-fi
Notes: 🍺 GREENE KING 👬 🐕 🍷 8

A 16th-century inn surrounded by countryside best appreciated on foot, so why not embark on one of the walks that start and end here. The Angel's interior is a blend of its original features and the contemporary; the beamed bar, for instance, has scrubbed pine tables, warmly decorated walls and an attractive fireplace with a wood-burning stove. It's often packed with locals, dogs by their sides, discussing everything from the local shoots to the price of beer. Exposed brickwork and antique dressers add a rustic feel to the more formal dining areas. The talented kitchen team produce an ever-changing menu to reflect the excellent West Country larder. As much as possible, produce is locally sourced – local steaks are a firm favourite.

From an imaginative menu, a choice for dinner may be duck egg with caramelised apple and black pudding Scotch egg; or white onion and cheddar soup, followed by rack of Wiltshire lamb, Lyonnaise potatoes, runner beans and port sauce; or sea bass, cod and ginger fishcake with coconut creamed spinach, with perhaps Calvados crème brûlée, mint apple pie and cider sorbet; or trio of chocolate – brownie, mousse and ice cream – to finish. Alternatively, for a quick bite just pop in for a plate of home-cooked ham with chunky hand-cut chips and salad.

Recommended in the area

Stonehenge; Old Sarum; Longleat

The Lamb at Hindon

★★★★ ◉ INN

Address: High St, HINDON, Salisbury, SP3 6DP
Tel: 01747 820573
Email: info@lambathindon.co.uk
Website: www.lambathindon.co.uk
Map ref: 2 ST93 **Directions:** From A303 follow
Hindon signs. At Fonthill Bishop right onto B3089 to
Hindon. Pub on left
Open: all day all wk 7.30am-mdnt 🍴 🍴 **L** all wk
12-2.30 **D** all wk 6.30-9.30
Rooms: 13 en suite (3 GF) **S** £115 **D** £175
Facilities: Garden Parking Wi-fi
Notes: ⊕ BOISDALE 🍴 🍴 ⊽ 10

The Lamb is set in the centre of a charming
village just 20 minutes from Salisbury. It began
trading as a public house as long ago as the 12th
century and by 1870 it supplied 300 horses to pull
coaches on the London-West Country route. The
inn is part of the Boisdale group, with two other
establishments in London, and this is reflected in
the distinctive interior design and in the quality
of the food and wine. The building still has plenty
of historic character, with beams, inglenook
fireplaces, and wood and flagstone floors, all set
off by fine antique furniture, old paintings and open
fires. Food is served from breakfast to dinner in
the dining room or the intimate Whisky and Cigar
Bar. Dishes are prepared from carefully sourced
ingredients, including fresh fish and game in season.
A dinner menu might feature main courses such as
Macsween haggis; Gloucester Old Spot sausages
with Beaune mustard mash and gravy; and the
'famous Boisdale' burger; plus a fish of the day
and pie of the day. The Meeting Room, in a sunken
area just off the main dining room, is available for
private dining or meetings. Each bedroom is richly
decorated and has an LCD screen.

Recommended in the area

Longleat; Stonehenge; Stourhead House & Gardens

The George & Dragon

★★★★ ◎◎ RESTAURANT WITH ROOMS

Address: High St, ROWDE, SN10 2PN
Tel: 01380 723053
Email: thegandd@tiscali.co.uk
Website: www.thegeorgeanddragonrowde.co.uk
Map ref: 2 ST96 **Directions:** 1m from Devizes,
take A342 towards Chippenham
Open: Mon-Sun L ⬛ ⓘ☉ **L** Mon-Fri 12-3, Sat-Sun 12-4
D Mon-Sat 6.30-10
Closed: Sun eve
Rooms: 2 en suite **D** £55-£115
Facilities: Garden Parking
Notes: ⊕ FREE HOUSE ⬆⬆ ⚲ ⚱10

Successfully combining the charm of a 16th-century inn with the relaxed atmosphere of a modern gastro-pub, The George and Dragon is located on the high street, a stone's throw from the Kennet and Avon Canal and the dramatic Caen Hill flight of locks. In summer the lawned garden is a delight, with its cottage-style flower borders and seating for an alfresco meal or a quiet drink; during winter there are welcoming log fires in the panelled bars and dining room and an interesting original feature is a carved Tudor rose on a beam in the restaurant. Seafood delivered directly from Cornwall is the speciality of the house, so diners can take their pick from the latest catch. The choice is huge, and may comprise sea bass, lobster, lemon sole, John Dory, mackerel, scallops, turbot and mussels. Blackboards above the bar list the fish dishes of the day, while the carte offers a range of local meat and game options. The emphasis of the award-winning food is on home-made delicacies, and this extends from the bread served at the start of the meal, to the delicious desserts and ice creams, and the chocolate fudge served with coffee. Draught beers include Butcombe Bitter, Milk Street Brewery ales and Bath Ales Gem. Three bedrooms, each full of character, are available.

Recommended in the area

Bowood House & Gardens; Lacock Abbey, Fox Talbot Museum & Village (NT); Avebury

The Somerset Arms

★★★★ INN
Address: High St, SEMINGTON, BA14 6JR
Tel: 01380 870067
Website: www.somersetarmssemington.co.uk
Map ref: 2 ST86
Directions: A361 from Devizes towards Trowbridge, right at 2nd rdbt into Semington
Open: all day all wk 🍴 **L** all wk 12-3 **D** all wk 6.30-9 🍽 **L** all wk 12-3 **D** Sun-Thu 6.30-9, Fri-Sat 6.30-9.30
Rooms: 3 en suite **S** fr £70 **D** fr £80
Facilities: Garden Parking Wi-fi
Notes: ⊕ FREE HOUSE 🍴 🐾 ♟ 16 🍷

A fine old coaching inn, the 17th-century Somerset Arms has a muted green and cream interior bringing out the best in its long-acquired character. Named after the Duke of Somerset, once a big noise round here, it is run by James, Darren and a strong team who together create an infectious atmosphere. The chefs use local ingredients as much as possible, all their meats, vegetables and dairy produce coming from local farms, their fish delivered fresh. A seasonally changing carte might well feature potted partridge with figs and rosemary brioche; home cured charcuterie; steamed vegetable suet pudding with cheddar mash and mustard sauce; and Thai marinated sea bass, tempura tiger prawns with coriander and chilli noodles. But although recognised as one of the best restaurants in the area, it hasn't forgotten its roots as a free house, and real ale lovers wouldn't fault its policy of supporting only breweries located within 50 miles of Semington, such as Bath Ales, Box Steam, Hopback, Stonehenge and Milk Street. Beer and cider festivals are regularly held here. Three boutique-style en suite B&B rooms are decorated with elegant wallpapers and fabrics.

Recommended in the area

City of Bath; West Kennet Long Barrow; Lacock Abbey, Fox Talbot Museum & Village (NT)

Marco Pierre White
The Pear Tree Inn

Address: Top Ln, WHITLEY, Melksham, SN12 8QX
Tel: 01225 709131
Email: info@wheelerspeartree.com
Website: www.wheelerspeartree.com
Map ref: 2 ST86
Directions: A365 from Melksham towards Bath, at
Shaw right onto B3353 to Whitley, 1st left
Open: all wk 🍴⊙ **L** Mon-Sat 12-3 (Sun 12-4)
D all wk 6-9.30 (Sun 6-9)
Facilities: Garden Parking Wi-fi
Notes: ⊕ HORATIO INNS 🚶🐾

When restaurateur Marco Pierre White's name is
linked with somewhere, you can reckon on great
things. In early 2011 he added this very pretty,
18th-century village pub to his ever-growing
portfolio and, while you do indeed get the expected
fine-dining experience, you also get the feel of a
nicely laid-back rural hostelry too. In the bar are
flagstone floors, beams, log fires and real ales like
Butcombe Gold, The Governor, an all-malt beer
brewed for Mr White by the J W Lees Brewery, and
named after his family greyhound, plus Governor's
Cider by Westons. Carefully selected wines come
from all over the world, and malt whiskies are from
all over Scotland. Stewart Langdell and his kitchen
team diligently source produce from locally based,
trusted suppliers to offer a stylish and great value
for money menu by Wheeler's of St James's (with
whom Mr White also has an involvement) featuring
smoked eel, Wheeler's potato and egg salad;
potted duck with prunes d'Agen; wing of skate with
winkles; grilled spatchcock of poussin à la chipolata;
Scottish rib-eye steaks presented in various ways -
à l'escargot with herbs, and à la Boston with oysters
being just two; and a selection of English and
French puddings such as soufflé of raspberries, or
Box Tree Eton mess. Outside, there is Marco's newly
created garden, with over 100 pear trees.

Recommended in the area

Lacock Abbey (NT); Avebury; Silbury Hill

Silbury Hill near Avebury

Worcestershire

Elgar's statue in Worcester

The Boot Inn

★ ★ ★ ★ ⬭ INN

Address: Radford Rd, FLYFORD FLAVELL, WR7 4BS
Tel: 01386 462658
Email: enquiries@thebootinn.com
Website: www.thebootinn.com
Map ref: 2 SO95
Directions: A422 from Worcester towards Stratford. Turn right to village
Open: all day all wk ⬭ ⚘ **L** 12-2 **D** 6.30-10
Rooms: (2 GF) **S** £50-£65 **D** £65-£95
Facilities: Garden Parking Wi-fi
Notes: ⬭ PUNCH TAVERNS ⬭ ⬭ ⬭ 8

An inn has occupied this site since the 13th century, though 'The Boot' itself, as it is called locally, dates from the Georgian period. It provides an ideal base for anyone wishing to explore Stratford-upon-Avon, the Cotswolds or the Malvern Hills. The award-winning inn has undergone modernisation, yet it has managed to retain much of its historic charm. The comfortable bedrooms in the converted coach house, furnished in antique pine, are equipped with practical extras such as tea- and coffee-making facilities, Freeview TV with a CD player and iPod dock, free Wi-fi and all have modern bathrooms; two rooms have disabled access. Guests can relax and indulge in the range of options available at this family-run pub, which prides itself on its friendly staff and lively atmosphere. Traditional ales and an extensive wine list complement the varied and imaginative menus, which are adapted according to availability of ingredients, with everything from sandwiches to bar meals to full carte on offer. The excellent food here, made from fine local produce, can be enjoyed in the cosy public areas, which include an attractive restaurant, a light and airy conservatory and a shaded patio area especially suited to summer dining.

Recommended in the area

Worcester Cathedral; Stratford-upon-Avon; Evesham

North Yorkshire

Ruins of St Hilda's Abbey

The Black Bull Inn

Address: 6 St James Square, BOROUGHBRIDGE,
Nr York, YO51 9AR
Tel: 01423 322413
Website: www.blackbullboroughbridge.co.uk
Map ref: 7 SE36
Directions: A1(M) junct 48, B6265 E for 1m
Open: all day all wk 11-11 (Fri-Sat 11am-mdnt, Sun
noon-11) 🛏 🍴 **L** all wk 12-2 **D** all wk 6-9
Facilities: Parking
Notes: 🍺 FREE HOUSE 🍴 🐾 🍷 11

Built in 1258, The Black Bull was one of the main
watering holes for coaches travelling what is now
the A1, and Dick Turpin allegedly stayed here.
Back then it had stables and a blacksmith's shop
attached; and these days, it still retains plenty of
original features, including old beams, low ceilings
and roaring open fires, not to mention the supposed
ghost of a monk. Traditional pub fare is the order
of the day here, with extensive menus covering all
the options. Starters such as chicken liver pâté with
Cumberland sauce; and Scottish smoked salmon
are sure to whet the appetite. The main courses
might include rump of English lamb with rosemary
and olive mashed potato; fish options and a
selection of very substantial steak dishes. Desserts
include banoffee meringue roulade with toffee
sauce; and dark chocolate truffle torte; apple pie
with custard. Sizeable bar snacks range from pork
and chive sausage with onion gravy, and deep-fried
prawns, to Thai beef strips with egg noodles and stir
fry vegetables. Among the array of sandwiches are
hot roast pork and apple sauce; and cold smoked
salmon with dill mayonnaise. Yorkshire beers are
available, and there is a selection of 17 malts.

Recommended in the area

Newby Hall & Gardens; Mother Shipton's Cave;
Ripon & cathedral

Crown Inn Roecliffe

★★★★★ ◉ INN

Address: Roecliffe, BOROUGHBRIDGE, YO51 9LY
Tel: 01423 322300
Email: info@crowninnroecliffe.co.uk
Website: www.crowninnroecliffe.co.uk
Map ref: 7 SE36
Directions: A1(M) junct 48, follow Boroughbridge
signs. At rdbt follow Roecliffe signs
Open: all wk 12-3.30 5-12 🍴 ◉ **L** Mon-Sat 12-2.30,
Sun 12-7 **D** Mon-Sat 6-9.30, Sun 12-7
Rooms: 4 en suite **S** £82-£90 **D** £97-£120
Facilities: Garden Parking
Notes: ⁺◊ ◊ ⚲ 30

Someone once described Roecliffe as "possibly the prettiest village in England". He or she may well have been right because pretty it certainly is, and from its position overlooking the village green this 16th-century coaching inn can admire the view. It was in a sorry state when owner and chef Karl Mainey first saw it, but he and his wife Amanda spent six months restoring it, making sure nothing compromised the authenticity of the beams, stoneflagged floors and other original features. Yorkshire place names litter the menu; Knaresborough asparagus with butter, sea salt and baked duck egg; Newby Hall Estate 30-day-aged sirloin steak; Middleton-on-the-Wolds duck breast with roasted figs, pak choi, purple endive and fresh plums; Great Ouseburn venison medallions with thyme rösti, wild girolles, gin and blackcurrants. From off the coast comes Yorkshire cod loin, served with Singapore-style noodles and baby brown shrimps, and other daily blackboard fresh seafood specials. Vegetarians have their own menu. County namechecks continue among the desserts with hand-made Yorkshire cheeses. Each en suite bedroom overlooks the village green. A new smokehouse sells kippers and smoked salmon (they're from Yorkshire too).

Recommended in the area

Newby Hall & Gardens; Fountains Abbey & Studley Royal; Aldborough Roman Site

Malt Shovel Inn

Address: BREARTON, Harrogate, HG3 3BX
Tel: 01423 862929
Email: bleikers@themaltshovelbrearton.co.uk
Website: www.themaltshovelbrearton.co.uk
Map ref: 7 SE36
Directions: A61 (Ripon to Harrogate) onto B6165
towards Knaresborough. Left, follow Brearton signs.
1m, right to village
Open: Wed-Sun L ⬛ ⏺ Booking required **L** Wed-Sat
12-2, Sun 12-3 **D** Wed-Sat 6-9
Closed: Sun eve, Mon-Tue
Facilities: Garden Parking
Notes: ⊕ FREE HOUSE ⅰ 🍷 14

At the heart of the picturesque village of Brearton
lies the Malt Shovel, a fine family-run 16th-century
inn. Although the pub is surrounded by rolling
farmland, it is just 15 minutes from Harrogate and
within easy reach of both Knaresborough and Ripon.
One of the oldest buildings in an ancient village, it
was taken over by the Bleiker family some five years
ago and they transformed it into an atmospheric
venue for eating and drinking, with open fires
in winter, flagstone floors and pianos in the bar
and conservatory. Swiss-born Jürg's innovative
cooking specialises in fresh fish – there's an on-site
smoking kiln – classic sauces and well-sourced local
produce, and diners can choose from the lunchtime
and early evening bistro menu or opt to eat à la
carte. The family bring their wealth of experience
in food, hospitality and entertainment to create an
ambience that combines elegance and theatricality
– Anna and D'Arcy Bleiker are international opera
soloists, and it's not unheard of for the odd aria
to be served up at dinner. However it's their
commitment to great food, fine wine, impeccable
cask ales and the warmest of welcomes that bring
customers back again and again.

Recommended in the area

Ripley Castle; Fountains Abbey (NT); Yorkshire Dales
National Park

The Bull

Address: BROUGHTON, nr Skipton, BD23 3AE
Tel: 01756 792065
Email: enquiries@thebullatbroughton.com
Website: www.thebullatbroughton.com
Map ref: 6 SD95
Directions: 3m from Skipton on A59, on right
Open: Tue-Sat noon-11pm (Sun noon-10.30pm)
⭐ **L** Tue-Sat 12-2, Sun 12-8 **D** Tue-Thu 5.30-8.30,
Fri-Sat 5.30-9, Sun 12-8 **Closed:** Mon, 25 Dec
Facilities: Garden Parking
Notes: FREE HOUSE

Long one of the county's landmark pubs, The Bull takes its name from the surrounding 3,000-acre Broughton Hall estate's famous herd of Shorthorns. Summer offers alfresco dining on the patios overlooking this parkland, which is often used for location filming; winter means eating and drinking warmed by blazing log fires. Real ales include Timothy Taylor Landlord and the unusual Saltaire Raspberry Blonde. The restaurant is acclaimed chef and star of the BBC's *Great British Menu*, Nigel Haworth's first venture into Yorkshire (he honed his skills in Lancashire!). He loves working with the region's farmers, growers and fine food suppliers to create dishes strong on local tradition, thus it should be no surprise to find a menu offering Yorkshire game pudding, forager's mash potato, roasted root vegetables and game sauce; The Bull North Sea fish pie; and Taste Tradition rare breed 10oz sirloin steak. An option among the hot and cold sandwich fillings is 'real' chips cooked in dripping – your waistline has been warned! Desserts include warm Skipton pudding with Lane Ends Farm organic cream; traditional English pancakes; and home-made organic ice creams and milkshakes.

Recommended in the area

Yorkshire Dales National Park; Malham Cove; Haworth

The Durham Ox

Address: Westway, CRAYKE, York, YO61 4TE
Tel: 01347 821506
Email: enquiries@thedurhamox.com
Website: www.thedurhamox.com
Map ref: 7 SE57
Directions: From A19 through Easingwold to Crayke. From market place left up hill, pub on right
Open: all wk 12-11 ⓑ ⓘ Booking required
L Mon-Sat 12-2.30, Sun 12-3 **D** Mon-Sat 5.30-9.30, Sun 5.30-8.30
Closed: 25 Dec
Facilities: Garden Parking Wi-fi
Notes: ⓦ FREE HOUSE ⌁ ♟ 10

Three hundred years old, and family-owned for the last thirteen, The Durham Ox is an award-winning traditional pub with flagstone floors, exposed beams, oak panelling and roaring fires. Situated in historic Crayke, with breathtaking views over the Vale of York on three sides, and a charming view up the hill (reputedly the one the Grand Old Duke of York's men marched up and down) to the church. A print of the eponymous ox – and a hefty beast it was too – hangs in the bottom bar. The Ox prides itself on serving good pub food, using the best locally sourced ingredients when possible for the seasonal menus and the blackboard specials. Dishes likely to be found are Ox prawn cocktail with home-made bread; spicy vegetable fritters, chick pea and ginger houmous, yoghurt and cucumber dip; rib-eye steak with béarnaise sauce; or venison and root vegetable casserole, Mount St John horseradish dumplings and red wine sauce. On Sundays, traditional rib of beef and Yorkshire puddings, fresh fish and other dishes are complemented by delicious desserts. Snacks include eggs Benedict, or Florentine, with bacon; chargrilled Ox burger; and a variety of open sandwiches. Four converted farm cottages and one studio suite provide overnight accommodation.

Recommended in the area

Castle Howard; Scampston Hall & Gardens; Byland Abbey

The Blue Lion

Address: EAST WITTON, Nr Leyburn, DL8 4SN
Tel: 01969 624273
Email: enquiries@thebluelion.co.uk
Website: www.thebluelion.co.uk
Map ref: 6 SE18
Directions: From Ripon take A6108 towards
Leyburn
Open: all day all wk 11-11 🍴 ⊗ **L** all wk 12-2.15
D all wk 7-9.30
Closed: 25 Dec
Facilities: Garden Parking Wi-fi
Notes: ⊕ FREE HOUSE 🍴 🐕 🍷 12

A sympathetically renovated country inn, built towards the end of the 18th century for coach travellers and cattle drovers journeying through Wensleydale. The bar, with an open fire and flagstone floor, is a beer drinker's heaven with a range of hand pulled beers, while the freshly prepared food in the highly praised candlelit restaurant uses mainly Yorkshire ingredients. A meal might start with warm salad of pigeon with black pudding, apples and Calvados, or Lincoln poacher Welsh rarebit with pickled red onion salad and tomato chutney, followed by pan-fried fillet of cod with a pancetta and thyme risotto; or cassoulet of duck leg, Toulouse sausage and belly pork and mash, then iced liquorice terrine with caramel sauce; or treacle sponge and custard. Bar meals are listed on a blackboard. This makes an ideal base from which to explore this lovely area, including Jervaulx Abbey, and nearby Middleham, home to some of the country's leading race horse trainers, and the spa towns of Ripon and Harrogate. If walking is your pastime then you'll be delighted to know there's a series of walks on the doorstep, ranging from a gentle stroll to a ten-mile challenge. Fifteen traditional and contemporary bedrooms are available.

Recommended in the area

Yorkshire Dales National Park; Jervaulx Abbey; Hardraw Force Waterfall

The Bridge Inn

Address: GRINTON, Richmond, DL11 6HH
Tel: 01748 884224
Email: atkinbridge@btinternet.com
Website: www.bridgeinngrinton.co.uk
Map ref: 6 SE09
Directions: Exit A1 at Scotch Corner onto A6108,
through Richmond. Left onto B6270 towards Grinton
& Reeth
Open: all day all wk
Facilities: Garden Parking Wi-fi
Notes: ⊕ JENNINGS BROTHERS PLC ♦ ⌐

With a host of activities such as walking, fishing, horse riding and mountain biking all on the doorstep, and a range of rooms available to stay in, The Bridge Inn makes a good base for those in search of country pursuits. Situated on the banks of the River Swale in the heart of the Yorkshire Dales National Park, this fine former coaching inn dates from the 13th century. Now with its beamed ceilings and open fires tastefully restored, the inn is fast becoming known for its great food and ales. Customers are invited to sample Jennings award-winning cask ales, or try something a little different from a micro-brewery; there is also an extensive wine cellar. Menus are based on seasonal local produce under the experienced eye of resident chef John Scott, and flavoured with herbs from the pub's own garden. Light snacks such as hot or cold baguettes and jacket potatoes are served in the bar, while in the restaurant, typical dishes could be a starter of ham hock terrine, followed by lamb shank in red wine and rosemary; or spiced parsnip pie with herby pastry. For those with room to spare, the dessert menu includes a daily choice of old-fashioned traditional puddings such as Liz's ginger sponge pudding.

Recommended in the area

Yorkshire Dales National Park; Reeth;
St Andrew's Church

The General Tarleton Inn

★★★★★ ◎◎ RESTAURANT WITH ROOMS

Address: Boroughbridge Rd, Ferrensby,
KNARESBOROUGH, HG5 0PZ
Tel: 01423 340284
Email: gti@generaltarleton.co.uk
Website: www.generaltarleton.co.uk
Map ref: 7 SE35 **Directions:** A1(M) junct 48 at
Boroughbridge, take A6055 to Knaresborough. Inn
4m on right **Open:** all wk 12-3 6-11 🍴 **L** all wk 12-2
booking required **D** all wk 6-9.15 🍴 **L** Sun 12-1.45
D Mon-Sat 6-9.15 **Rooms:** 14 en suite (7 GF)
S £75-£107 **D** £129-£150 **Facilities:** Garden Parking
Wi-fi **Notes:** ⊕ FREE HOUSE 🍴 🍷 11

A tastefully redesigned old coaching inn owned and run by John and Claire Topham. Sir Banastre Tarleton, after whom it was named, allegedly fired on surrendering troops during the American War of Independence and became known as "Bloody Ban"; he later became a Liverpool MP. The inn's low-beamed ceilings, rustic walls, log fires, cosy corners and modern black-and-white still lifes create welcoming surroundings. With two AA Rosettes, knowledgeable, friendly and professional staff serve honest British food using seasonal and local produce in an intimate and inviting atmosphere. The General Tarleton's reputation for fresh seafood partly depends on daily calls from fishing boat skippers; within hours perhaps mussel chowder or John's signature dish of seafood parcels in lobster sauce available in the bar brasserie or restaurant. In the latter you might well find Nidderdale oak-roast hot smoked salmon with Bloody Mary dressing; slow-braised Yorkshire beef and Black Sheep ale suet pudding; and trio of rhubarb - brûlée, crumble and compôte. Home-made dishes on the children's menu have been road-tested by the Topham offspring. Dine outdoors in the garden or covered courtyard in summer.

Recommended in the area

Fountains Abbey (NT); Ripley Castle; Yorkshire Dales National Park

Sandpiper Inn

Address: Market Place, LEYBURN, DL8 5AT
Tel: 01969 622206
Email: hsandpiper99@aol.com
Website: www.sandpiperinn.co.uk
Map ref: 6 SE19
Directions: A1 onto A684 to Leyburn
Open: 11.30-3 6.30-11 (Sun noon-2.30 7-10.30)
 L all wk 12-2.30 **L** all wk 12-2.30 **D** all wk
6.30-9.30
Closed: Mon & occasionally Tue
Facilities: Garden Wi-fi
Notes: FREE HOUSE

Handy for Wensleydale and many other Yorkshire attractions, this 17th-century, ivy-clad inn occupies the oldest building in Leyburn, but has only been a pub for some 30 years. Inside is the bar and snug, with a roaring, wood-burning stove in colder months, where you can enjoy a pint of Copper Dragon, or your pick from 100 single malts. Owners Jonathan and Janine Harrison have established an excellent reputation for modern British food using the finest ingredients; everything is made in house, from the organic bread through to the ice creams. Head for the restaurant to peruse the list of exciting and varied traditional and international dishes such as a starter of seared scallops with caramelised rare-breed belly pork, celeriac purée

and apple; or ham hock and rabbit terrine with home-made piccalilli. Follow this with locally sourced, aged Dexter rib-eye with béarnaise sauce; or pressed Dales lamb, savourade potato and mint and cranberry sauce. Lunch brings the likes of omelette Arnold Bennett; Sandpiper burger with thin fires; and Masham sausages with mash and onion gravy. Children are not only welcome - they get to choose from their own menu of home-made dishes, perhaps mini gammon and eggs followed by banana split.

Recommended in the area
Wensleydale Railway; Forbidden Corner, Tupgill Park; Theakston Brewery & Visitor Centre, Masham

The Lister Arms

★★★★ INN

Address: MALHAM, BD23 4DB
Tel: 01729 830330
Email: relax@listerarms.co.uk
Website: www.listerarms.co.uk
Map ref: 6 SD96
Directions: In town centre
Open: all day all wk
Rooms: 9 en suite **S** £70-£104 **D** £76-£110
Facilities: Garden Parking Wi-fi
Notes: ⊕ THWAITES INNS OF CHARACTER
♦♦ ➤ ♟ 8

It was Thomas Lister of Gisburne Park, created the first Lord Ribblesdale in 1797, who gave his name to this beautiful old stone coaching inn. Right on the village green, it's a good place to stop for morning coffee or a pint of Thwaites Wainwright bitter, named after Alfred, famous for his pictorial guides to the Lakeland Fells. Food from chef/patron Terry Quinn's kitchen is seasonal, local and always freshly prepared, with daily 'Lister Loves' dishes hanging from a board above the fireplace in the main bar. For lunch try a hot chargrilled steak sandwich, or pappardelle pasta with cherry vine tomatoes. For dinner start with a terrine of pork, pistachios and garden herbs known as Harrogate loaf; then pan-roasted breast of Nidderdale chicken with bacon, mash and creamy wild mushroom; and finish with Yorkshire Dales ice cream. Children can choose from their own menu, tuck into complimentary fresh fruit, top up their soft drinks free and receive a goodie box. Well-behaved dogs, muddy boots and cycles are also happily tolerated. Wake up to a full Yorkshire breakfast following a night in one of the en suite guest rooms, from some of which you can see the distant rock amphitheatre of Malham Cove.

Recommended in the area

Malham National Park Centre: Yorkshire Dales Falconry & Wildlife Conservation Centre; Skipton Castle

Fox & Hounds Country Inn

★★ 82% ◉ HOTEL

Address: Sinnington, PICKERING, YO62 6SQ
Tel: 01751 431577
Email: fox.houndsinn@btconnect.com
Website: www.thefoxandhoundsinn.co.uk
Map ref: 7 SE78 **Directions:** 3m W of town, off
A170 between Pickering & Helmsley
Open: all wk 12-2 6-11 (Sun 12-2 6-10.30)
🍽 Booking required **L** all wk 12-2 **D** all wk 6.30-9
Closed: 25-26 Dec
Rooms: 10 (4 GF) **S** £59-£89 **D** £70-£130
Facilities: Garden Parking
Notes: ⊕ FREE HOUSE 🍴 🎯

Set in a pretty village with a river running by, and
a large green with a small pack-horse bridge, this
18th-century inn offers good drinking, imaginative
modern cooking, and ten well-designed, en suite
bedrooms. Adjacent to the North York Moors
National Park, this area is very popular with by
walkers, cyclists and nature lovers. After exploring
the area, the inn's lounge bar, with its oak beams
and central woodburner, makes the ideal place for
a pint of Copper Dragon or Wold Top best bitter,
or a glass of wine from a selection of eight house
wines. At lunch, in addition to the carte menu,
lighter options are offered; perhaps a little fish pie
with spinach, or a black pudding and bacon salad
together with sautée potatoes and a poached
egg. The carte menu has something for everyone
including twice baked cheddar soufflé, watercress
and sun blushed tomato, followed by beef steak
suet pudding with mash, or the fish platter of tuna
niçoise, king scallop with peas and pancetta, little
fish pie and mini fish and chips. The contemporary
restaurant is candlelit in the evening which creates
an intimate and more formal dining option.

Recommended in the area

North Yorkshire Moors Railway; Rievaulx Abbey;
Nunnington Hall (NT)

The Buck Inn

★★★ INN

Address: THORNTON WATLASS, Ripon, HG4 4AH
Tel: 01677 422461
Email: innwatlass1@btconnect.com
Website: www.buckwatlass.co.uk
Map ref: 7 SE28
Directions: From A1 at Leeming Bar take A684 to
Bedale, B6268 towards Masham. Village in 2m
Open: all wk 11-mdnt ♨ ⑩ **L** Mon-Sat 12-2, Sun
12-3 **D** all wk 6.30-9 **Closed:** 25 Dec eve
Rooms: 5 en suite (1 GF)
Facilities: Garden Parking
Notes: ⊕ FREE HOUSE ♀♂

A traditional, well run, friendly institution that has been in experienced hands of Michael and Margaret Fox for over 20 years, who have no trouble in maintaining its welcoming and relaxed atmosphere. This is a quintessential Yorkshire village in a glorious area where much of the television's *Heartbeat* was filmed. The inn doesn't just overlook the village green and cricket pitch; players score four runs for hitting the pub wall, and six if the ball goes over the roof! There are three separate dining areas - the bar for informality, the restaurant for dining by candlelight, and on busy days the large function room is opened. The menu ranges from traditional, freshly prepared pub fare to exciting modern cuisine backed by daily changing blackboard specials.

Typical bar favourites are Masham rarebit; steak and ale pie; oven-baked lasagne; and beer-battered fish and chips. Main courses include dishes like grilled smoked haddock with buttery mash, saffron cream and crisp onion rings; venison sausages with Lyonnaise potatoes and rosemary gravy; or pan-fried duck breast with stir fry vegetables and hoi sin sauce. There's a choice of five real ales and 40 different malts to try, and most Sunday lunchtimes there's live jazz music.

Recommended in the area

Lightwater Valley Theme Park; Theakson Brewery Visitor Centre; Yorkshire Dales National Park

Steam train in Cropton Forest

West Yorkshire

Brönte Waterfall

Shibden Mill Inn

★★★★ ⑧⑧ INN

Address: Shibden Mill Fold, HALIFAX, HX3 7UL
Tel: 01422 365840
Email: enquiries@shibdenmillinn.com
Website: www.shibdenmillinn.com
Map ref: 6 SE02 **Directions:** From A58 into Kell
Ln. 0.5m, left into Blake Hill
Open: all wk noon-2.30 5.30-11 (Sat-Sun noon-11)
🍴 **L** Mon-Sat 12-2, Sun all day **D** Mon-Sat 6-9.30
🍽 **L** Sun 12-7.30 **D** Fri-Sat 6-9.30 **Closed:** 25-26 Dec
eve & 1 Jan eve **Rooms:** 11 en suite (1 GF)
S £81-£133 **D** £100-£158 **Facilities:** Garden Parking
Wi-fi **Notes:** ⊕ FREE HOUSE 👬 🐾 🍷 12

The waters of Red Beck once powered a spinning mill, for the Shibden Valley used to be an important wool production area. Those days are gone, but the low-beamed mill remains tucked away in a wooded glen that makes one forget that Halifax is only a spit away. Now with two AA Rosettes, it's the restaurant that particularly draws people in with food prepared from trusted local growers and suppliers. From a seasonal menu, on which newly conceived dishes share space with the regulars, two starters to consider might be rolled crispy Yorkshire lamb breast with asparagus and Woodall's ham salad; and duo of Calderdale rabbit. Then for a main course, perhaps grilled line-caught Peterhead mackerel with handmade scallop and coriander ravioli, celeriac and apple rémoulade, and caper velouté; or braised English veal breast with white polenta mash, oven-dried tomatoes, gremolata crust and game jus. Game, incidentally, features strongly (no pun intended) in the autumn. Such highly creative dishes are balanced by a good selection of simple old favourites, such as diced steak and Shibden ale pie; and Yorkshire goats' cheese ciabatta. Individually designed luxury bedrooms provide free Wi-Fi, flat-screen TV, DVD and access to a DVD library.

Recommended in the area

Shibden Hall; Eureka! The National Children's Museum; Bankfield Museum

Drummond Castle Gardens, Crieff

SCOTLAND

Tigh an Truish Inn

Address: CLACHAN-SEIL, Oban, PA34 4QZ
Tel: 01852 300242
Website: www.tighantruish.co.uk
Map ref: 9 NM71
Directions: 12m S of Oban take A816. Onto B844
towards Atlantic Bridge
Open: all wk 11-11 (Mon-Fri Oct-Mar 11-2.30 5-11)
L all wk 12-2 **D** all wk 6-8.30 (Apr-Oct)
Closed: 25 Dec & 1 Jan
Facilities: Garden Parking
Notes: ⊕ FREE HOUSE 👬 🐕

Following the Battle of Culloden in 1746, the final confrontation of the failed Jacobite Rebellion, Seil islanders heading to the mainland were supposed to swap their outlawed kilts for the hated British trousers. This is why the inn's Gaelic name means 'house of the trousers'. It overlooks the ambitiously named Bridge over the Atlantic, a tiny hump-backed construction, which crosses what is actually the narrow Clachan Sound, but an arm of the ocean nevertheless. Kilt removal having now become unnecessary, people stop here today for the wide selection of single malts, regularly changing real ales from the Atlas brewery in Kinlochleven and Fyne Ales of Cairndow, and a menu that includes plenty of seafood. Salmon and mussels are from

Argyll; smoked mackerel pâté is served with Scottish oatcakes; and lobster and prawns are caught by local fishermen working the Firth of Lorne. There are simpler options: at lunchtime the menu offers soup and light bar meals, such as filled baguettes and toasted sandwiches, and homemade beefburger; at dinner, macaroni cheese, and homemade steak and ale pie. Families are welcome and a separate lounge bar contains children's books and a high chair. The waterfront beer garden is hard to resist.

Recommended in the area

Arduaine Garden; Carnassarie Castle; sea boat charter to Corryvreckan whirlpool

The Inn at Inverbeg

★★★★ 🏨 🍽 INN

Address: LUSS, G83 8PD
Tel: 01436 860678
Email: inverbeg.reception@loch-lomond.co.uk
Website: www.innatinverbeg.co.uk
Map ref: 9 NS39
Directions: 12m N of Balloch
Open: all day all wk Mon-Thu & Sun 11-11 (Fri-Sat 11am-mdnt) 🛏 🍴 **L & D** all wk 12-9
Rooms: 12 en suite (5 GF)
Facilities: Parking Wi-fi
Notes: ⊕ FREE HOUSE ♂♀ ☍ 30

Many first-time visitors to this former AA Pub of the Year for Scotland are surprised at how close Loch Lomond is to Glasgow. This is an advantage for many reasons, not least that a stay at this contemporary inn, first opened in 1814, but given a multi-million pound refit some three years ago, puts guests within easy reach not only of the city but the West Highlands too. Mr C's, the fish and whisky bar/restaurant, with leather furniture and a big roaring fire, has been going since 1942 and is renowned for its award-winning fish and chips, over 200 whiskies, 30 wines by the glass and a good range of real ales. Also on the menu, on which you tick your choices for the kitchen, are starters of battered black pudding and haggis fritters; Cullen skink; and West Coast oysters. Other options include fresh Mallaig langoustines; Buccleuch sirloin steak; and Thai-style fish or chicken curry. Musicians play traditional Scottish folk music on Friday and Saturday evenings from April to November. Within the main building guests stay in comfortable, modern accommodation, while more spacious, loch-side Beach House rooms have four-poster beds, chaises longues and balconies looking across the water to the mountains.

Recommended in the area

Argyll Forest Park; Boat trip on Loch Lomond; Hill House, Helensborough (NTS)

The Jigger Inn

Address: The Old Course Hotel, ST ANDREWS, KY16 9SP
Tel: 01334 474371
Email: reservations@oldcoursehotel.co.uk
Website: www.oldcoursehotel.co.uk
Map ref: 11 NO51
Directions: M90 junct 8, A91 to St Andrews
Open: all day all wk 11-11 (Sun noon-11)
🛏 🍽 **L & D** all wk 12-9.30
Facilities: Garden Parking
Notes: ⊕ FREE HOUSE ♦ ♟ 8

This whitewashed, former stationmaster's lodge on a long-dismantled railway line stands now as the unique 19th hole in the grounds of the most famous golf course – The Old Course. St Andrews is renowned, of course, throughout the world as the Home of Golf. Therefore, don't be surprised by the abundant golfing memorabilia, and golfers comparing their scorecards as they warm themselves in front of a crackling, open-hearth fire cradling a pint of Jigger Ale – a brew in the style of a classic Scottish Ale that is as unique as the Jigger Inn itself and available for consumption only within the pub's ancient walls. This traditional Scottish pub is always busy and offers warm hospitality at its very best. All-day availability is one advantage of the short, simple menu that lists soups and salads such as Cullen skink and Caesar salad, or triple-decker sandwiches and wraps. For something more substantial, there is St Andrews Ale beer-battered fish with chunky chips, Speyside rib-eye steak, Jigger cheese and bacon burger, or garden vegetable pie and chips.

Recommended in the area

St Andrews Cathedral; West Sands Beach; Fife Folk Museum

Cawdor Tavern

Address: The Lane, CAWDOR, Nairn, IV12 5XP
Tel: 01667 404777
Email: enquiries@cawdortavern.co.uk
Website: www.cawdortavern.co.uk
Map ref: 13 NH85
Directions: A96 onto B9006, follow Cawdor Castle
signs. Tavern in village centre
Open: all wk 11-3 5-11 (Sat 11am-mdnt Sun
12.30-11) all day in summer ⌷ ❍❘ **L** Mon-Sat 12-2,
Sun 12.30-3 **D** all wk 5.30-9
Closed: 25 Dec, 1 Jan, 2wks mid Jan
Facilities: Garden Parking
Notes: ⊕ FREE HOUSE ♦♦ ♔ ⚑ 9

Tucked away in the heart of Cawdor's pretty
village, the Tavern's near neighbour is the castle
where Macbeth held court. Nairn's pretty wooded
countryside slides away from the pub, offering
umpteen opportunities for easy rambles before
retiring to consider the welcoming mix of fine
Scottish food and island micro-brewery ales that
makes the pub a destination in its own right. There's
an almost baronial feel to the bars, created from
the Cawdor Estate's joinery workshop and featuring
wonderful panelling which originated in the castle;
log fires and stoves add winter warmth, as does the
impressive list of Highland and Island malts. A highly
accomplished menu balances meat, fish, game and
vegetarian options, prepared in a modern Scottish
style with first class Scottish produce. Settle in with
a pint of Raven Ale from the respected Orkney
Brewery and contemplate a starter of seafood
platter; or trio of Scottish puddings – black pudding,
haggis and white pudding, appetizers for mains
covering pan-fried fillet of sea bream served on
spinach crayfish-tail risotto, fillet of Moray pork in
a sage and onion mousse; Speyside pigeon breast,
apple fritter, crispy bacon and red wine jus; or local
brie, cranberry and chestnut risotto. Children have
their own extensive menu to choose from.

Recommended in the area

Cawdor Castle; Fort George; Culloden Battlefield

The Plockton Hotel

★★★ 75% SMALL HOTEL

Address: Harbour St, PLOCKTON, IV52 8TN
Tel: 01599 544274
Email: info@plocktonhotel.co.uk
Website: www.plocktonhotel.co.uk
Map ref: 13 NG83 **Directions:** A87 towards Kyle
of Lochalsh. At Balmacara follow Plockton signs, 7m
Open: all day all wk 11am-mdnt (Sun 12.30pm-
11pm) 🍽 **L** all wk 12-2.15 **D** all wk 6-10
Closed: 25 Dec, 1 Jan
Rooms: 15 (1 GF) **S** £55-£90 **D** £80-£130
Facilities: Garden Wi-fi
Notes: ⊕ FREE HOUSE 🍴

The award-winning Plockton Hotel sits right next
to the gently lapping waters of Loch Carron, a
sheltered sea loch warmed by the Gulf Stream and
fringed with palm trees. It is the only waterfront
hostelry in this lovely National Trust village,
the location for the cult film *The Wicker Man*.
The breathtaking view, across the bay to the
Applecross Hills, is enjoyed by many of the hotel's
comfortable en suite bedrooms. Converted from
a ship's chandlery in 1913, this establishment has
been run by the Pearson family and their staff for
more than 20 years. Menus are based on the very
best of Highland produce, with seafood a major
strength: expect to find locally caught langoustines,
shellfish from Skye, fresh fish landed at Gairloch
and Kinlochbervie, and smoked fish from Aultbea.
Products from the smokehouse feature in one of
the hotel's specialities – cream of smoked fish soup.
Other starters may include Talisker whisky pâté and
fresh Plockton prawns. Top quality Highland beef
appears in flamed peppered whisky steaks from the
charcoal grill. Other main courses include casserole
of Highland venison, haggis and tatties, and wild
boar burger with salad and fries. A fine range of
malts is offered.

Recommended in the area

Isle of Skye; Eilean Donan Castle; Applecross
Peninsula

Plockton Inn & Seafood Restaurant

Address: Innes St, PLOCKTON, IV52 8TW
Tel: 01599 544222
Email: info@plocktoninn.co.uk
Website: www.plocktoninn.co.uk
Map ref: 13 NG83
Directions: A87 towards Kyle of Lochalsh.
At Balmacara follow Plockton signs, 7m
Open: all day all wk ⓑ **L** all wk 12-2.30 **D** all wk 6-9
⦿ **D** all wk 6-9
Facilities: Garden Parking Wi-fi
Notes: ⊞ FREE HOUSE ⦿ ⦿

Just 100 metres from the harbour, this attractive stone-built free house is run by Mary Gollan, her brother Kenny and his partner, Susan Trowbridge, who have turned it into an inveterate award-winner, the ladies sharing the role of chef, while Kenny runs the bar. An easygoing atmosphere is apparent throughout, with winter fires in both bars, and a selection of over 50 malt whiskies. A meal in the reasonably formal dining room, or the more relaxed lounge bar, is a must, with a wealth of freshly caught local fish and shellfish, West Highland beef, lamb, game and home-made vegetarian dishes on the set menu, plus daily specials. Martin, the barman, lands the Plockton prawns (langoustines here) himself, then Kenny takes them and other seafood off to

his smokehouse, to feature on the menus later. Starters include a vegetable or fish-based soup; oysters with vodka, tomato juice and herbs. Among the mains are those langoustines Martin caught in Loch Carron; Scottish salmon fillet; hand-dived king scallops; lamb shank; pork goulash; and lentil and hazelnut roast. Desserts include cranachan ice cream, and Scottish cheeses. The public bar is alive on Tuesdays and Thursdays with music by local musicians, and winter Fridays feature laid-back pub quizzes.

Recommended in the area

Eilean Donan Castle; Lochalsh Woodlands (NTS); Strome Castle (NTS)

Moulin Hotel

★★★ 75% HOTEL

Address: 11-13 Kirkmichael Rd, Moulin,
PITLOCHRY, PH16 5EH

Tel: 01796 472196

Email: enquiries@moulinhotel.co.uk

Website: www.moulinhotel.co.uk

Map ref: 13 NN95 **Directions:** From A924 at
Pitlochry take A923. Moulin 0.75m

Open: all day all wk 11-11 (Fri-Sat 11am-11.45pm
Sun noon-11) 🍴 **L** all wk 12-9.30 **D** all wk 12-9.30
🍽 **D** all wk 6-9 **Rooms:** 15 **S** £45-£77 **D** £60-£92

Facilities: Garden Parking Wi-fi

Notes: ⊕ FREE HOUSE ᛙ 🐾 ⚐ 25

Built in 1695 at the foot of Ben Vrackie on an old
drovers' road, this great all-round inn is popular as
a walking and touring base. As the excellent home-
brewed beers, Ale of Atholl, Braveheart, Moulin Light
and Old Remedial are not available anywhere else
many enthusiasts are drawn to the hotel's bar to try
them, and on weekdays the brewery, just over the
road, is open to visitors. The interior boasts beautiful
stone walls and lots of cosy niches, with blazing
log fires in winter; while the courtyard garden is
lovely in summer. Menus offer the opportunity to
try something local such as mince and tatties; Skye
mussels; venison pan-fried in Braveheart beer; and
Vrackie Grostel – sautéed potatoes with smoked
bacon topped with a fried egg. You might then
round off a meal with Highland honey sponge and
custard, or raspberry crumble. A specials board
broadens the choice further. If you decide to stay
over there are 15 quiet, individually styled en suite
bedrooms. This makes the ideal base for exploring
this lovely area, and visits to Blair Castle, Castle
Menzies and Scone Palace, or a drive along the
famous Whisky Trail all make for interesting and
enjoyable days out.

Recommended in the area

Edradour Distillery; Scottish Hydro Electric Visitor
Centre, Dam & Fish Pass; Blair Castle, Blair Atholl

CRE U·C
FEL·GW
O·H WR

Millennium Centre

WALES

Caesars Arms

Address: Cardiff Rd, CREIGIAU, CF15 9NN
Tel: 029 2089 0486
Email: info@caesarsarms.co.uk
Website: www.caesarsarms.co.uk
Map ref: 2 ST08 **Directions:** M4 junct 34, A4119
towards Llantrisant/Rhondda. 0.5m right at lights
signed Groesfaen. Through Groesfaen, past Dynevor
Arms. Next left signed Creigiau. 1m, left at T-junct,
pass golf course. Pub in 1m **Open:** noon-2.30 6-10
(Sun noon-4) 🍴 **L** Mon-Sat 12-2.30 🍽 **L** Mon-Sat
12-2.30, Sun 12-4 **D** Mon-Sat 6-10 **Closed:** 25-26
Dec, 1 Jan, Sun eve **Facilities:** Garden Parking
Notes: 🛢 FREE HOUSE 👫 🐾

Just ten miles outside Cardiff, Caesars Arms sits
tucked away down winding lanes offering fine
views of the surrounding countryside from its
heated patio and terrace. The restaurant has a
vast selection of fresh fish, seafood, meat and
game taking pride of place. The emphasis here is
on locally sourced food, displayed on shaven ice.
Starters might include imaginative choices such as
Bajan fishcakes, or cherry-smoked duck breast with
organic beetroot. Main courses take in hake, halibut,
Dover sole and lobster, as well as a show-stopping
Pembrokeshire sea bass baked in rock salt, which
is cracked open and filleted at your table. But it's
not all about fish – other choices include steak from
Carmarthenshire plus lamb and venison from the
Brecon Beacons and free-range chickens from the
Vale of Glamorgan. Home-grown organic herbs,
salads and vegetables are all used as much as
possible, and the inn has its own smokery. Another
attraction is the farm shop, which provides a range
of home-produced honey, free-range eggs, Welsh
cheeses, home-baked bread and chef's ready-
prepared meals.

Recommended in the area

Castell Coch; Llandaff Cathedral; St Fagans: National
History Museum

White Hart Thatched Inn & Brewery

Address: LLANDDAROG, Nr Carmarthen, SA32 8NT
Tel: 01267 275395
Email: bestpubinwales@aol.com
Website: www.thebestpubinwales.co.uk
Map ref: 1 SN51
Directions: A48, 6m E of Carmarthen towards
Swansea, onto B4310 signed Llanddarog
Open: 11.30-3 6.30-11 (Sun noon-3 7-10.30)
†◎ǀ **L** Thu-Tue 11.30-3 inc wknd **D** Thu-Tue 6.30-11 inc
wknd **Closed:** Jan, Wed
Facilities: Garden Parking
Notes: ⊕ FREE HOUSE ♦♦

Interesting legends surround this family-run, ancient thatched building, thought to be built to house stone masons who built the first church next door. Dylan Thomas often visited on his way west. 'Cwrw Blasus' (meaning tasty ale) is always available along with different cask conditioned ales, made from top quality ingredients – malted barley, whole hop cones and yeast - including water from 300 feet beneath the inn. The pub's 14th-century origins can be seen in the thick stone walls, heavy beams and cosy log fire. The restaurant is situated in a converted barn, and has views to the open-plan kitchen where the chefs can be seen preparing your food. The family-run business is now a member of Prince Charles' exclusive Welsh lamb club as they use only best Welsh lamb. They also serve pedigree Welsh Black beef on the menu. The specials board is likely to include beef and ale pie, and beef and ale with cauliflower cheese double pie; trio of Welsh pork sausages, peas and mash; half duckling sizzling in orange sauce; and home-made lasagne. In summer, the flower-filled patio garden is perfect for alfresco dining. Children will enjoy the play area and seeing the pigs, chickens, ducks and turkeys on the small home farm.

Recommended in the area

Folly Farm; National Botanic Gardens of Wales; Aberglasney House

The Groes Inn

★ ★ ★ ★ ★ ⊚ INN

Address: CONWY, LL32 8TN
Tel: 01492 650545
Email: reception@groesinn.com
Website: www.groesinn.com
Map ref: 5 SH77
Directions: Exit A55 to Conwy, left at mini rdbt by
Conwy Castle onto B5106, 2.5m inn on right
Open: all wk 12-3 6-11 ⓛ ⓣ❍ⓛ **L** all wk 12-2
D all wk 6.30-9
Rooms: 14 en suite (6 GF) **S** £91-£190 **D** £115-£220
Facilities: Garden Parking Wi-fi
Notes: ⊕ FREE HOUSE ⋈ ♟ 14

One of Wales' oldest pubs (first licensed in
1573), the creeper-clad inn nestles between the
easternmost summits of the Carneddau mountain
range and the rich riverside pastures of the verdant
Conwy Valley; Snowdonia at its most benign, with
extraordinary views from the flowery gardens
one good reason to linger, another is the range
luxuriously appointed yet ultra traditional bedroom
suites. Rambling rooms, beamed ceilings, careworn
settles, military hats (there's a connection to the
Duke of Wellington here), historic cooking utensils,
a stag's head over an open fire – this inn has plenty
to point out and even snigger over (namely, the
saucy Victorian postcards) – but don't expect a
jukebox, gaming machines or pool table. The team
of talented chefs create award-winning menus
a distinctly Welsh tilt, with lamb and game from
nearby estates and an infinitely varied selection of
fruits of the sea; try lamb's liver and onions with
mustard mash; the seafood pie, a medley of fresh
market fish, or perhaps some renowned Conwy
mussels. The chalk board specials denote the ever-
changing quality dishes of the day, whilst the beers
are mostly from the Great Orme micro-brewery. The
staff offer a warm welcome whether you're calling
in for a pint or staying for a night or two.

Recommended in the area

Snowdonia; Bodnant Gardens; Conwy Castle

The Queens Head

Address: Glanwydden, LLANDUDNO JUNCTION,
LL31 9JP
Tel: 01492 546570
Email: enquiries@queensheadglanwydden.co.uk
Website: www.queensheadglanwydden.co.uk
Map ref: 5 SH77 **Directions:** A55 onto A470
towards Llandudno. At 3rd rdbt right towards
Penrhyn Bay, 2nd right into Glanwydden, pub on left
Open: all wk 11.30-3 6-10.30 (Sat-Sun 11.30-10.30)
🍴❤️ **L** Mon-Fri 12-2, Sat-Sun 12-9 **D** Mon-Fri 6-9,
Sat-Sun 12-9
Facilities: Garden Parking
Notes: ⊕ FREE HOUSE ♟ 10

The village of Glanwydden is just five minutes' drive
from the Victorian seaside resort of Llandudno,
its shops and grand, curving beach. In the other
direction lie the countryside and the mountains,
making this 18th-century country pub and
restaurant, once the wheelwright's cottage, well
placed for both. Previous winners of the AA's Pub of
the Year for Wales, Robert and Sally Cureton have
created this smart pub with appealing menus, good
selection of wine and beers, and a team of attentive
staff. In winter the bar's log fire will be blazing, while
in summer you can take your drinks out on to the
pretty terrace. At any time of the year your fellow
evening imbibers might, following their pre-theatre
dinner, be heading for the town's Venue Cymru.

Typically, a meal could be smoked salmon and trout
mousse, then chargrilled Welsh rump steak, and
raspberry and amaretto trifle to finish. Lighter dishes
include salmon and coriander fishcakes, and fresh
asparagus risotto, while more hearty are Jamaican
chicken curry, and sautéed lamb's liver and crispy
bacon. There's more of the same, as well as roasts,
on Sundays, while the wine list offers plenty of
choice too.

Recommended in the area

Conwy Castle; Great Orme Heritage Coast;
Bodelwyddan

Penhelig Arms Hotel & Restaurant

Address: Terrace Rd, ABERDYFI, LL35 0LT
Tel: 01654 767215
Email: info@penheligarms.com
Website: www.penheligarms.com
Map ref: 5 SN69
Directions: On A493, W of Machynlleth
Open: all day all wk ⬛ **L** all wk 12-2
D all wk 6-9 ⭐❗ **L** all wk 12-2 **D** all wk 7-9
Facilities: Parking Wi-fi
Notes: ♿ S A BRAIN & CO LTD 👫 🐕 🍷 20

The Penhelig Arms has been in business since 1870 and offers spectacular views over the tidal Dyfi estuary. Indeed, in the summer months the Penhelig's own seating area opposite is the place to enjoy the fine views. In winter a welcoming log fire burns in the wood-panelled Fisherman's Restaurant – the perfect place to relax and unwind after a hard day's fishing, playing golf, walking or sightseeing and to enjoy a pint of Brains Reverend James or Thatchers Katy cider. Great food is served in both the Fisherman's Bar and the waterfront restaurant, and the menus are strong on fresh fish - crab, bass and bream arriving straight from the quay - backed up by Welsh beef and lamb. In the restaurant kick things off with a glass of champagne then choose from dishes such as pan-fried scallops with chilli, ginger and garlic butter; or fillets of sweet cured herring, beetroot and red onion salad, followed by grilled sea bass fillets with chive hollandaise; or roast rack of lamb, roast butternut squash and red wine sauce. Leave room for a tempting dessert, perhaps lemon posset or warm poached pear, fudge sauce and chocolate ice cream. The accommodation includes spacious suites with patios or balconies. Snowdonia National Park is within easy reach.

Recommended in the area

Centre for Alternative Technology; Tal-y-Llyn Railway

The Greyhound Inn

Address: LLANTRISANT, Usk, NP15 1LE
Tel: 01291 672505 & 673447
Email: enquiry@greyhound-inn.com
Website: www.greyhound-inn.com
Map ref: 2 ST39 **Directions:** M4 junct 24, A449 towards Monmouth, exit at 1st junct signed Usk. 2nd left for Llantrisant. Or from Monmouth A40, A449 exit for Usk. In Usk left into Twyn Sq follow Llantrisant signs. 2.5m under A449 bridge. Inn on right
Open: all day 11-11 🛌 🍽️ **L** all wk 12-2.15
D Mon-Sat 6-10 **Closed:** 25 & 31 Dec, 1 Jan, Sun eve
Facilities: Garden Parking Wi-fi
Notes: 🍺 FREE HOUSE 👬 🐕 🍷 10

A sensitively restored 17th-century Welsh longhouse with two acres of award-winning gardens, this establishment combines the charm and atmosphere of a traditional family-owned inn offering delicious home-cooked meals with very comfortable accommodation. In winter enjoy several roaring log fires or in summer dine alfresco in the beautiful gardens. Lovers of real ale will find an interesting range complemented by an impressive wine selection. Nick Davies, The Greyhound's owner for over 30 years, heads a kitchen team that prepares deliciously cooked food for customers in the candlelit dining room or any of the three other eating areas. They source locally the ingredients for well-established favourites – steak and ale pie, lamb shank in red wine, liver and bacon, Welsh sirloin steak, freshly grilled local trout, freshly battered cod, chilli con carne, lasagne verde, venison in season and vegetarian dishes such as Brazil nut and spinach roast. More unusual dishes occupy the daily specials board so you will be spoilt for choice. You will receive a very warm welcome whether you want to spend the evening drinking and chatting in the 'locals' bar, enjoying an informal meal or snack in the lounges or eating in the dining room. Ten en suite bedrooms, with all modern facilities, are housed in the converted barn.

Recommended in the area

Tintern Abbey; Raglan Castle; Big Pit, Blaenavon

The Lion Inn

Address: TRELLECH, Monmouth, NP25 4PA
Tel: 01600 860322
Email: debs@globalnet.co.uk
Website: www.lioninn.co.uk
Map ref: 2 SO50 **Directions:** From A40 S of
Monmouth take B4293, follow Trellech signs. From
M8 junct 2, straight across rdbt, 2nd left at 2nd rdbt,
B4293 to Trellech **Open:** 12-3 6-11 (Fri-Sat noon-
mdnt Sun 12-4.30 Mon eve 7-11pm Thu eve 6-mdnt)
🍽 **L** Mon-Fri 12-2, Sat-Sun 12-2.30 **D** Mon 7-9.30,
Tue-Sat 6-9.30 **Closed:** Sun eve
Facilities: Garden Parking
Notes: ⊕ FREE HOUSE 🕴 🐾 🍺

This popular and well-established free house is
opposite St Nicholas's Church. Guests are greeted
by welcoming real fires in the winter months, while
in the summer drinks and meals can be served in
the garden, which overlooks fields and features a
stream and large aviary. The former brew house has
won many accolades for its food and hospitality
over the years, and its reputation is growing.
Visitors aiming to explore the nearby walking trails
and notable historic buildings, or visit Trellech's
own archaeological dig, will find it a useful staging
post. The extensive pub menu caters for all tastes,
from bar snacks and basket meals to blackboard
specials, including fresh fish dishes. There is also
an adventurous menu featuring wild and hedgerow
ingredients, such as nettles and wild mushrooms.
Real ales include Bath Ales, Wye Valley Butty Bach,
Rhymney Best, Cottage Brewery and many more
regularly changing brews. Anyone who wants to
extend their visit to The Lion can stay overnight in
the pub's one-bedroom cottage, which is suitable
for up to three guests. It features an en suite
bathroom and kitchenette. Dogs are allowed at the
pub, and water and biscuits are provided for them.

Recommended in the area

Tintern Abbey; Chepstow Castle;
Wye Valley Forest Park

The Swan Inn

Address: Point Rd, LITTLE HAVEN,
Haverfordwest, SA62 3UL
Tel: 01437 781880
Email: enquiries@theswanlittlehaven.co.uk
Website: www.theswanlittlehaven.co.uk
Map ref: 1 SM81 **Directions:** B4341 from
Haverfordwest. In Broad Haven follow seafront/Little
Haven signs, 0.75m to inn
Open: all day 11am-mdnt ⓛ ⓘⓞⓘ **L** all wk 12-2
D all wk 6-9 (closed Sun out of season)
Closed: 3 Jan-18 Feb **Facilities:** Garden
Notes: ⊕ FREE HOUSE ⓘⓘ ⓘ

This historic seaside inn, a previous winner of AA
Pub of the Year for Wales, has been impeccably
renovated but retains its rustic charm thanks
to the beams, blazing log fires, old settles and
exposed stone walls. It was built by a fisherman
and is literally just a stone's throw from the beach,
offering great Pembrokeshire views from some
tables. Cooking, with the emphasis on seasonal,
local produce, is modern British in style, and is very
accomplished, though informal. Diners can eat in
the elegant contemporary upstairs dining room, or
in the intimate restaurant below. Seafood is the star
here, be it pan-fried scallops with chorizo, whole
roasted sea bass with caper butter and samphire,
mussels in Welsh ale and herbs or beer-battered

fish and chips. St Brides Bay crab and home smoked
mackerel feature with other seaside favourites such
as a pint of prawns and moules marinière. For the
carnivores there may be Welsh fillet steak, local
lamb or venison, as well as home baked bread and
Welsh cheese. The busy bar serves a range of bar
snacks and well-kept real ales, and there are many
wines available by the glass, all to be enjoyed in one
of the leather armchairs.

Recommended in the area

Pembrokeshire Coast National Park; Skomer Island

The Stackpole Inn

Address: STACKPOLE, nr Pembroke, SA71 5DF
Tel: 01646 672324
Email: info@stackpoleinn.co.uk
Website: www.stackpoleinn.co.uk
Map ref: 1 SR99
Directions: From Pembroke take B4319, follow
Stackpole signs, approx 4m
Open: 12-3 6-11 🛏 †◎† Booking required **L** Mon-Sat
12-2, Sun 12-2.30 **D** all wk 6.30-9
Closed: Sun eve (winter)
Facilities: Garden Parking Wi-fi
Notes: ⊕ FREE HOUSE †† 🐾 🍷 12

Location, location, location. The meaning of the phrase becomes crystal clear in the context of this 17th-century inn, standing in beautiful gardens within the Pembrokeshire Coast National Park. Nearby are stunning cliffs, bays and beaches, and the huge natural arch known as the Green Bridge of Wales. It's a freehouse, and there's always a guest from elsewhere to accompany three Welsh ales. Warmth is provided by a wood-burning stove set within the stone fireplace. Produce from the local countryside and coastal waters plays a major part in the home-cooked repertoire. At lunchtime, for instance, Thai style fish cakes on sticky vegetable rice with soy reduction; steamed Bantry Bay mussels in garlic and Parmesan cream;

and a vegetarian dish of the day. Evening starters include Perl Las (organic Welsh blue cheese), bitter leaf salad, pickled walnuts and grapes poached in Sauternes; and chicken liver, toasted hazelnut and roast garlic parfait. Typical mains are slow-roast shoulder of Welsh lamb on fennel confit with light rosemary jus; and baked field mushroom, spinach and red lentil gâteau with rich wild mushroom gravy. Mackerel, fresh lobster and sea bass tend to feature as specials. Wines come from around the world, including Wales.

Recommended in the area

Pembrokeshire Coastal Path; Caldey Island;
Gower Peninsula

The White Swan Inn

Address: Llanfrynach, BRECON, LD3 7BZ
Tel: 01874 665276
Email: lee.havard@hotmail.co.uk
Website: www.the-white-swan.com
Map ref: 2 SO02
Directions: A40, 3m E of Brecon onto B4558 follow Llanfrynach signs
Open: 11.30-3 6.30-11.30 🍴 🍽️ **L** Wed-Sat 12-2, Sun 12-2.30 **D** Wed-Sun 7-9
Closed: 25-26 Dec, 1st 2wks Jan, Mon & Tue (ex summer, Dec & BH)
Facilities: Garden Parking
Notes: ⊕ FREE HOUSE 👬 🍷 8

Set opposite the ancient church of St Brynach, this smartly-converted row of white-painted stone cottages enjoys the awesome backdrop of the Brecon Beacons. Originally a coaching inn in the 17th century, it is now an unpretentious gastro-pub with character and atmosphere, featuring stone walls, exposed oak beams, stone-flagged floors, wooden furniture and bar counter, plus log fires, leather sofas, atmospheric lighting, and a warm and cosy feel. Eat in the spacious Flagstone Restaurant, or more informally in the bar, which also offers a lighter snack menu and Brains Bitter on hand pump. With imaginative menus changing monthly, enjoy crisp, honest dishes in the unpretentious gastro-pub mould, all freshly prepared using locally sourced produce, with daily fish specials listed on the chalkboard. Lunch might be a crispy Thai style spring roll with tempura battered scallops, sweet and sour apple and Thai dressing, followed by traditional Welsh lamb cawl with Welsh cheese and freshly baked bread. Typical evening dishes include Chinese spiced Gressingham duck breast with spiced sweet potatoes, roast plums and sweet and sour sauce, and peppered local venison haunch with potato and celeriac mash and red wine jus. There's also a selection from the grill.

Recommended in the area

Brecon Beacons National Park; South Wales Borderers Museum; Hay-on-Wye book shops

Nantyffin Cider Mill Inn

Address: Brecon Rd, CRICKHOWELL, NP8 1SG
Tel: 01873 810775
Email: info@cidermill.co.uk
Website: www.cidermill.co.uk
Map ref: 2 SO21
Directions: At junct of A40 & A479, 1.5m W of Crickhowell
Open: noon-3 6-11 ⅼ ⏺ **L** Sun 12-2.30 **D** Fri-Sat 6.30-9.30
Closed: Mon (ex BH), Sun eve Oct-Mar
Facilities: Garden Parking
Notes: ⊕ FREE HOUSE ⅰ 🖈 🍷 10

Originally a drovers' inn, this family-run, 16th-century inn lies at the foot of the Black Mountains. Until the mid-1960s, it was well known for its cider; the old mill wheel and original press, still in working order, are in the oak beamed Mill Room Restaurant, once used as an apple store. There's room to eat in the bars too where local real ales and draught and bottled ciders, including a mulled offering in the winter, are served. Recognised as a great food destination, the inn successfully combines the traditional values of the great British pub with Mediterranean influences. Menus are full of choice – wild game from nearby estates, Welsh beef and lamb, hearty casseroles, pot roasts, puddings and pies. Other possibilities include home-cured meat and smoked fish platters, lamb cawl (soup), rib-eye steak and free-range duck. The daily specials board is always structured around the best line-caught fish and shellfish in season, but is also likely to include starters such as game broth, and warm salad of Madgett's Farm chicken livers with smoked bacon and black pudding. Among the desserts might be apricot bread and butter pudding, sticky toffee pudding and a slate of Welsh cheeses.

Recommended in the area

Brecon Beacons National Park; Big Pit, Blaenavon; Brecon Mountain Railway

The Castle Coaching Inn

Address: TRECASTLE, nr Brecon, LD3 8UH
Tel: 01874 636354
Email: reservations@castle-coaching-inn.co.uk
Website: www.castle-coaching-inn.co.uk
Map ref: 2 SN82
Directions: On A40, W of Brecon
Open: all wk Wed-Sun noon-3, Mon-Sat 6-11
 L Wed-Sun 12-2 **D** Mon-Sat 6.30-9, Sun 7-9
Facilities: Garden Parking Wi-fi
Notes: ⊕ FREE HOUSE ♦♦ ♒

Once a Georgian coaching inn on the old London to Carmarthen coaching route, The Castle sits right on the northern edge of the Brecon Beacons/ Black Mountain area, with myriad streams flowing down to join the River Usk nearby. The inn retains lovely old fireplaces, a remarkable bow-fronted bar window and has a peaceful terrace and garden. A good selection of real ales is on offer, including Fuller's London Pride, Breconshire Brewery Red Dragon and Timothy Taylor Landlord. Food can be eaten in the bar or more formally in the restaurant, and bar lunches feature tempting, freshly-cut sandwiches (maybe roast beef, turkey or Stilton), a ploughman's with cheese or perhaps duck and port pâté, and hot crusty baguettes with fillings such as

steak with melted Stilton or bacon with mushrooms and melted mature Cheddar. Of the more substantial offerings, specialities include mature Welsh 12oz sirloin steak served with mushrooms and onion rings; home-made lasagne; and supreme of chicken with a Marsala and mascarpone sauce. The tempting desserts are worth saving room for, and might include hot jaffa puddle pudding, or Dutch chunky apple flan. Or perhaps sample the fine selection of Welsh farmhouse cheeses. There is a separate children's menu.

Recommended in the area

Dan-yr-Ogof The National Showcaves Centre; Brecon Beacons National Park; Usk Reservoir

County Map

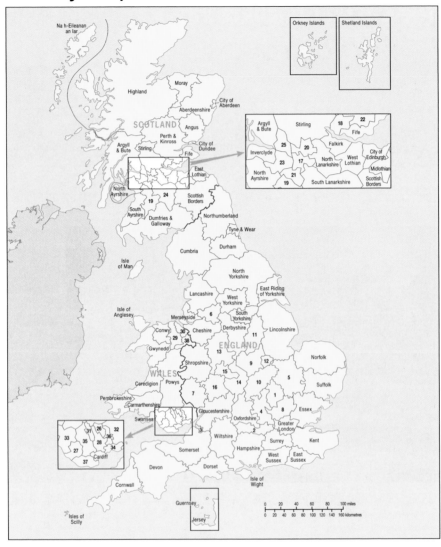

England
1. Bedfordshire
2. Berkshire
3. Bristol
4. Buckinghamshire
5. Cambridgeshire
6. Greater Manchester
7. Herefordshire
8. Hertfordshire
9. Leicestershire
10. Northamptonshire
11. Nottinghamshire
12. Rutland
13. Staffordshire
14. Warwickshire
15. West Midlands
16. Worcestershire

Scotland
17. City of Glasgow
18. Clackmannanshire
19. East Ayrshire
20. East Dunbartonshire
21. East Renfrewshire
22. Perth & Kinross
23. Renfrewshire
24. South Lanarkshire
25. West Dunbartonshire

Wales
26. Blaenau Gwent
27. Bridgend
28. Caerphilly
29. Denbighshire
30. Flintshire
31. Merthyr Tydfil
32. Monmouthshire
33. Neath Port Talbot
34. Newport
35. Rhondda Cynon Taff
36. Torfaen
37. Vale of Glamorgan
38. Wrexham

Maps

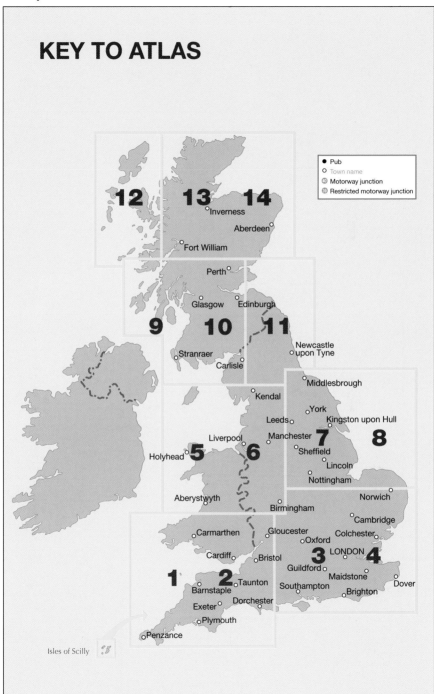

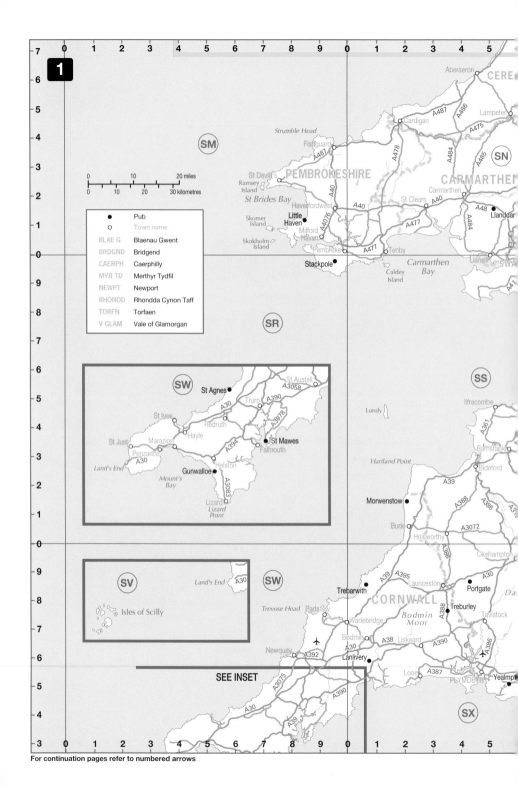

1

CERE

Aberaeron

Lampeter

Cardigan

A487

A486

A475

A478

A484

A485

SN

Strumble Head

Fishguard

SM

St David's

Ramsey Island

St Brides Bay

Skomer Island

Skokholm Island

PEMBROKESHIRE

CARMARTHE

Carmarthen

Haverfordwest

Little Haven

Milford Haven

Pembroke

A4076

A40

A477

Tenby

St Clears

A40

A48

Llanddar

A484

Stackpole

Caldey Island

Carmarthen Bay

Llane

SWA

	Pub
○	Town name
BLAE G	Blaenau Gwent
BRDGND	Bridgend
CAERPH	Caerphilly
MYR TD	Merthyr Tydfil
NEWPT	Newport
RHONDD	Rhondda Cynon Taff
TORFN	Torfaen
V GLAM	Vale of Glamorgan

0   10   20 miles

0   10   20   30 kilometres

SR

SW

St Agnes

St Austell

A3058

Truro

A390

SS

Ilfracombe

St Ives

Redruth

A30

A3078

Lundy

St Just

Marazion

Hayle

A394

St Mawes

Penzance

A30

Land's End

Gunwalloe

Helston

Falmouth

Mount's Bay

A3083

Lizard Lizard Point

Hartland Point

Morwenstow

Bude

Holsworthy

A39

Barnstaple

A361

Bideford

A39

A388

A386

A3072

Okehampton

SV

Isles of Scilly

Land's End

A30

SW

Trevose Head

Padst

Wadebridge

Bodmin

Newquay

A392

A30

A38

Lanlivery

Trebarwith

CORNWALL

Bodmin Moor

Liskeard

A39

A395

Launceston

A388

A30

Portgate

Da

Treburley

Tavistock

A390

A386

Looe

A387

PLYMOUTH

Yealmpt

SEE INSET

A3075

A390

A30

A29

SX

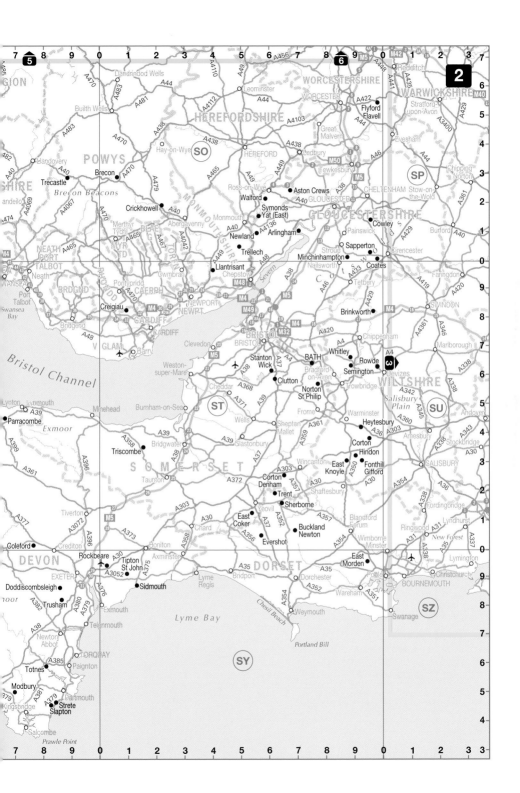

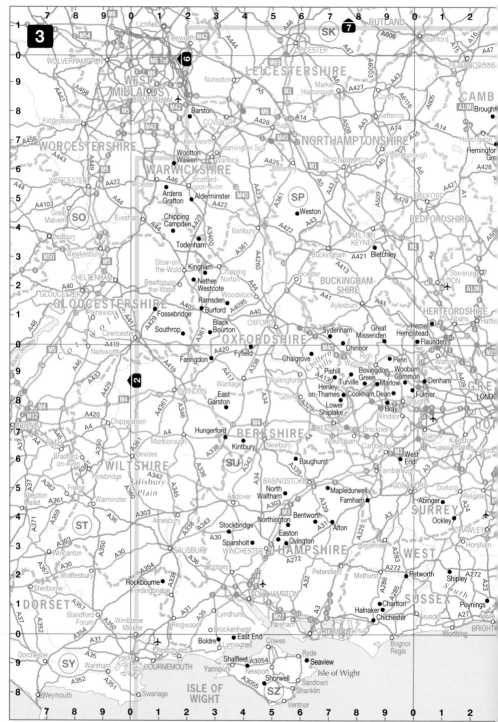

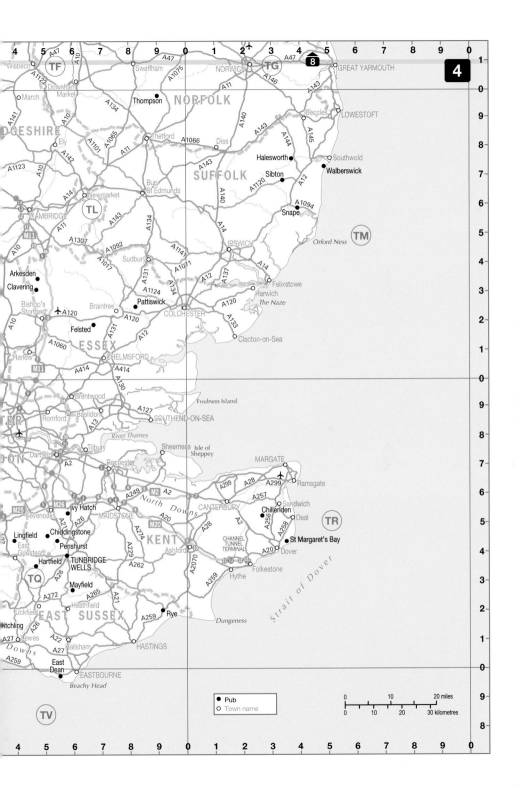

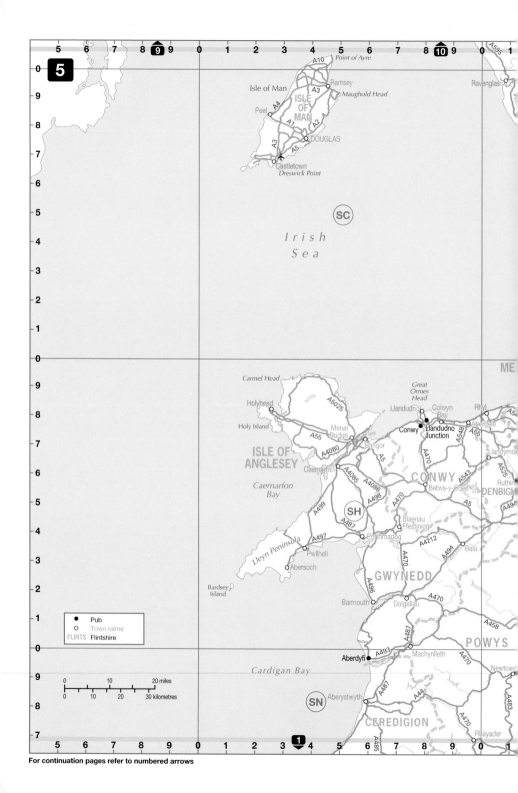

A10

Point of Ayre

Isle of Man

Ramsey
Maughold Head
A3

Ravenglass

ISLE
OF
MAN

Peel A4

A1 A2

A3 DOUGLAS

Castletown A5
Dreswick Point

SC

*Irish
Sea*

ME

Carmel Head

Great
Ormes
Head

Holyhead

A5025

Llandudno Colwyn
Bay
Rhyl
A5

Holy Island

Menai
Bridge

Conwy Llandudno
Junction

Abergele

A55

A55

A4080

A5

Llandyno

ISLE OF
ANGLESEY

Caernarfon

A4085

A4086

CONWY

A543

Ruthin

Betws-y-Coed DENBIGH

A525

*Caernarfon
Bay*

SH

A499

A498

A470

A5

A494

A487

Blaenau
Ffestiniog

Lleyn Peninsula

A497

Porthmadog

A470

A4212

A494

Bala

Pwllheli

Abersoch

GWYNEDD

Bardsey
Island

A496

Barmouth

Dolgellau

A470

A458

	Pub
○	Town name
FLINTS	Flintshire

A487

POWYS

A470

Aberdyfi

Machynlleth

Newtown

Cardigan Bay

0		10		20 miles
0	10	20		30 kilometres

SN

Aberystwyth

A487

A44

A470

A483

CEREDIGION

Rhayader

A485

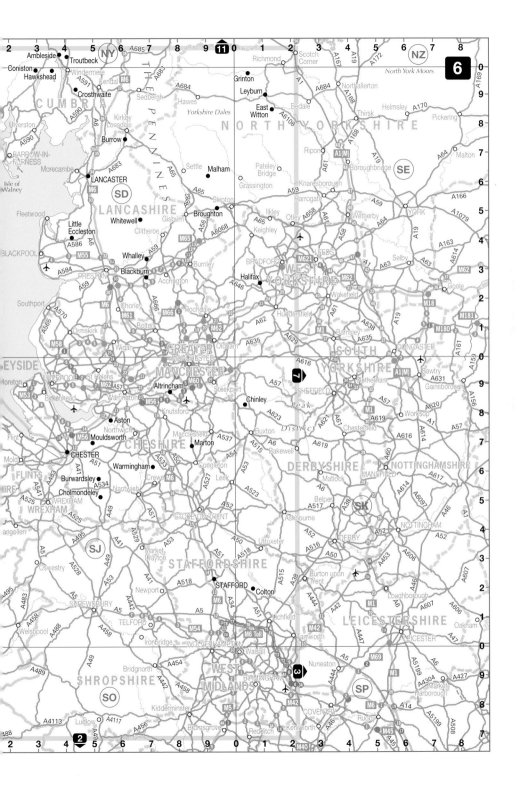

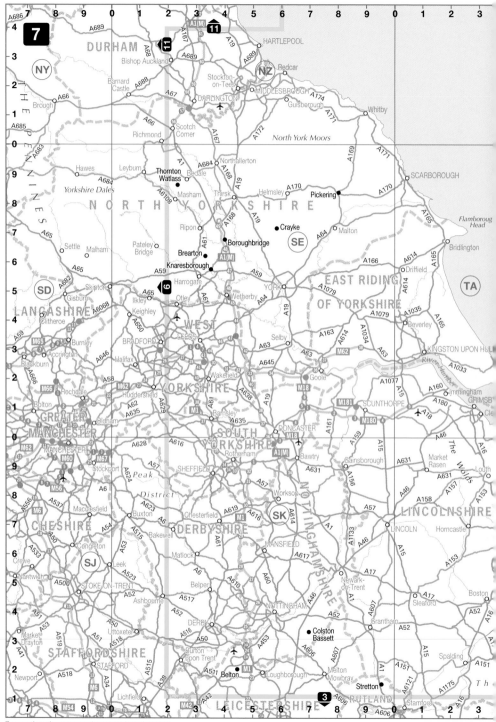

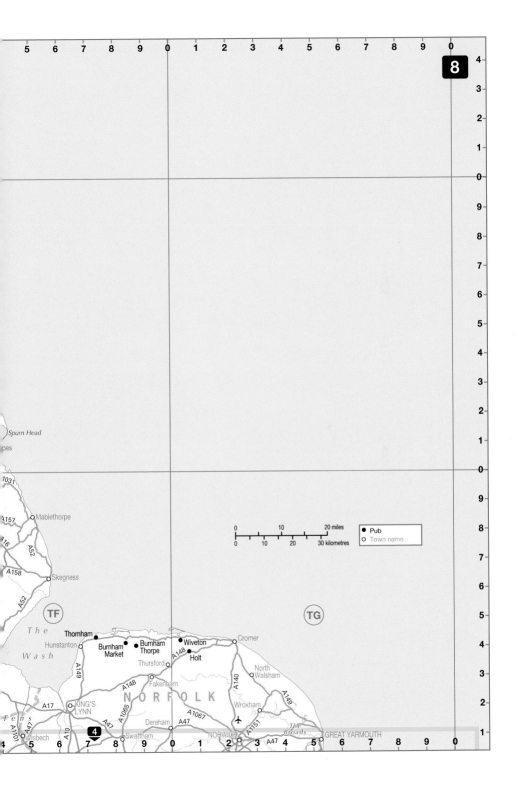

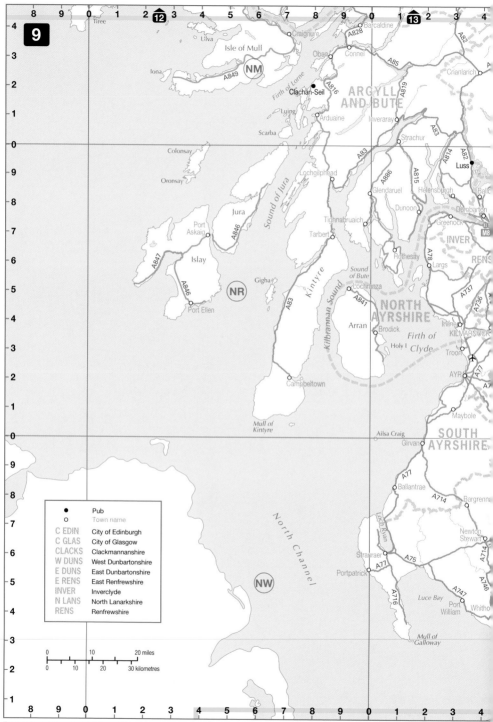

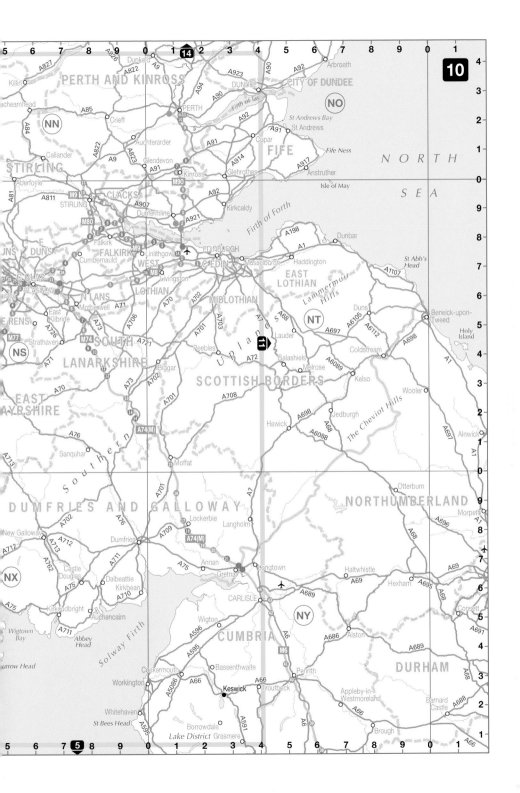

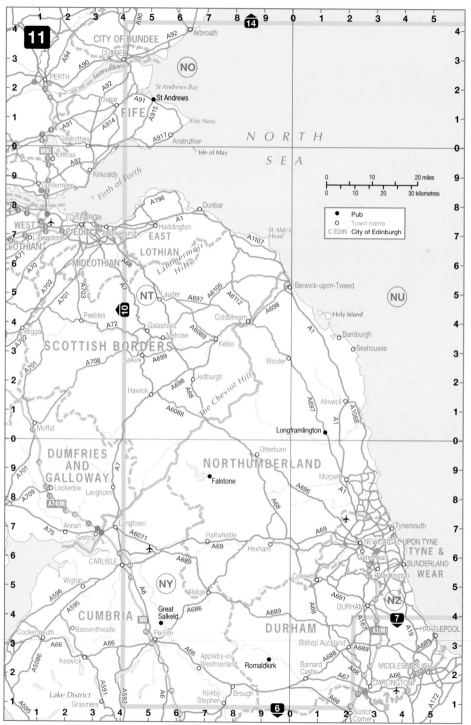

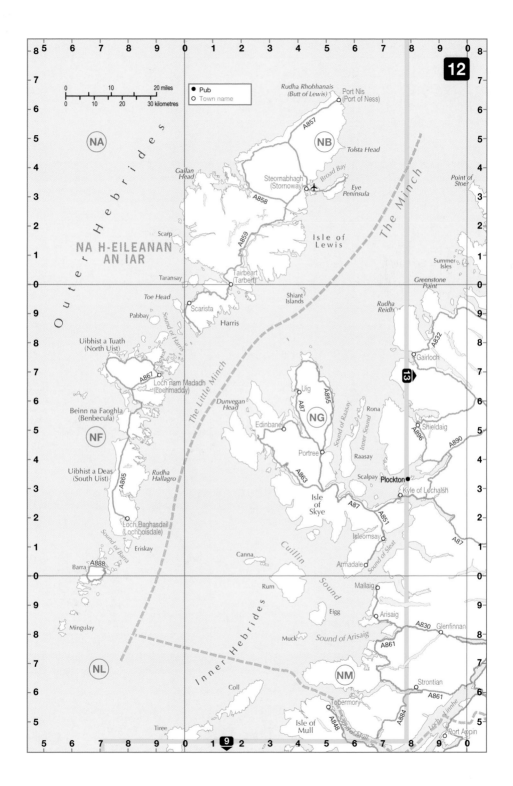

Location Index

Establishment Index

Acknowledgements

The Automobile Association would like to thank the following photographers, companies and picture libraries for their assistance in the preparation of this book.

Abbreviations for the picture credits are as follows – (t) top; (b) bottom; (c) centre; (l) left; (r) right; (AA) AA World Travel Library.

4 The Feathered Nest Inn; 5t Courtesy The Trout at Tadpole Bridge; 5b Courtesy Gaggle of Geese/Jon Gooding; 9l Photodisc; 9r Courtesy The Bell/Robert Dowell; 12t Courtesy The Print Room; 12b Courtesy The Mill Race; 14 Courtesy The Chequers Brasserie; 16/17 AA/Anna Mockford and Nick Bonetti; 18 AA/James Tims; 24 AA/Michael Moody; 34 AA/Laurie Noble; 37 AA/Laurie Noble; 38 AA/John Mottershaw; 46 AA/Adam Burton; 54 AA/Tom Mackie; 63 AA/Roger Coulam; 64 AA/Tom Mackie; 66 AA/Adam Burton; 82 AA/Andrew Newey; 88 AA/Roger Coulam; 90 AA/Neil Setchfield; 95 AA/Neil Setchfield; 96 AA/David Hall; 109 AA/David Hall; 110 AA/S Beer; 112 AA/Michael Moody; 126 AA/Caroline Jones; 130 AA/Michael Moody; 133 AA/James Tims; 134 AA/Laurie Noble; 141 AA/Laurie Noble; 142 AA/David Clapp; 150 AA/James Tims; 152 AA/James Tims; 155 AA/James Tims; 156 AA/S & O Matthews; 163 AA/Tony Souter: 164 AA/M Birkitt: 166 AA/Jo Hunt; 169 AA/Jo Hunt; 170 AA/James Tims; 172 AA/James Tims; 185 AA/Caroline Jones; 186 AA/M Birkitt; 188 AA/James Tims; 196 AA/Caroline Jones; 199 AA/Caroline Jones; 200 AA/Tom Mackie; 205 AA/Tom Mackie; 206 AA/James Tims; 212 AA/Laurie Noble; 219 AA/Laurie Noble; 220 AA/John Miller; 227 AA/Laurie Noble; 228 AA/Caroline Jones; 232 AA/Caroline Jones; 234 AA/Andrew Newey; 238 AA/Michael Moody; 248/249 AA/Michael Moody; 250 AA/Caroline Jones; 252 AA/Mike Kipling; 265 AA/Mike Kipling; 266 AA/James Tims; 268/269 AA/Jonathan Smith; 277 AA/Jonathan Smith; 278/279 AA/Rebecca Duke

Every effort has been made to trace the copyright holders, and we apologise in advance for any unintentional omissions or errors. We would be pleased to apply any corrections in a following edition of this publication.